Epistles of a
PROLIFIC PONTIFF

New
Updated
2nd Edition
2024

M.K.SUDARSHAN

BLUEROSE PUBLISHERS
India | U.K.

Copyright © M. K. Sudarshan 2024

All rights reserved by author. No part of this publication may be reproduced, stored in a retrieval system or transmitted in any form or by any means, electronic, mechanical, photocopying, recording or otherwise, without the prior permission of the author. Although every precaution has been taken to verify the accuracy of the information contained herein, the publisher assumes no responsibility for any errors or omissions. No liability is assumed for damages that may result from the use of information contained within.

BlueRose Publishers takes no responsibility for any damages, losses, or liabilities that may arise from the use or misuse of the information, products, or services provided in this publication.

For permissions requests or inquiries regarding this publication, please contact:

BLUEROSE PUBLISHERS
www.BlueRoseONE.com
info@bluerosepublishers.com
+91 8882 898 898
+4407342408967

ISBN: 978-93-6452-767-5

Cover Design: Sadhna Kumari
Typesetting: Pooja Sharma

First Edition: June 2023
Second Edition: June 2024

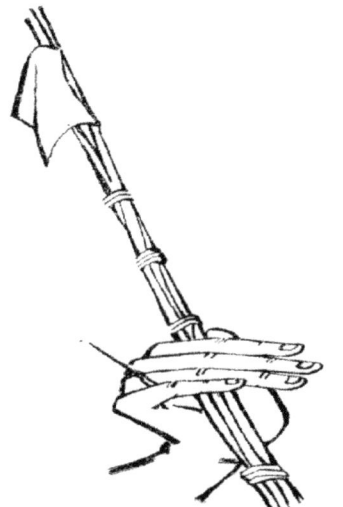

Epistles of "Srimathe Srivann Satagopa Sri Vedanta Desika Yathindra Mahadesikan" Translations into English from the Tamil original

"The Prolific Pontiff"
(New & Updated Second Edition 2024)

Epistles of
Srimathe Srivann Satagopa
Sri Vedanta Desika Yathindra Mahadesikan
(His Holiness, 44th Azhagiyasingar and Spiritual Head of Sri Ahobila Math)

Translated into English from the Tamil original
By
M.K. Sudarshan

Published with the permission of
The "Sri Nrsimha Priya Charitable Trust", Chennai, India
Sponsored by Smt.Mani Krishnaswami Foundation, Chennai

(1895-1992)

His Holiness, Sri Lakshminrsimha Paduka Sevaka Srimathe Srivaan Satagopa Sri Vedanta Desika Yathindra Mahadesikan 44th Azhagiyasingar, the Pontiff of Sri Ahobila Math

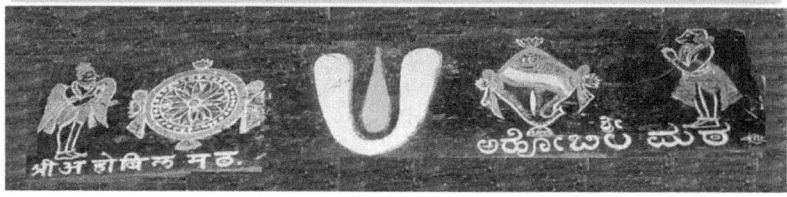

This book has been blessed by

HH Srimathe Srivan Satagopa

Sri Ranganatha Yathindra Mahadesikan

The 46th Azhagiyasingar and present Pontiff of Sri Ahobila Math

Translator's Note on Second Edition-2024

"Sri Lakshmi Narasimha Parabrahmane namah"

The First Edition of this book was published and made available for sale in April 2023.

The Epistles of a Prolific Pontiff, since then has been welcomed by readers of both the worldwide Sri Vaishnava community at large as well as by the general Hindu public belonging to *Sanatana Dharma* faith.

The book has also received critical acclaim through reviews in journals like *"Sri Nrisimha Priya"* (English). It has also elicited the appreciation of several religious scholars, *"aasthika*-s" and distinguished philanthropists. The eminent industrialist and benefactor of several Sri Vaishnava Temple establishments in the State of Tamil Nadu, **Sri. Venu Srinivasan**, *Chairman Emeritus of the TVS Motor Company* conveyed his thoughts on the book to the Translator:

"The Epistles that you have so carefully translated, covers a range of topics, from spiritualism, philosophy, and social ethics that define Sri Vaishnavism, one of the oldest and most revered traditions of India, propounded by the great Sri Ramanujacharya.... Thanks to your translation, we are now able to partake of this timeless wisdom and dip into this vast ocean of knowledge. This book is sure to appeal to all those who wish to have a deeper experience and understanding of Vedantic Philosophy...."

The need for a **Second Edition** of this book coming so early on the heels of the First after just a year was felt due mainly to the following two reasons:

(A) The First Edition comprised an anthology of **sixteen** carefully selected *"arul mozhi-s"* in Tamizh authored by *His Holiness Srimad*

"*Mukkur Azhagiyasingar*" sometime in *circa.* 1970s and 1980s, all duly translated into English. Since, its publication, however, it was felt that **five more** excellent epistles of great topical value to readers, especially the young, ought to be added to the wonderful bouquet turning it into an anthology of **twenty-one** splendid *"arul-mozhis"* republished as **Second Edition**. Following are their titles which have been inserted appropriately in the *Table of Contents*:

1. *"**Daana mahimai**"* : Charity's Value
2. Six ***Bhaktha*-s** in a ***Divya Desam***
3. Desire
4. Nuggets of Vedanta
5. Eight Maxims of Life

(B) The First Edition, furthermore, needed to be corrected for minor proofing errors which have now been duly carried out in the new Second Edition.

The Translator in all earnestness has undertaken the task of publishing this new Edition with the sole aim of further expanding the popular reach of ***Srimad Mukkur Azhagiyasingar's*** deep Vedantic knowledge amongst his vast following of disciples and students living today and who still remember him for it. All through his life (1895-1992 CE), he sought to spread his rare wisdom through the widely read and appreciated, lucid, and very illuminating epistles he wrote copiously.

It is hoped this book will be wholeheartedly welcomed by *"aasthika*s", their families and extended circles of relatives, friends and acquaintances in very large numbers. The income-proceeds of this second edition of the book, as in the case of the first one too, will also accrue to *Sri Nrisimha Priya Charitable Trust.*

"Srimathe Sri Ranganatha Yathindra Mahadesikaya namah"

Daasoham

M.K.Sudarshan

June 2024

Chennai

From
SRI KARYAM
SRI AHOBILA MATH
ஸ்ரீ அஹோபில மடம்

HH 46th Jeer

We have every reason to be proud of our lineage of great and glorious Acharyas (preceptors)who have adorned the spiritual pontifical throne of Sri Ahobila Matham. Each of these mahatmas has catered to the spiritual wellbeing of disciples in their own unique way and style, with the view to liberate the suffering souls from this transmigratory ocean of samsara. Thus, right from the revered founder of the Sri Ahobila Math, Sri Adivan Satakopa Swami, to the present Pontiff Sri Rangantha Yatindra Mahadesikan, every Acharya has deemed it his life's mission to emancipate suffering souls.

Special mention must be made here about Mukkur Srimad Azhagiasingar, the 44th Pontiff of Sri Ahobila Matham, whose upanyasams (discourses), Kalakshepams (traditional teaching), writings and conversations were entirely devoted to Vedanta vichaaram (philosophical inquiry). All these reflected his mastery over all aspects of Vedanta (*Vedanta vijnaana sunischitaartthaa.*). He had acquired such prodigious scholarship through devoted service to his Acharyas, especially the 39th, 40th, 41st, 42nd and 43rd Srimad Azhagiasingars, all of whom were scholars of renown.

Mukkur Srimad Azhagiasingar's compulsive generosity is known to everyone. He was hailed as *Kalivuga Karnan* for his munificence towards beneficiaries, irrespective of caste, lineage or scholarship. Such generosity was not confined to donations of cash, kind and food to deserving people, but extended to sharing his boundless wisdom with disciples and others through his innumerable discourses, kalakshepams and essays. The last-mentioned were mostly his messages to readers of **Sri Nrisimhapriya**, under the banner of **Arulmozhi**. It is no exaggeration to say that all that one needs to know about the Sampradaya could well be gleaned from these *Arulmozhis*.

It is therefore essential that these Arulmozhis are translated into other languages too, for the edification and enlightenment of those who are not conversant with Tamizh. I am happy to note that Sri Madabushi Sudarshan, a disciple of Sri Matham and an author of books on the SriVaishnava sampradaya, has come forward to translate these wonderful nuggets of wisdom into English and that several of these translations which appeared serially in *Sri Nrisimhapriya* (English) are now being brought out in book form. Prakrutam HH Srimad Azhgiasingar too, whose devotion to his Acharya Mukkur Srimad Azhagiasingar knows no bounds, expressed happiness at the endeavour and conveyed his blessings for its success.

The present pontiff, His Holiness Sri Ranganatha Yatindra Mahadesikan, felt very happy about the efforts of Sri Madabushi Sudarsan in his efforts and blessed him for his total prosperity.

Place: Selaiyur (E.Tambaram)   By the order of HH the Jeer of Sri Ahobila Math

Date : 24.04. 2023

Parutthipattu Vangipuram Devanarvilagam

Dr. Padmanabhacharya

Sri Karyam (Principal Secretary to HH the Jeeyar of Sri Ahobila Mutt)

SRI KARYAM
PRINCIPAL SECRETARY TO
HIS HOLINESS THE 46TH JEER
OF SRI AHOBILA MATH

Editor's Note to the First Edition: "A Word with You..."

Spiritual and religious scholars are of various types. Some delight in using their erudition to find fault with the writings of others. Some adopt a highfalutin writing style comprehensible only to their peers and superiors (and sometimes only to themselves). Some are prolific in writing but when asked to address an audience, become dumbfounded. Contrarily, there are versatile speakers who tie themselves up in knots before penning a page. It is thus difficult to find scholars who are equally at home with speaking and writing, whose words, spoken or written, are entirely devoted to the upliftment of the spiritually unlettered, and whose endeavors are prompted solely by the precious milk of human kindness and the desire to do good without the expectation of a *quid pro quo*. Rarely do we find scholars who are ready to share their learning with all those who desire it, with absolutely no material motives. And when you apply your grey matter to the search of such an altruistic scholar, nay, spiritual giant, who has brought about a silent revolution in the thought processes of innumerable devotees, you find that the sole figure that comes to your mind is that of **HH Mukkur Srimad Azhagiasingar, the 44th Pontiff of Sri Ahobila Matham.**

Trained as he was by the best of scholars, **Mukkur Srimad Azhagiasingar** acquired formidable scholarship in all fields of the Sri Vaishnava Sampradaya. Having performed *Vedadhyayanam*, acquired expertise in *Divya Prabandas*, mastered Samanya Sastras like *Nyaya* and *Mimamsa* and undergone *kalakshepam* in *Sri Bhashyam, Sri Gita Bhashyam, Bhagavad Vishayam* and *Srimad Rahasyatraya Saram*, HH was eminently equipped for his spiritual responsibilities, which included the dissemination of spiritual wisdom to disciples. The nature of HH's study of these texts was so prodigious that he had instant recall of all the key concepts. Additionally, through intensive study, he had mastered the nooks and corners of the texts, which inculcated in him absolute confidence. His study was therefore not only extensive, but intensive too.

And his thoughts were constantly immersed in Vedanta *Vichara*, the contemplation of the Ultimate, the lines of the *Brahma Sutras* and Sri Ramanuja's wonderful commentary thereon constantly running through his mind, such that all matters were crystal clear to him—*Vedanta vijaana sunischitaartthaa:* HH took very seriously Sri Ramanuja's diktat *Sri Bhashyattai vaasittu pravarttippittal (*It is every Sri Vaishnava's sacred duty to not only learn the *Sri Bhashya*, but to propagate it too). Additionally, if the claim of Swami Desikan, of having grown old and his head having become fully white with the study of Sri Ramanuja's works, (*Yatipravara bharati rasa bharena neetam vaya: praphulla phalitam sira:*) could be applied to anyone else, it was **Mukkur Srimad Azhgiasingar**, who not only learnt *Sri Bhashyam* in his teens, but honed his wisdom and understanding by attending all the sessions of seminars and scholarly conclaves (*vidwat sadas*) over several years.

HH's erudition shone through in his discourses even before he adorned the ochre robes. He was very much in demand for his spiritual discourses, both in the public domain and in private, traditional settings (*kalakshepam*). He had a phenomenal recall of apt and pertinent quotes to astound the audience. His logic was clear, convincing and irrefutable.

The exceptional learning of HH has been summarized by **Sri Kaa. Sree. Sree** in the following verses:

Vede Vedanta yugme Raghuvara charite Brahmasutraadi bhaashye

Bhavye Divya Prabande Shrutisikhara guro: vaangmaye ananya krishti:

Loke bhaktim vidhaaya Achyuta pada kamala dikshu vikhyaata bhoomaa

Raakaa saahasradarsee budha mahitam ahe bhaati Vedanta Yogi.

This verse tells us how *Mukkur Mahan* acquired inimitable scholarship in *Vedas, Vedanta, Brahma Sutras, Divya Prabandas, Itihasas,* the nectarine works of **Sri Alavandar, Sri Ramanuja and Swami Desikan** and as a result, developed enviable mastery over them, such that he was able to capture the hearts of listeners with his gripping discourses, sowing the seeds of devotion in them and earning renown in all the lands.

As I have lamented elsewhere too, it is indeed a pity that no records of HH's innumerable discourses are now available, but for a solitary one on **Saranagati**. I must say that we have lost an invaluable treasure through our negligence of not recording and preserving these discourses, each of which was indeed a gem. Listening to him, one was reminded of Sri Rama's tribute to Maruti during their first encounter—*ucchaarayati kalyaaneem vaacham hridaya haarineem* (He speaks well and in a manner which steals the listeners' heart). His rendering of Sri Rukmini Kalyanam was a classic and extremely popular too. The hundreds of *upanyasams* HH must have rendered at *Dolotsavams* never had an element of duplication in them. With his masterful command over *Itihasas* and *Puranas*, HH could enliven the narrative with appropriate gestures too, bringing the scene graphically before the listeners' eyes. And interspersed in the narrative would be extremely pertinent homilies, instilling the right thought and conduct in the listener. A majestic voice, clear and firm diction and comprehensibility made the discourses extremely popular and listened to by masses with rapt attention.

However, we have a measure of compensation in having preserved his writings. Most of these were in the form of *Arulmozhis* contributed to the Mutt's monthly journal *Sri Nrisimhapriya*.

HH's writings are in a class of their own. They are couched in extremely simple words, devoid of the jargon scholars use to flaunt their erudition. The emphasis was on conveying the message to the reader with clear and unambiguous diction. And despite being simple, the words were extremely evocative and many a time, brought tears to the reader's eyes. Complex concepts from *Sri Bhashyam*, gems from *Aruliccheyal*, parables from the Puranas, distilled wisdom from the Vedas—all these in turn formed the subject of the **Arulmozhis,** sowing the seeds of erudition even in lay readers and nurturing the fledgling shoot of devotion growing in the cracks of the hard rocks that our minds are. HH was capable of putting even complex concepts in simple words, with homespun examples, for the comprehension of readers. It was indeed a gift HH was blessed with, that of elucidating esoteric and intricate matters in unpretentious words.

These gems are in Tamizh and have catered to a vast audience of all ages, over the last almost seven decades. Currently, however, we are facing a rather unusual situation of a whole lot of people, whose mother tongue is Tamizh, being more comfortable in English, due to their education, vocation, location, etc. This segment of the population comprises people of all ages, particularly youth. However, their anglicized reading habits have not reduced their hunger for spiritual education, provided it is encapsulated in the appropriate language. While initially, only those settled abroad had such a predilection for spiritual wisdom through the medium of English, today's position is that many of the youth in India are in the same boat.

This population segment is too large and too important to ignore. Recognizing this need, spiritual institutions have started over the last decade to bring out English versions of hallowed spiritual journals- *Sri Nrisimhapriya* is an example.

It was to cater to such an audience that I requested **Sri Madabushi K. Sudarshan**, who has been writing on matters relating to Sri Vaishnavism in English for several decades now, to translate these *Arulmozhis* into English. Given the erudition of **Mukkur Srimad Azhagiasingar**, the nature and range of the topics covered by his *Arulmozhis*, etc., it is a difficult task for anyone. However, to my surprise, Sri Sudarshan readily agreed and got on the job with admirable alacrity. And what is more, the translations he turned out were eminently readable, because he was able to capture the spirit of each *Arulmozhi* and tell the story in his own words, words which display a nice turn of phrase and make for a smooth, seamless narrative. As one with a little translation experience, I can understand how difficult an endeavour it is to render a spiritual work from Tamizh to English, especially the work of a scholar *nonpareil* like **Mukkur Srimad Azhagiasingar**. It is evident that this has been a labour of love for Sri Sudarshan, who deems it as an act of service (*kainkaryam*) to the *Sampradaya* to bring the wonderful words of this spiritual giant to the English-speaking readers without detracting a bit from the tone, tenor and spirit of the original.

These translated articles have been appearing in *Sri Nrisimhapriya* for more than a year now and evoked excellent response from readers spanning all age groups, which proves wrong all the Cassandras who predict that the younger generation being what it is, our *Sampradaya's* years are numbered. In view of all this encouraging response, Sri Sudarshan felt that these translated articles would serve a larger audience in book form, as the reader-attention span of a monthly journal is rather limited. It is indeed a good idea to make these treasures available in the form of books/e-books, for perusal and repeated perusal, all at one's convenience.

When the proposal was mentioned to **His Holiness Srimad Azhagiasingar HH Srivan Satakopa Sri Rangantha Yatindra Mahadesikan**, present Pontiff of Sri Ahobila Mutt, he was graceful enough to convey his immediate approval. Sri J.S. Vasan, trustee of *Sri Nrisimhapriya*, copyright holder for the ***Arulmozhis***, readily agreed to the proposal.

As forewords go, this might be lengthy, but when you think of the innumerable nuggets of wisdom embedded in the enclosed pages, you would forgive my having waxed eloquent, to give the reader an idea of how invaluable each of these articles is and how glorious the scholarship of the author. Here you can find all the wisdom you will ever need, brought to you in a nutshell, sparing you the impossible task of having to delve through all the original works in chaste Tamizh and Sanskrit, which are beyond the reach of today's average reader. The wonderful concept of **Saranagati** runs through all these articles as a common thread, piquing the reader's interest to learn more and be blessed with the ultimate in all things to aspire for— **Liberation.**

It is my sincere hope that this collection of essays acquires the popularity it deserves and encourages the translator to bring out more such volumes periodically. And dear readers, this book is all the more deserving of your patronage when you learn that the translator has pledged the sale proceeds to fund charitable and spiritual causes espoused **by Sri Ahobila Mutt**, a venerated seven-century-old institution.

5th April 2023

K. Sadagopa Iyengar -- Editor, *Sri Nrisimha Priya*

Translator's Note to the First Edition

In the year 2020, when the world was reeling under devastation caused by the Covid pandemic, and with people everywhere seized by mortal fear and despair, I felt my own spirit sinking too into deep depression. There was no way then to tell when the pandemic would pass nor when, if ever at all, would our lives be restored to normalcy. A great pall of sadness descended upon the world and people everywhere.

It was in those dark days when one's spirit was afflicted with a nameless angst that one day a glimmer of hope and solace seemed to stream into my life.

One morning, I suddenly received a telephone call from **Sri. K. Sadagopan**, the editor of *"Nrsimha Priya* (English)". To my utter surprise he requested me to accept to undertake at once a translation-assignment for the magazine. My job was to translate into English a select series of Tamil epistles of *Srimadh Azhagiasingar*, the **44ᵗʰ Pontiff of Sri Ahobila Math, Srivan Satagopa Sri Vedanta Desika Yathindra** (popularly known as ***"Mukkur Swamy")*** which had been compiled and published earlier as a book titled, *"Arul Mozhi"*. The epistles before being published as a book under copyright of the *Sri Nrsimha Priya Trust* had appeared as serialized articles in the monthly issues of the Tamil edition of *"Sri Nrisimha Priya"*.

The task assigned to me by Sri. Sadagopan at first seemed incredibly daunting to me for more than one reason. Firstly, amidst the death and despair being witnessed all around me in the wake of the worldwide pandemic – not to mention the harrowing experiences of seeing near and dear ones pass away suddenly, of mass hospitalization and of being forced to stay quarantined at home under general curfew conditions for months -- the state of my mind was not quite so happy as to make me feel well disposed towards taking up a task involving literary effort.

Secondly, as I told Sri Sadagopan too then, I did not also feel adequate to the task. I had no confidence in my abilities to translate Mukkur Swami's works which were renowned for rare, insightful wisdom and deep, scholarly content. I neither possessed thorough knowledge of the various subjects of *"Sri Vaishnava Sampradaaya"* that *Azhagiyasingar's* epistles discoursed upon nor the requisite mastery in Tamil language to be able to effectively render into English the profundity of the Pontiff's thoughts and thought-processes.

Although initially I baulked at his suggestion, Sri. Sadagopan succeeded in goading and prevailing upon me to take up the assignment.

In the ensuing two years – 2021 and 2022 – sixteen of the *"arul mozhigal"* in Tamil of *Mukkur Swamy* (all carefully selected by Sri Sadagopan) were translated into English by me and were published serially in the monthly issues of the English editions of both **"Nrisimha Priya"** and **"Vainavan Kural"** magazines. The main themes of the epistles pertained to *"Sri Ramanuja siddhaanta"* and the school of *"Sri Desika sampradaaya"*. They cover many of the philosophical principles, theological doctrines and religious practices of Sri Vaishnavism so lucidly and elegantly yet so powerfully explained by His Holiness.

As I began the translations of Azhagiyasingar's epistles, I suddenly began to feel the pall of depression lift from my spirit! The pandemic was forgotten. Instead, I found myself immersed in an extraordinary spiritual self-learning experience. As I read the Tamil originals, reflected on the *"arul mozhi"* of Mukkur Swami, and then understood and internalized their deep meaning and wisdom, I realized that translating them was actually opening my eyes to verities and nuances of Sri Vaishnava *"sampradaaya"* which hitherto I had either been utterly blind to or else had failed to appreciate in full measure.

In the following year and half that I spent diligently translating, page after page of each of Azhagiyasingar's epistles, I realized the experience was turning out to be a rich reward in itself for me, personally. The painful lessons of life, death and grief that the pandemic had taught me were cathartic but, more importantly and impactfully, it was the privilege I was enjoying of translating the *"arul mozhi*" which was truly therapeutic for my saddened soul. The whole effort in the end, I realized, had helped my mind overcome a state of depression and pessimism. The epistles lifted my spirits. The words of wisdom of the Acharya were soothing balm and solace to my mind.

Today, thank God, the deadly pandemic is behind us all… Our country and people after recovering remarkably well are moving on. At a personal level, I can say without any doubt that my own recovery from the two-year trauma of the pandemic is to be attributed to the God-sent opportunity given me to translate the works of Mukkur Swamy. I profited from it emotionally, spiritually and intellectually.

***

The title of this book of translations has been chosen to be **"The Prolific Pontiff"**. It is tribute to the versatile qualities of Mukkur Swamy. He was a brilliant Vedic scholar specialized in abstruse *"meemaamsa"* and *"tarka saastra"* as well as in Ramanuja's *Sri Bhaashya* and Vedanta Desika's *"Rahasya Traya Saaram"*. He was an expositor par excellence of the great scriptural epics of *Srimadh Ramayana* and *Srimadh Mahabharatha*. His discourses on the *Bhagavath Gita* were a delight to audiences of all ages. He was an exceptionally gifted writer. Besides his scholasticism, Mukkur Swamy was also a visionary and indefatigable institution-builder. Three monumental achievements during his lifetime in large-scale project-management are proof indeed of the fact:

(i) the expansion of the *Madurantakam Veda-paatashaala* (a school for Vedic seminarians) which he supervised and completed

(ii) instituting the forum of *"vidwat sadas"* for Sri Vaishnava scholars to assemble at academic conclaves to workshop, debate and exposition upon matters of Sri Vaishnava *"siddhaantham"* and *"sampradaaya"*

(iii) building the magnificent temple-tower, the awesome *"rajagopuram"* of Sri Rangam, whose construction over nine long years he personally oversaw and completed, even while exerting himself to extremes of physical endurance even at the age of ninety, showing astounding will-power, stamina and energy! So much did this *"sannyaasi"* achieve in a lifetime with so little resources at his command and that too in such a short time. There is perhaps no better word that can aptly describe this pontiff than "***prolific***"!

It is my sincere hope that these sixteen translations into English of **Srimadh Mukkur Azhagiyasingar's** *"arul mozhigal"* will serve the useful and important purpose of reaching the Pontiff's message, so full of spiritual wisdom and brilliant Vedantic insights, to the farthest corners of the world wherever the Sri Vaishnava laity live, embrace practice and cherish their faith.

"Srimathe Sri Lakshminrisimha Parabrahmane namah!"

M.K. Sudarshan

March, 2023

Contents

"*Sri Raamaanuja Siddhaantham*": Philosophy of Sri Ramanuja 1

Sri Nigamantha Mahadesikan's "*Paramatha Bhangam*" 15

"Desire ("*aasai*") 28

"Breaking Out of Bondage" 33

A Session of Questions & Answers 47

The essence of the 13th Chapter of Srimadh Bhagavath Gita 56

Nuggets of Vedanta 72

The Questions of Yaksha and The Answers of Dharmaputhra 88

"Praise The High-Souled" 107

"The 9-Stepped Stairway to *Parama-Padam* Sri Desikan Built" ... 114

Six Traits of The Salvation Seeker 128

Six "*Bhaktha-s*" in a "*Divya-Desam*" 137

Tamizh "*Upannyaasam*" On "*Saranaagathi Tattvam*" 155

"*Sri Vaishnava Sampradaaya*": Clarification of a Few Doubts on Doctrine 183

The Good That Virtuous Women Do 193

A Tiff Over Tiffin! ("*Saapaatu Sandai*") 210

On Forbearance and Patience 217

"*Daana Mahimai*": Charity's Value 229

"*Daaney Dvishantho Mithraa Bhavanthi*": Charity 248

On the Glorious Significance of "*Govinda Naama*" 261

Eight Maxims of Life 274

Acknowledgements 286

About the Translator 287

-1-
"*Sri Raamaanuja Siddhaantham*": Philosophy of Sri Ramanuja

Synopsis: *The fundamental metaphysical concepts in Visishtadvaita Philosophy such as the "tattva traya", "cit" or "jivatma", "acit" or "prakruti", and "Isvara" or "paramaatma" are explained along with other ontological phenomena such as Time (kaala), the genesis of creation and cosmic dissolution.*

The tenets found in this Philosophy are Truth. This philosophy has been established by a long lineage of preceptors, such as the **Azhwars, Sri.Alavandaar, Sri. Raamaanjuja** and **Sri. Vedanta Desikan**, underpins the faith that this *"siddhaantam"* upholds and contains the same truths that the *Veda, Vedaanta, Itihaasas, Puraanas* and *Smriti*-s reveal. Therefore, what is said in the following pages should be read and studied by all of you diligently, even more than once if needed, so that you can absorb and understand it all thoroughly.

(Courtesy: R.Chithralekha)

I am writing this piece imagining myself to be delivering my sermon to you all in person. If you were to take up self-study on your very own about the matters that I am about to write about hereinafter, it is possible that you might all incur the grave and mortal risk of erroneous understanding (*"dosham"*). That risk however can be avoided if you follow carefully and grasp fully what I am going to present to you.

It is improper for a preceptor – an anointed *Achaarya* like me – to proceed to instruct disciples at his own behest, without them expressly requesting him to do so. Since, a few good-hearted ones amongst you have come forward and appealed to me to address you all on the matters I am about to deal with below, there is no risk of any impropriety (*"dosham"*) on my part as an Acharya either. Therefore, rest assured and, without any anxiety of any sorts, please pay heed and attention closely to what is written below and assimilate it fully.

1. **Srimann Naaraayana** is the Supreme Being (*"parabrahman"*), or God Almighty (*"kadavull"*). His Consort, **Sri:** is *His equal in all respects*…i.e., *Lakshmi* too, like Him, possesses all the excellences that He does. She too, exactly like Him, is *all-Pervasive.* Thus, these two inseparable entities indeed together constitute the **Supreme Beings** of the entire universe.

2. Individual souls (*"jeevaatma"*) are ontological entities endowed with Intelligence; they are indestructible and, in that respect, they resemble **Bhagavaan** *(Naaraayanan).* They are monads i.e., they are atomic in form and nature, indivisible and unitary in the absolute sense. These *jeevaatma-*s are inestimably countless in number. Not only are they too innumerable to estimate by humans but they are also said to be beyond count by the Almighty even.

   2.1 The revealed scriptures (*"saastra"*) classify *"jeevaatmas"* into three distinct groups. They name each of them as "**Bonded souls**" (*baddha-*s), "**Souls that have attained Liberation**" (*"muktha-s"*) and "**Souls that are eternally liberated**" (*"nithya-suri-s"*).

   2.2 The bonded souls – the *"baddha-s"* -- are infinite in number. The numbers of the *"muktha-s"* and *"nithya-suri-s"* too are likewise infinite and it is said that even *Bhagavaan* finds their numbers inestimable.

   2.3 Pay close attention to me now as I am about to describe to you the nature of the class of *Jeevaatmaas* which amongst the three aforementioned ones above is known as *"baddha"*. The scripture (*saastra*) describes these souls as being mired in the mortal experience of "***punnya***m" and "***paapam***" (where *"punnya"* are <u>rewards of happiness</u> resulting from the good deeds and *"paapa"* are the <u>retribution of sufferings</u> that result from all evil or unnatural deeds done). These *jeevaatmas* generally experience sufferings (*dukkha*) much more, in fact, than they experience happiness (*sukha*). They experience also states of limbo where there is neither.

2.4 It is thus that all beings in the universe --- beginning with the divinities such as *Brahma-deva* (the primordial Creator), *Shiva (cosmic Destroyer), Indra, Suryan, Chandran,* the "three-hundred-thirty- three million" *Devas, Asuras, Raakshasaas, Maharishis* as well as *Humans*; and similarly, earthly creatures too such as the house-fly, ant, insect, mosquito, worm, and furthermore, countless number of invisible micro-organisms; flora and fauna, plants, creepers and other botanical creations etc. too -- all possessing mortal bodies – all these do experience both happiness and sufferings, existential rewards and retribution alternately... They are all collectively said to be "*baddha*" souls by the scriptures.

2.5 Let me next tell you about who the "*muktha jeevaatmaa-s*" are. It is imperative that we get to know about them and understand them well since it is in emulating them that we too can seek and attain everlasting happiness. So please pay careful attention to this matter which the *saastra-s* have elaborated upon clearly.

2.6 Amongst the population of souls that remain in earthly bondage -- chained as it were to their existential condition by the iron-shackles of "*punnya*" and "*paapa*" and of temporal happiness and sufferings -- there are also some "*jeevaatmas*" who by dint of their own virtuous efforts manage to break free from the oppressive tyranny of both "*paapa*" and "*punnya*". They do so either by earning the Grace of God directly, or else through divine redemption. Thereby, eventually, they secure a place for themselves in the abode of *Bhagavaan* called **Sri Vaikuntam** where they enjoy everlasting happiness. Their relentless efforts first begin with an inner awareness of their pathetic condition of earthly bondage and suffering; then being taken hold of a deep desire to escape from the despair such bondage causes they go about seeking lessons and illumination from men of deep wisdom. They then transition to a plane of existence called "*moksham*", which they are fully convinced is the sole means of attaining and enjoying everlasting Happiness. Thereafter, their efforts continue forth until they attain true knowledge itself --- i.e., the *"tattva"*, the doctrine which reveals that in the age of Kali, the road to everlasting happiness indeed lies nowhere else than in the path shown by Sri Krishna's proclamation **"*maamekam sharanam vraja, aham tvaa sarva paapebhyo moksha-ishyaami*"** *("There is a way leading to "moksham" and you can be certain of travelling to it if you renounce everything else and surrender yourself unto Me...").* That knowledge of the *"tattva"* is gained and experienced when the seeker approaches a *"sadhaachaarya"* – a guru or preceptor – and faithfully follows his guidance and precepts right along the pathway of *"saranaagathi"*. Finally, either with the aid of the guru or else through his intercession, the seeker's efforts all culminate in earning *Bhagavaan's* everlasting grace and Happiness.

2.7 So far, out of the three classes of *"jeevaatmas"* mentioned, I have explained the nature of two of them, the *"baddha"* and *"muktha"*. Now, let me proceed to explain the nature of the last of the three *"jeevaatmas"* known as *"nithya-suri"*. Please pay keen attention.

2.8 As explained above, because of their innumerable *"paapam"*, souls floundering about in mortal bondage (*baddha*) to earthly birth and death remain imprisoned there under decree of the divine order of the *"paramaathma"*. This is revealed by the scripture in the expression: *"pasavah: paasitaah: poorvamparamena svaleelalayaa"* ....

2.9 Then there are souls (*muktha-s*) that having redeemed themselves from their *"paapam"*, and having received absolution and the pardon of *Bhagavaan*, are able to free themselves from the jail of mortal coils and return to their true home in the abode of *Bhagavaan* in *Sri Vaikuntam* where they enjoy everlasting happiness.

2.10 Souls that are *"nitya-suris"* however are *"jeevaatmas"* that are sinless and ever free of even a tiny taint of *"paapam"*. They are also souls that have been subjected to neither the perils of mortal birth nor death, nor have they ever had to endure any earthly or temporal ordeal. These souls also enjoy a state of being that is verily an imitation in God's own image. As the scriptural expression reveals, *"savayasa iva yay nithya nirdosha gandhaah:"* in such a state of pristine imitation of the Almighty, they closely resemble him and his qualities in many respects. The imitative aspect of *"nithyasuris"* can be understood through analogy – of how in a group of friends flocking together as *"birds of a feather"* one might broadly resemble each other in age, physical looks, pedigree, manners and social status.

2.11 These *"nithya-suris"* are thus absolutely blemish less souls who congregate at all times around the divine Lord Almighty *Bhagavaan* and who share with him, *and in him*, his own eternal beatitudes. In the assembly of such glorious *"nithya-suris"* are to be found the pantheon of other gods and goddesses such as *Bhoomi-Devi* (mother Earth), *Neela-Devi* (the youngest consort of *Bhagavaan*), *Adi Seshan* (the divine serpent-bed of *bhagavaan*), *Garudan* (the divine avian vehicle of *bhagavaan*), *Vishvaksena* (the celestial commander-in-chief of the divine legionaries of *bhagavaan*), *Dvaarapaalaas* (the guardian gate-keepers of the heavenly realms), *Parichaarakaas* (the corps of divine courtiers), *Sevars* (the corps of divine servitors), *Ganaapathis* (heavenly goblins), *Sainnyaas* (the corps of divine infantry), *Apsaraas* (heavenly nymphs), avian flocks of divine nature such as the *Hamsa* (swans), pride of divine lions (*Simham*) and a host of other celestial beings. Collectively, they all constitute the community of *"jeevaatmas"* known as *"nithya-suris"*. For an even more exhaustive description of these *"nithya-suris"*, you may all please read (Sri Raamaanuja's work of poetic mysticism in Sanskrit), the **"Sri Vaikunta Gadyam.** If you memorize the *"mantras"* that are chanted while There is a daily Vedic rite to be performed daily, called *"aadhaara-shakti tarpanam"*. If you memorize the mantras that are to be chanted in that rite, you will never forget the names and natures of these exalted *"nithya-suris"*.

3. We must now proceed to examine three more specific concepts (of Sri Ramanuja's Philosophy). They are **"prakruthi"**, **"kaalam"** and **"suddha-sattvam"**.

   3.1 First, let me explain what is meant by *"prakruthi"*. That ontological entity that is cause of all elements of nature to be created and from which they emanate too viz. *Space, Fire, Wind, Water and Earth* is called *"prakruthi"*.

   3.2 Milk, curd, butter, ghee etc. are all mere derivatives of a single substance, aren't they? Do you know that substance? Let me tell you. It is nothing but grass or hay upon which cows feed and they are verily the origin of all dairy products like milk etc. Likewise, that from which the natural elements, *Spatial Ether, Fire, Water, Earth* and *Wind* all emanate is called *Prakruthi*.

   3.3 Let me tell you a bit more about *Prakruthi* …. Listen with rapt attention please.

   3.4 Everything that exists in the universe, right from the high heavenly realms of *"brahmaloka"* down to our lowest terrestrial domains, without any exceptions, all become extinct at a certain point in time. During that time of cosmic dissolution, there exist an infinite number of souls which are yet to attain *"moksha"*. The souls attach themselves to a primordial ontological substance just as one might imagine tiny particles of gold-dust fastening to a big ball of molten wax. That primordial substance, *moola-prakruthi* that is thus admixed with such an assortment of all unredeemed soulful entities is known as **"Tamas"**. *Tamas*, while remaining bereft of association with unredeemed souls (*baddha jeevaatmaa*-s), is known as *"prakruthi"*.

   3.5 From one part of *"prakruthi"* is caused an entity called *Mahat*. From *Mahat* gets created an entity called *"Ahankaaram"* or the Ego (i.e., the primordial sense of "**I-ness**"). It is from the Ego that are then caused the physical and facultative human sense organs (eyes/ sight, ears/hearing, nose/smell etc. and the mind) which are eleven in number.

3.6 From another part of *"prakruthi"* emerges – in the way as we all know fresh curd emerges from milk in fermentation -- an entity which in its nascent state is called *"aakaasa"* or Spatial Ether. From the *nascent state of Ether* emerges another state that is *evolved Ether*. From the evolved ethereal state then emerges *nascent natural element*, Wind (*vaayu*), and from which, in turn, emerges the *evolved element* of Wind... And from there, again similarly emerges *nascent and evolved* Fire (*agni*), *nascent* Water and *evolved* Water (*jala*), *nascent* Earth and *evolved* Earth (*prithvi*).

3.7 It is through such cosmic process of successive *creation and evolution* of the natural elements that *Bhagavaan* causes the *twenty-four different "tattva-s" or "realities"* to emerge and constitute the substrata of all existence in the universe.

3.8 It is from the substratum of the primordial 24 *"tattvas'* that every *"jeevaatmaa"* (*baddha*) comes into being once again in Creation. In both form and character, the soul acquires the earthy incarnation it deserves by dint of its own unredeemed past deeds viz. its own legacy of an accumulated, unexhausted karmic stock of both *"paapa"* and *"punnya"*: evil and good deeds. *Bhagavaan* himself thus inheres into all bodily forms and remains universally immanent within all souls, as their sole protector.

4. Next, let me explain the metaphysical entity called *"suddha sattvam"* which you must all try to understand by exerting your intellects a bit.

4.1 The entity called *"prakruti"* that has been explained above comprises three fundamental spiritual essences or qualities called *"guNa"*. There are 3 such primordial *"gunas"*: **Sattva, Rajas** and **Tamas**. The ontological entity called *"suddha-sattva"* is that which is entirely devoid of both *"rajas"* and *"tamas"* and is replete with the *"sattva guna"* alone. That is precisely why this entity has come to be termed *"suddha sattva"* – the spiritual-essence that is absolutely pristine.

4.2 Every being or thing that exists in *Sri Vaikuntam* (the abode of *Bhagavaan*) is made up of this very same absolutely pristine spiritual-substance called *"suddha-sattva"*. In other words, all heavenly beings such as *nithya-suri-s, jeevaatmaa-s* that have attained liberation (*mukthi*), *Bhagavaan* himself, as well as all heavenly establishments such as the towers, ramparts, mansions, hallways and all manner of heavenly structures there –all those are constituted wholly and solely by this supra-ethereal *"suddha-sattvam"*.

5. Next, let me proceed to explain yet another metaphysical reality, *"kaala"* or Time. Time is apprehended by us in terms of its conceptual divisions such as *seconds, minutes, hour ("muhurtham"), day, night, fortnight, month, season, solstice ("ayanam"), year* and so on and so forth.

   5.1 No part of what is the primordial substance called *"moola-prakruthi"* is to be found in the realm of *Sri Vaikuntam* which is pervaded wholly and solely by *"suddha-sattva"* alone. Conversely, the supra-ethereal substance called *"suddha-sattva"*, which is verily the warp-and-woof of the heavenly realm of *Sri Vaikuntam*, is never to be found in the terrestrial worlds.

   5.2 However, Time, in its ontological form called *"kaala"*, prevails both in the terrestrial worlds as well as in *Sri Vaikuntam*.

6. All that I have explained through metaphysical concepts so far, you ought to be able to grasp and absorb clearly and fully. On the basis of what thus far has been explained, there are a few more related ideas you all ought to know which the *"saastra-s"* have enunciated and about which I now expatiate below.

7. Outside those universal realms pervaded entirely by *"suddha-sattva"* do lie the realms where it is *"prakruthi"* that is all pervasive. And *vice versa*, wherever in the cosmic spaces *"prakruthi"* does not pervade, there it is *"suddha-sattva"* that is all-pervasive.

   7.1 Of the three different classes of souls, we spoke about, it is the *"muktha-aatma-s"* and *"nithya-suri-s"* alone who dwell in *Sri Vaikuntam* in everlasting bliss in the divine presence of *Bhagavaan Srimann Naaraayana*. They never have to suffer the fate that befalls the mortal souls on earth and are perennially subject to a cycle of mundane birth and death, creation and dissolution.

7.2 As "*baddha jeevaatmaas*", or souls in earthly bondage, we of course always have the opportunity, through surrender unto *Bhagavaan*, to rid ourselves of all sin (*paapam*) and join the great celestial assembly of "*nitya-suri-s*" and "*mukthaatma-s*" in *Sri Vaikuntam* and enjoy there equally with them the same heavenly bliss that they do.

7.3 A very rare one amongst those "*baddha jeeva-s*", after having undergone several millions of lives on earth and faithfully worshipped *Bhagavaan*, finally earns the reward of being anointed by the Almighty as **Brahmma, the Creator**, who then carries out the cosmic function of creating everything in the universe in accordance with *Bhagavaan's* own will and command.

7.4 Similarly, a very rare one amongst the "*baddhaa-s*", after having performed innumerable sacrificial rites ("*yagnya*") in millions of lives undergone on earth, finally earns the reward of being anointed as "***deva-devan***" (**Mahadeva**), who then carries out the cosmic function of destruction (*samhaaram*), again in accordance with *Bhagavaan's* own will and command. That deity is called "*parama shiva*".

7.5 Again, in similar fashion, one amongst the "*baddhaa-s*", after having performed a hundred "*ashwamedha yagnya-s*" (the formidable Vedic "*Horse-Sacrifice*"), gets anointed as **Indra,** the celestial Lord of the Three Worlds (*Earth, Celestial* and the *Heavenly* ones).

7.6 Furthermore, there are other "*baddha jeevaatmaa-s*" who gain the reward of ascending to the lower-order heavenly paradise of "*svarga*", "*devaloka*" and "*brahmaloka*" and remaining denizens there. There are other "*baddhaa-s*" who gain the heavenly '*svarga*' as reward for their having faithfully performed several sacrificial rites of "*yagnya*" on earth; but after having enjoyed briefly the joys of paradise, and upon exhausting their heavenly tenure there, they return to terrestrial bondage again, taking bodily forms in accordance with their respective pre-existing residual stock of "*paapam/punnyam*".

7.7 Then there are other "*baddha-jeevaatmaa-s*" on earth who continue performing severe penance and austerities as "*tapas*". They are renowned as the great "*rishi-s*" or seers of the world --- such as the sages *Vasishta, Paraashara, Vyaasa, Suka et al.*

7.8 There are other "*baddhaa-s*" too on earth who, in dogged pursuit of salvation, are engaged in the practice of arduous "*bhakthi-yoga*" – the path of devotion towards God.

7.9 Some "*badddhaa-s*" after performing "*saranaagathi*", and absolutely surrendering their selves unto *Bhagavaan*, they await the end of their lives on earth when they are able to attain salvation.

8. There are souls on earth who are disbelievers in God, scripture or the wisdom of the ancestors or sages and live their lives in willful self-conceit. They find themselves heading towards hell (*Naraka*).

   8.1 Then again, there are some "*baddhaa-s*" who despite being guilty of living a life of sin, however, repent for it in time. They then turn a new leaf, and repose their faith in the sage counsel of wise preceptors. They expiate their sins (*praayachittam*) and thereafter strive for a life of virtue.

   8.2 There are also souls that live their youthful days in wicked ways, but later realizing that their mundane existence on earth is evanescent, and fearing the unknown fate that awaits their souls in the after-world, they quickly mend their ways, turn God-fearing and carry on in life performing at least a modicum of good deeds such as "*sandhyaavandanam*" etc.

   8.3 There are some souls here on earth who perform "*saranaagathi*" (self-surrender unto *Bhagavaan*) as a matter of hedging against chance… They tell themselves, "*If the "saastra" happens to be true about "saranaagathi" and if "saranaagathi"* too happens to be a true pathway to salvation, why not perform it and play safe?' That is the attitude of such *"baddhaa*-s" (<u>Translator's note</u>: This attitude is redolent of the famous *"Pascal's Wager"* that the 17th century CE French philosopher, Blaise Pascal wrote about).

8.4 A few *"baddhaa*-s" think to themselves: *It is commonly seen that through the chant of specific powerful mantras, it is quite possible to remove the deadly toxins injected by scorpion or snake bites. Why then should it not be also possible to remove the toxins of sin that infest my soul through duly performing "saranaagathi" unto the Almighty?* Thinking thus such souls whole-heartedly surrender at the feet of our Lord Sri Lakshminarasimhan. Some others similarly perform *"saranaagathi"* to the Deities at *Sri Rangam, Kanchipuram* or *Tirumala* and live out their time faithfully abiding by the tenets of their faith as laid down by their respective venerable Acharyas.

8.5 Those souls that perform *"saranaagathi"* with absolute faith do finally realize *"moksham"* at the end of their mortal existence on earth and attain the bliss promised by *Bhagavaan*. Those who perform it however without absolute faith and rather who only perfunctorily do so, they too attain salvation even if not in their current lifetime at least eventually in some future life when their faith evolves sufficiently to absolutely abide in the doctrine of *"saranaagathi"*. Their efforts in earlier lifetimes are never wasted.

9. *Bhagavaan* is all-pervasive, and as the *saastra* has revealed in the expression: *"antar bahischa tat sarvam vyaapya naaraayaana stithah:"* he inheres in all things and all beings in the world --- i.e., within all the three classes of *"jeevaatmaa*-s", within *"prakruthi"*, *"suddha-sattva"* and *"kaala"*.

9.1 Having inhered himself into all beings, *Bhagavaan* makes them all function according to his own will and for his own purpose. Therefore, all things existent in the universe serve and function only as a bodily instrument of *Bhagavaan*. This is what has been attested to by scriptural authority found in the Vedantic Upanishad: *"yasya atmaa sareeram, yasya prithivee sareeram".*

10. Thus, to sum up, Goddess Lakshmi and Srimann Naaraayana are *"paramaathma-*s". Countless are the number of *Baddha, Muktha* and *Nithya jeevaatmaa-*s. Countless too are the mortal entities within *Prakruthi* which serve and function as bodily instruments for the *Baddhaa-*s of the world; the very same purpose and function for *Bhagavaan's* consort, Lakshmi, and for all the *Nithya-suri-s* too is served by the entity called *Suddha-Sattvam*. Finally, there is *Kaala*, or Eternal Time, which too serves the Divine purpose that constitutes setting out, every now and then, but across the endless horizon of time, the best and most auspicious moments for Man to perform duties that advance and promote his spiritual evolution through *"yagnya"* (great sacrificial rites), to faithfully perform daily and preordained obligations to the gods such as *"sandhyaavandanam"* etc., *"bhagavath tiruvaaradanam"* (personal and household worship of God) and to conduct other such sacramental deeds.

10.1 Thus, the five 5 primordial ontological entities of *jeevaatma-*s, *paramaatmaa, prakruthi, kaalam, suddha-sattvam* are all eternally existent realities. The consciousness of all *jeevaatmaa-*s i.e., that *"gnyaana"* which is an inseparable part of them …. That *gnyaana* too is eternally existent reality. All other existent beings and entities in the universe undergo endless change and seeming flux in terms of *creation, dissolution, mutations of form, shape* and *name*. For instance, both *darkness* and *smokiness* are merely different forms of the same reality or *"prakruti"* but given different names; *Smoke* possesses the quality of smell or aroma; while, *Darkness (tamas)* possesses the attribute of deep blue color.

With deep understanding of all the above concepts and tenets of our *"siddhaantham"* (i.e., Sri Ramanuja's philosophy), it is possible to attain the eternal bliss of *Sri Vaikuntam*, the eternal abode of *Srimann Naaraayana* through duly performing *"saranaagathi"* unto him and releasing ourselves thereby from the bondage of mortal coils called *"prakruthi"*.

It is to protect and redeem those souls that have surrendered unto him that, indeed, the Almighty of *Sri Vaikuntam*, from time to time, appears in various avatars in the mortal realms as Rama or Krishna. This is attested by the scripture as *"yadaa yadaa hi dharmasya glaanir bhavathi…"* (Bhagavath Gita). For the sake of all of us that are not privileged to live during the time of such avatars, Bhagavaan out of infinite compassion for us, inheres into his iconic images in sacred spots on earth such as **Sri Rangam** and other ***"divya-desam-s"***. On our part, by visiting and worshipping at the sanctum in such spots, we are enabled to earn his grace. Our great **Lord Lakshminarasimha** shows us, in fact, even more compassion in that he saves us the trouble of even journeying all the way to the *"divya-desam-s"*: His iconic form is ever ready to be conducted in joyous and ceremonial procession into our very own homesteads where we can all individually beseech him to grant us the infinite bliss of his eternal grace.

***

-2-
Sri Nigamantha Mahadesikan's "*Paramatha Bhangam*"

Synopsis: *The postulates, premises and principles of Visishtadvaita Philosophy as propounded and established by Sri Ramanujacharya differ variously from those of fifteen other schools of thought in the Vedantic tradition as well as in the heterodoxic and heretical systems of thought such as Buddhism and Jainism. In a famous treatise titled "**Paramatha Bhangam**" written by Sri Vedanta Desika, the relative merits of "**ramanuja siddhaantam**" compared with the demerits and deficiencies of the other schools of philosophy were masterfully elucidated. This epistle of Mukkur Swamy summarizes the salience of the treatise.*

The *siddhaanta* (philosophical system) of **Visishtadvaita** that Sri Ramanujacharya first propounded and then established came to be later further elaborated and lucidly expatiated upon by **Srimann Nigamantha Mahadesikan** in many of his scholarly works. One such treatise, the "***PARAMATHA-BHANGAM***" (written in *Manipravaalam* dialect), he wrote mainly for the benefit of posterity and to explain to it the salient features of other rival, heretical and heterodoxic schools of thought, thus ensuring it would not fall prey to them by either getting enchanted or led astray by their specious allure and ideas. There are 15 such heretical philosophies that he enumerated in the treatise and they are:

1. "*lokaayatheeya*"
2. "*Madhyamika*"
3. "*yogaachaara*"
4. "*sowthaanthreeka*"

5. *"vaibhaashika"*
6. *"pracchanna-bowtha"*
7. *"jaina"*
8. *"bhaaskara"*
9. *"vyaakarana"*
10. *"vaiseshika"*
11. *"naiyyaayika"*
12. *"neereeswara-meemaamsaka"*
13. *"saankhya"*
14. *"yoga-siddhaanta"*
15. *"paasupatha"*

Let me now briefly describe the essential tenets of each of the above philosophies *in seriatim*:

1. *"lokaayatheeya":* Reality is that alone which is perceptible to the human eye. The Body is verily the Soul. There is nothing that differentiates the Body from Soul. There is no other plane of existence anywhere other than that of this world. All that is experienced as Pleasure in this world verily constitutes what may be regarded as Heaven or Paradise (*svargam*); and similarly, whatever is experienced as pain or sorrow here in this world verily constitutes Hell (*narakam*); there is no other separate place called Hell. When this worldly experience of both bodily Pleasure and Pain/Sorrow finally ceases, then that state in itself verily constitutes Salvation (*moksham*). Those who are powerful enough to be able to rule over this world are to be regarded as Gods. There is no God other than them. The Body is nothing but an organism that gets formed when the elements such as the *Earth*, *Water*, *Fire* and *Wind* happen to combine; and it is out of such a combination that Intelligence and self-awareness (*buddhi*) is created. It is with such combination that the Body-Soul complex is enabled to proceed to act in and through life.

   This philosophy is said to have been imparted by *Brahmaa* (the Creator) to a daemon (*asura*) named **Virochana,** who in turn propagated it to all his race and progeny. That is how this philosophy of the *Asuraas* began spreading as a gospel amongst themselves and all of their kind too in the rest of the world.

2. ***"maadhyameeka"***: The central tenet of this school of philosophy is stated by its adherents as follows: **Buddha** is our preceptor. We consider him omniscient. Everything he spoke is Truth. We faithfully follow whatever he taught us to believe. What he told us, principally, is this: *"All this world is an illusion and so is the world beyond. It is futile to go seeking heaven (svarga) and salvation (moksha), since such things do not exist. Thus did our preceptor teach us"*, Buddha's followers say.

3. Next, the main tenet of the school of the ***"yogaachaara"*** philosophy is this*:*

"This world as Matter does not exist as Reality, and neither does any world beyond this one here and now. However, there does exist one reality which cannot be denied and it lies in the expression *"idam aham gnyaanaami"* (Sanskrit), *"idhai naan arigirane"* (Tamizh) or, *"This I am able to know or apprehend"*. This Cognition alone is Reality and it is a proposition that is tenable here is why: We say that it is by virtue of Cognition alone that **"I"** becomes Subject and **"This"** becomes Object. * (**Translator's note*: And this is, in fact, precursor to the cognitive paradigm of Descartes's *"cogito ergo sum"* i.e. *"**I know, therefore I am**"*).

Cognition, therefore, by itself verily constitutes what is known as *"aatma"*, the individual soul. This soul now exists as reality in one moment and in the very next moment, instantly, it ceases to be real. It thus goes from *Being onto Un-Being* in an endless cycle of *coming into existence* and *going out of existence*. Under the circumstances, only that which is perceptible to the eye in the very moment of instant perception can be said to be real; even such perceptive cognition is gained only through an element of inference (*anumaana*). Everything else lying outside the moment of such momentary cognition must therefore be unreal and non-existent – akin to whatever appears to exist in a dream but which really has no existence or reality outside the dream.

Such then is the belief of the followers of this school of philosophy.

4. **"sowthraantheeka"**: The fundamentals of this philosophy are: External reality or Matter is comprised of both perceptible and imperceptible particles (*padaarthangal*). It is not possible to cognize all Matter through perceptive faculties alone; and, since they are composed of countless monadic particles, they can, instead, be apprehended only through inferential cognition. The particles themselves undergo countless cycles of existence and non-existence and, hence, what may be either perceived or inferred about them can be momentary only and through a stream of consciousness. Eventually, the cognitive stream (*gnyaana*) too ceases. Cessation of '*gnyaana*' means absolute Void or Non-Being. Thus, it is Non-Being, or Nullity, which, verily, is *"moksha"* or Salvation. In other words, the central tenet of the followers of this school of thought is that Reality is a Void but cognition of what is only apparent reality is induced by *"brahmai"* – a hallucinatory projection of the senses.

5. **"vaibhaashika"** in a nutshell is this: Matter is reality but Cognition (*gnyaana*) itself is *Atma*, the Soul. Without *gnyaana*, there is no soul. All Matter exists one moment and ceases to exist the next moment. While the cause of all Matter is an atomic substratum (*parama-anu*), such substratum too undergoes constant change of existential condition i.e., it exists one moment but ceases to exist in another. There is indeed no other ontological reality other than this and a super-reality called *Isvara* does not exist. The absolute dissolution of Matter (and the consequent absolute negation of Cognition that ensues) alone may be held to be *Moksha*.

6. **"pracchanna-bowtha"**: the gist of this philosophy (which is antithesis of the aforesaid school of thought of Buddha) may be stated as follows: That proposition that all Matter is nothing but hallucinatory reality is accepted. Nonetheless, it is also to be acknowledged that despite being hallucinatory in nature, a rope, by analogy, still is seen to be as real as a serpent. Likewise, all inert matter as well as sentient beings too possess a semblance to the substrate of a reality. However, that reality is not apprehended by us through our own power of reasoning or

cognition (*buddhi*) alone. It can be apprehended only with the aid of what the Vedas reveal to us about it viz.:

Brahman that by its very nature is Pure Knowledge (*gnyaana-mayam*) is to be cognized as a being without any attributes. It is "*nirgunam*"; it is eternal; it is all-pervading; there is no other being similar to it. The reality of this Brahman however is veiled or shrouded by a timeless accompaniment called Ignorance or *Avidya*. It is *Avidya* thus which, in effect, produces the hallucinatory world of countless individual souls, of Matter, of the seas, the mountains and gods, and makes them all appear as though they were real, as if they are true ... as in "*tat satyam*".

Whereas, what is real, and the sole absolute reality, is Brahman alone and nothing else i.e., "*gnyaatha*", "*gneyam*" and "*gnyaanam*" (the *knower*, the *object of knowledge*, and the *knowledge* itself), all three are themselves revealed by the Vedas to be mere hallucination. This is what is asserted by the followers of this school of philosophy.

The unreal individual soul, the "*jivaatma*", through ceaseless contemplation upon its own unreal and non-existent nature, as well as about the unreal world of matter, can eventually rid itself of the veil of *Avidya* through *dhyaanam*.

Just as realization finally dawns upon one that the serpent is mere apparition and it is only the rope which is real and the truth, through "*dhyaanam*" is born "*gnyaana kann*" (the eye of realization) or the enlightenment of the self -- "*aham brahmaasmi*" – through which the unreal soul finally wakes up to the fact *"that my reality is not different from that of Brahman which alone is true reality, and therefore, I too am that Brahman alone and really nothing else"*. That "*gnyaana*" itself is what constitutes '*moksham*' or Salvation.

To say, however, that the individual soul in that state of "*moksha*" also separately experiences the Bliss of Brahman in some other separate plane of reality called **Vaikuntam** is false.

This philosophical position is what is called **Advaita** and its followers interpret the revealed truths of Vedanta metaphysics in this way.

7. *"jaina":* There lived one by the name of *Jeener* (i.e., **Mahaaveer**) who, like the Buddha, was greatly revered by his followers as being wise and omniscient. He propagated a system of belief whose important tenets can be summarized in the following way:

   Jeevaatma, individual souls, are all real. In accordance with their respective past deeds of virtue and sin (i.e., *punnya, paapa*), they take innumerable bodily forms in this world and therewith live or exist by alternately growing and dissolving in an endless cycle of birth and rebirth.

   The adherents of this philosophy abjure all forms of rituals and *"yaagaas"* since they believe it only involves needless violence (*himsa*) to many creatures and animals.

   This school is atheistic.

   It considers *"moksha"* to be a state of bodiless-ness, i.e., the state when the Body is completely rid of all its condition of *"punnya-paapa"*, that state is held to be salvation. To be able to rid the Body of its condition of *"punnya"* and *"paapa"*, this school of philosophy prescribed for its followers a method of penance or *"tapas"* that involved going into deep seclusion and beginning to meditate upon oneself by incessant chanting of the mantra, *"parama sukham, parama sukham"* ("Supreme Bliss! Supreme Bliss!"). While endlessly chanting that way, the meditator proceeds to deliberately pluck, one by one, every strand of hair upon his scalp by its root! And thus, by the time that the last strand of hair standing upon his head has been uprooted, all of the *'punnya'* and *'paapa'* of the meditator, along with the Body too, all get entirely extinguished through the penance. Once thus extinguished, the Body does not ever return to the world to retake any other bodily form, and such a state of ultimate bodiless-ness is what constitutes *"moksha"*. Thus, say his followers, has their preceptor, the *Jeener* spoken about *"moksha"* which is an utterly bliss-less state. (<u>*Translator's note*</u>: here the *"hair plucking"* is not to be taken too literally; it is only a form of analogy meant to convey the idea that the path to salvation in Jainism is an extremely long, hard and arduous one).

8. *"bhaaskara":* There is only one Reality and that is Brahman alone. It is omnipotent. It is self-illumined. It is *"sath"* or the Truth lying latent in the Word itself (i.e., the *Logos*). This Brahman is the substrate or source for all sentient and insentient beings. As gold in ore form transforms into other forms such as a golden ring etc. so does this Brahman manifest itself in sentient forms such as *'jeevaatma'*. Just as plain, misshapen clay transforms into the form of clay pot, so too does this Brahman transform into inert, insentient Matter (*prakkruti*) and which, in turn, then transforms into a variety of bodily forms, each as suited and appropriate to the purpose of each sentient-being.

   The adherents of this philosophy hold that even sensory faculties such as Speech (*vaak*) and physical faculties, such as limbs, are thus creations of Brahman and are dissolved by it too.

   It can, however, never be known when such creation and dissolution of sentient beings (*jeeva*) and insentient matter (*prakkruti*) originated since *jeevaas* have no beginning (*anaadi*). In course of time however, when *jeevaatma*-s come to realize that *"I am of the nature of Brahman but have been transfigured into a 'jeeva' and now having undergone all manner of grief and infirmities without cease, I continue to undergo repeatedly the same condition furthermore"*.

   After countless rebirths then, however, comes a time, when the *Jeeva*, at last, attains the realization of the truth *"That Brahman, I am that myself!"* (*"Brahma-bhaavam"*). And having attained such realization of *Brahma-bhaavam*, there is never any return to the state of mere *"jeevaatma"* again anymore. And that, according to the followers of this school of thought, is what constitutes *"moksham"*.

9. *"vyaakarana":* The followers of this school posit the existence of *"sabda brahmam"* ... i.e., a *Primordial Sound* from which all that exists in the universe is emanated. They call this primordial sound *"sphotam"*.

   They put forward the proposition that just as sound emanates when the two palms of the hand are clapped, so do the movements of the entire universe produce sounds which all emanate from the one primordial sound called *"sphotam"*.

All of the heavens and earth, in their view, are enveloped by "*sabda*", the humming of the universe, as it were, and all such sounds are but echoes of the one Primordial Sound, the "*sphota*", which verily is the Brahman that can be realized. This philosophy belongs to the school called "*maayaavaada*".

10. "vaiseshika": In this school of philosophy, it is accepted that *Isvara* (or *Brahman*) exists; He is omniscient, and it is He who has created the entire and vast universe. The reality of that Brahman need not necessarily be known only with the aid of the Vedas. Even by proper inference (*anumaanam*), the followers of *Vaiseshika* aver, it can be realized that since none amongst *jeevaatma*-s is able to cause such universal creation, there must necessarily therefore exist one Being who is much superior to every other being.

It is accepted by these followers, that the Vedas spring from *Isvara* alone and therefore it is infallible. Thus, they (proceed to take the words and meaning of the Vedas itself to) claim the context for the truth they espouse as follows:

Jeevaas, monadic souls, exist in countless numbers in the universe; each of them possesses the potential to assume huge bodily forms (*vibhu*) but by themselves they possess no intelligence (*arivu*); but when they take birth, together with the body, they come to possess intelligence too. Then, in time, the body perishes and along with it, intelligence too. What remains in the end is mere, inert matter... nothing more to it... and there is neither any joy nor sorrow to be had here. Such is the belief system of *Vaiseshika*.

11. "naiyyaayika": While Sage Vyaasa expounded the **principles** of Vedanta philosophy in his great work (the **Brahma Sutra**) of aphorisms, beginning with "*athaatho brahma jignyaasa:*" and concluding with "*anaavrutthi: sabthaat*", likewise, Sage Gautama too expounded the **dialectics** of Vedanta through his work of aphorisms which is the basis of this school of thought.

According to this school, *Isvara* is Reality, and He is the efficient Cause (*nimittakaaranam*) of the entire universe of existence and the giver of the Vedas.

Jeevaatma-s, atomic souls are infinite in number but possess no intelligence (*arivu*) or self-awareness. They pervade all of space just as ether (*aakaasa*) does. They are eternally existent. Due to their respective deeds of "*karma*", they come to incarnate various bodily forms in the world, including the human form; and when that happens, the souls beget intelligence and they become self-aware too. The experience of both joy and sorrow (*sukha-dukha*) of existence then ensues.

These embodied souls obtain their form by the mere combinations and permutations of various pre-existent natural elements and forces such as ether (*aakaasa*), earth (*pruthvi*), water (*jalam*), energy (*tejas*), wind (*vaayu*) etc. An entity or separate principle known as Matter (*prakkruthi*) does not exist. When, finally, a soul attains the state of "*moksham*" (salvation), the knowledge (*gnyaana*) it obtained previously is lost forever in cosmic dissolution. What remains of the soul then is plain, inert, rock-like (*paashaanam*) barren-ness, devoid of all qualities such as joy, sorrow and the like.

Nyaaya philosophy, despite being a branch of Vedanta, nevertheless contains many tenets that patently contradict the Vedas and that is why Sage Vyaasa himself characterized it as being "*tarkka-prathistaanaadapi*:

'தர்க்காப்ர திஷ்டாநாதபி'

He rejected it as a school of thought based on dialectical sophistry.

12. **"neereeswara-meemaamsaka":** This philosophy can be summed up as follows:

God does not exist, nor do any demigods and even if they did, they possess no personification. Thus, they cannot grant any kind of blessings or benefits to anybody.

However, this school believes that the various sacrifices, rituals and sacraments prescribed in the Vedas ought to be scrupulously performed without fail so as to remove all taint of human sin, and by which *jeevaatma*-s become wholly deserving of, and are able to reap, the rewards of heavenly bliss and enjoyment (*svargaanubhavam*). The heavenly realm (svargam) is here conceived as a lush, verdant, sylvan and beautiful idyllic place (like the *Nilagiri* valleys on earth!). Such is the philosophical outlook of these "*meemaamsaka-s*".

13. **"*neereswara-saankhya*":** The main tenets of this school of philosophy are these:

    The Vedas are eternally self-existent. On the question whether there exists an Almighty God (*kadavuL*), *Saankhya* is silent.

    Jeevaatma-s (monadic souls) exist in infinite numbers.

    There does exist an ontological principle known as Matter (*prakkruthi*) and it is the cause for *jeevaatma*-s taking bodily and manifest forms. In that sense, it is insentient Matter (*prakkruthi*) that is efficient and immanent cause for all existent entities.

    Matter when associated with *jeevaatma* gains by itself intelligence and self-awareness (*arivu*) too and thereby experience everything through agency.

    All 'jeevaatma-s" are of "*vibhu*" form (i.e., all-pervasive in size) but they possess no intrinsic attributes of any kind. If a *jeevaatma* contemplates constantly upon these truths about the immanence of Matter (*prakkruti*), it can rid itself of its bodily form and manifestation and, thereby, attain the experience of "*moksha*". There is nothing else to experience.

14. **"*Yoga-siddhaanta*":** Here is a gist of this school of philosophy: This "*siddhaantham*" was first propounded and propagated by the four-faced son of Almighty *Srimann Naaraayana*, **Brahmaa**.

    Naaraayana, the Omnipotent One, exists as supreme reality. He is to be known as the **Efficient Cause** (*nimitta kaarana*) of all Creation but he is not its **Material Cause** (*upaadaana kaarana*).

    The way to attain *Srimann Naaraayana* through the path of *Bhakthi* (i.e., *bhakthi-yoga*) is ineffective. There is another way to attain "*moksha*" which is our way and in it, salvation is gained when *jeevaatma* consummates the contemplation upon its very own true self and nature. There is no such similar experience to be gained through contemplation of Godhead. The four-faced

Brahmmaa, who it was that first propounded *Saankhya*, has spoken thus.

15. **"paasupatha":** This philosophy is said to have been propounded by **Lord Pasupathi**, a personification of god *"paramasivan"*. This *"paramasivan"* is a deity that is superior to even *Srimann Naaraayana* and is the true Efficient Cause of all Creation.

    Souls (*jeevaatma*-s) are monadic entities that exist in countless numbers. They are all able to attain *"moksha"* through constant contemplative worship of Shiva (*shivopaasana*) and having reached his abode, they too assume his own likeness in all respects, including that of being able to experience and enjoy the bliss that he enjoys himself (*sivabhogham*). It is Shiva alone, known as *"sadaashivan"*, from whom emanated all other gods such as *Vishnu, Brahmmaa, Indra* and others.

    Within this school of *Paasupatham*, there are four other sub-branches each with their own distinctive philosophical shades of thought. One of them upholds a certain discipline called *"sivadeekshai"*. Those who embrace and practice this discipline constitute a distinctively egalitarian community with no differences amongst themselves based on either caste, rank or birth status etc. According to this discipline, a *jeevaatma*, that is of atomic or monadic nature, upon attaining *"moksha"*, assumes a size and form that is of ethereal dimensions i.e., it attains cosmic immanence and pervasion much like the great formless one, Shiva himself, who, besides being all-pervasive and immanent, has really no personality other than that of being Pure Consciousness (*gnyaana-mayam*).

    After dissecting threadbare all the above schools of philosophy in his formidable treatise, our **Sri Nigamantha Mahadesikan** set out his conclusions as a comparative summation containing the quintessence of *Visishtaadvaita* Vedanta.

    Some of the philosophies adumbrated above clearly are opposed to the Vedas.

    While putting forth theories and speculations, that are both whimsical and fanciful in nature and construction, they have only tried to establish heresy as though it were an authentic system of thought. A few others amongst them, while accepting the authority of Vedic scriptural revelation, have postulated wholly erroneous interpretations of the same, only to suit their own theories and views. There are also a few amongst the above systems of philosophy that, even while following the orthodox schools – which posit *Srimann Naaraayana* as supreme deity to which all others are subordinate --nonetheless, at the same time, they also sanctify and glorify lesser god or demigods. They do so on the grounds that by propitiating them, through means prescribed in the Vedas as rituals and sacrifices (*karma*), those lesser gods confer great many earthly gains, material and even spiritual benefits upon souls -- quickly and very easily too.

It is for all the above reasons that it is possible, that with the passage of time, in this age and era of Kali Yuga, we will witness the mushrooming of many more philosophies, cults and false gods that would either befuddle and misguide or enthrall and captivate the minds of ordinary people (*saadhus*), but which, in fact, are only even more toxic and flawed in nature.

It in this context that we must view the treatise of **Sri Nigamantha Mahadesikan,** who after deep study and inquiry into the merits and demerits, into the inconsistencies and self-contradictions of each and every one of the philosophies or belief-systems he enumerated, was able to unravel, resolve and reconcile all the various disparate and dissonant viewpoints, fallacies and paradoxes that were inherent in them. This he accomplished based on the strength of sound and proven authoritative works, such as ***Sri Bhaashyam,*** which, propounded earlier by a long lineage of orthodox Achaaryas, sought to establish Veda and Vedanta on a firm and unassailable footing, now known to be **Visishtadvaita.**

16. In the illuminative treatise of his titled "***PARAMATHA BHANGAM***", Sri Nigamantha Mahadesikan has clearly, succinctly and comprehensively expatiated upon the profound verities of Visishtadvaita axioms, principles, concepts and reasoning for our own edification. They include: the nature of

paramaatma, the nature of *jeevaatma*, the nature of *Matter*, its cause and ontological adjuncts, the nature of *Time* and its adjuncts, the nature of divine and pure essence (*suddha-sattvam*) and how it defines and characterizes the plane of highest blissful existence known as *Sri Vaikuntam*, the relationship between *paramaatma* and *jeevaatma*, between body and soul, between sentient, insentient and *Isvara* principles, the doctrines of *bhakthi-yoga* and *prapatthi* as means of aspiring for and attaining "*mukthi*" or temporal liberation, the kinship between God and Devotee (*bhagavath-bhaagavatha sambandham*) through *Bhakthi*... etc.

All the above "*lakshanam*-s" --- fundamental tenets --- of *Visishtadvaita* have been lucidly set out in the great treatise of our **Acharya Sri Nigamantha Mahadesikan** which he has passed on to us as his compassionate legacy for posterity.

I have penned this epistle of mine (*arul mozhi*) in response to many of you known to me in the ordinary, day-to-day secular world (*loukeekam*), who had, for quite some time, been expressing a yearning for a concise and easily comprehensible digest of this great work of our Acharya. In writing the "***PARAMATHA BHANGAM***", our *Acharya* had complete faith that it was firmly based on the verities established by his predecessor lineage of great preceptors and gurus who had delved deep and surely into the depths of the Vedas and Vedanta. And he was sure too that his treatise would therefore serve us all as invaluable aid and guide that will help us journey forth, without facing any significant obstacles on the way, to that great realm called **Sri Vaikuntam**.

***

-3-
"DESIRE ("*aasai*")

Synopsis: *In this succinct but thought-provoking epistle, Srimadh Mukkur Azhagiyasingar essays the nature of Human Desire and how it drives behavior. He alludes to very evocative tales from the purana and itihasa to drive home his message.*

"Kanaka-kaladhowtha-shaila-prabruthibhir-api poorana-kshipthaih:
Trishne! Bhajathi samriddhim bhooyo bhooyasthvaadare kaarshyam"

("sankalpa-suryodayam" of Vedanta Desika)

"Were that pit of the great stomach called DESIRE to be filled with mountains of gold, silver and precious gems, still would it remain empty", says Swami Desikan.

Desire is an innate human quality. None is there in the world that has no desire. So powerful is the force of Desire that it impels one to go to any lengths in life to satiate it. To satisfy Desire one can be driven to commit even unethical deeds. Even then the flame of Desire does not abate. On the other hand, it only increases further.

Let me give you a few illustrations of this fact:

An utterly penurious man desires no more than a hundred rupees at first thinking it will give him happiness in life. Thereafter he begins setting his eyes upon saving up a thousand rupees. After that, he aspires for hundreds of thousands of rupees! Then he who lords over hundreds of thousands of rupees starts nursing ambitions to become a king. After becoming a king, the desire to become a lord of the celestials seizes him. Next, the desire to become verily the lord of the gods takes hold. Indra aspires to become *Brahma*. Then *Brahma* aspires to become *Shiva* and *Shiva* in turn desires to ascend to the state of *Vishnu*! It is in this ceaseless way that, as a poet has described it, a little desire when satiated soon gathers an ever growing and increasing momentum on its own.

It is in the above manner that an errant one driven by naked, irrepressible desire goes on committing grave misdeeds and even lands himself in jail. Even after being released from jail, the desire to again amass wealth does not cease and he relapses to his old, wicked ways again. The term of imprisonment perhaps only reinforces and does not in any way diminish the power of evil desire that taken hold of him.

It is a common sight to see that even with the onset of age, a man's desire does not cease. The body might be withering away, the man may be fast balding, even the dentures may be falling away, why, the man may even be unable wrap a decent-sized *"veshti"* (*dhothi*) around his emaciated waist and may be pottering around in only a skimpy one... hobbling about on a walking-stick! Even in that decrepit state the man's ravenous appetite will not stop him from gorging down on all kinds of rich food without any restraint! We see in the world so many such old men consequently suffering from all kinds of gastric ailments, don't we?

There once lived a king named **Yayati**. He had two wives. The elder one was the daughter of **Rishi Shukracharya**, **Devayani**. She gave birth to two sons. The younger wife, **Sharmishta**, gave birth to three sons. This at once aroused Shukracharya's ire and by a terrible curse which he wreaked upon Yayati; the king instantly turned into a doddering old man! The contrite Yayati then beseeched the irate sage Shukracharya to show due understanding and relieve him of the curse. To which the sage demurred saying, *"My curse once hurled is irreversible. However, if you can find any other man in the world who would be willing to exchange his youthfulness with you, you can regain then your own youth through such a trade"*.

Yayati then summoned his sons and sought to know which one of them would come forward to willingly give up their youth and bestow it upon him at once. In exchange for such favor granted to him, Yayati promised the donor son the inheritance of his entire empire after a period of a thousand years had elapsed and by when, Yayati said, he on his own would take back then from the son the decrepitude of age.

Four of his five sons refused point-blank to oblige their father's rather strange wish. It angered him and thereupon he wreaked a terrible curse on each one of them. The curse on the eldest one was that he and his progeny would never ascend to the royal throne and enjoy its power or glory. It was as a result of this curse that the Yadava clan could not ever rule over a kingdom. Yayati then cursed the three other sons to lose their noble caste and all attendant birthrights. One son was condemned to the status of a *"mleccha"*, and the other two were consigned to status of *"Yavana"* and *"bhoja"* -- all belonging to the lowest of low orders of society in a caste-hierarchy.

The last son, **Puru**, however, came forward to fulfill his father's desire. In an instant, the old king turned into a youth while the young son transformed into an aged man. Yayati heartily thanked the son and blessed him. He also solemnly promised to bequeath to Puru his throne and all his empire.

Thereafter for a thousand-year reign King Yayati lived a life of carnal enjoyment with his wives. Despite it all, the fire of lust he felt remained untamed. It was then that Wisdom dawned upon him:

Na jaathu kaama: kaamaanam upabhogena shaamyathi I

Havishaa krishnavarthmeva bhooya evabhirvardhate II

Tasmaadetaam aham tyakthvaa brahmannyaadhaaya maanasam

Nirdvandho nirmamo bhoothva charishyaami mrugaisaha II

"To give in to Lust or Desire is to condemn oneself to a perennial state of unfulfillment. One will never be able to say, *"Enough, my desire has been sated now, and I need no more of this indulgence!"*. Just as the ghee poured into the ritual fire as libation makes the flames leap only higher, so too does the fire of Desire rage more with every indulgence".

"I now resolve that from this day onwards I shall renounce all my desires and submit them all at the feet of Bhagavan. Henceforth I shall let my mind dwell upon Him alone. I shall go forth to submit to him alone and offer worship to him alone. I am going to retire to the forests and live there amongst wandering animals, devoting myself to penance, austerity and meditation".

Thus did King Yayati resolve firmly. He then threw off his youthful garb and bestowed it upon his son. Reverting to his old, decrepit form and self, Yayati thenceforth began to meditate upon Bhagavan alone.

The moral of the story is thus only this:

The Desire for mere material things of life or hankering after unworthy objects of lust and greed should never be allowed to take root in our heart. If we fail to rein in such desires, the consequences will only lead us to ruination.

If one is wise, then one's desire in life will always be only towards opportunity to serve the will of **Bhagavan** and to serve his devotees. This does not mean that one should not cultivate any desires in life at all. The desire to serve Bhagavan's Will leads to fruition of other virtuous desires which one might regard otherwise as unattainable. Such desire that we can nurture and nourish in our heart for Bhagavan is precisely what is called **Bhakthi**. It is the power of such Desire, such Bhakthi that the *Gopikas* won over the heart of Bhagavan Krishna – "*kaamaath gopyah:....*".

In the same way, why do even to this day we venerate **Anjaneya**? It is only because he showed the world how solely by virtue of extraordinary love or the *bhakti* that he had cultivated for Rama, he had earned the everlasting privilege of being able to enjoy immersion in the delight of listening to the Ramayana wherever in the world it happens to be narrated...

The founder of our ***Sri Visishtadvaita "Siddhantha"***, **Sri Bhaashyakaara (Sri Ramanuja)** in his Sanskrit hymn, "***Sri Vaikunta Gadyam***" gave vent spontaneously to his own intense *bhakti* in the following soul-stirring words:

"When will ever get to be blessed to experience the bliss of being able to behold with my own eyes Bhagavan Narayana stand before me as a clear object, as my mother, my father and my very own deity?! When will the moment arrive when I shall lovingly bear the lotus-like sacred feet of Bhagavan upon my head?! When will that hour arrive when all desires shall be forever rid from

my heart besotted as it will then be with the sole Desire of serving at the feet of Bhagavan alone?! When will the time arrive when I shall have earned the privilege of being the eternal servitor Bhagavan and shall be able to look upon it as my supreme blessing? When will the moment arrive when Bhagavan will at last cast his benevolent eyes upon me and command me in sweet words then in his majestic presence to serve him? When will I be drawn into that beatific presence in which my love and devotion for him and my desire to remain in his service shall keep getting only ever more intense? When will the time come when I too shall be immersed in Bhagavan's presence and along with Adi Sesha and Goddess Lakshmi be able to experience everlasting Bliss?!"

To conclude, it is thus that one should truly yearn within one's heart for servitude to Bhagavan. One should yearn for such yearning to keep ever intensifying too. Therefore, it becomes imperative for us that we forsake all desires for objects that can only end in endless misery and instead strive to embrace that paramount desire of all – the *Desire for Bhagavan* – which alone can secure for us everlasting bliss.

***

-4-
"Breaking Out of Bondage"

Synopsis: *In Visishtadvaita Philosophy the ideas of Sin ("paapam") and Virtue ("punnyam") are very subtle, closely related as they are to notions of spiritual evolution and advancement. The ideas are posited within a broader and more comprehensive system of ethics relative to the framework of the Theory of Karma. This epistle is a lucid explication of "paapam" and "punnyam" and how each either hinders or advances the human journey to redemption and salvation.*

There are only two things that can be said to perennially accompany us throughout our lifetime and are the real causes for all the joys and sorrows that we experience in this world. When the spirit finally takes leave of the body, it has to perforce leave every bit of all its belongings behind. Except for the two things mentioned, nothing else whatsoever is ever possible to be taken along. The truth of this matter has been expressed so beautifully in an aphorism by a wise *"maharishi"* (sage). Everyone with an intelligent and discerning mind should now listen carefully to me explain what belongings do accompany us in death and what possessions can never go along with us.

"arthaa gruhey nivartantey smashaaney mitrabaandhava: I
Sukrtham dushkrtham chaiva gacchanthamanugacchathi II

For a moment let us imagine a man who, using his intelligence and all his skills, has toiled for several long years, struggled hard by way of frugal living – i.e., *keeping his belt ever tightened* and *his tongue ever restrained at his job* -- and has finally earned and saved up enough at last in life to be able to afford building for himself a fine home. When the time arrives for him to shed his mortal body and depart from the world, does the home that he so painstakingly built also go along with him? The answer is **No!** Not only does the house not accompany him but we see that the house itself, as it were, seems to want to evict him *post-haste*.... or, expel his lifeless body forthwith in the very moment he is declared dead!

While alive, he kept always fussing over the upkeep of his house: he fitted it with all kinds of beautiful lamps and lights, took care to paint its walls, festooned it with frippery, and arranged for daily fresh "*kolam*" (elaborate floral designs) to decorate the frontage-floors... All the care and fuss taken for the upkeep of his house however get forgotten in a trice! They become all naught in the very instant he is no more and his lifeless body no longer has any place inside the house and must get disposed of at once!

When his lifeless body is carried on the way out of the house, none of his personal effects and precious possessions that he had worked so hard and so long to earn and acquire – like all of his valuable silverware, for instance – do not go out too along with him. Nor do his diamond ear-studs walk out with him; nor does the remaining cash stashed in his safe-vaults set out with him; nor do the herds of cattle that he had acquired for the comfort his homestead, follow him. The grand bedstead he slept on now does not follow him out of the home. The priceless rings that bejewel his fingers now do not go with him.... All of precious stuff on his person thus gets stripped off his lifeless body, one by one, well before he is vacated out of the house! Even his new or usually well-worn, fine clothes in his wardrobe are all stripped down and whisked away! What remains of his mortal body is then clothed with a freshly purchased mere strip of fabric no more than one-and-half yard long... but then even that gets eventually stripped away too from him in the end....

The same fate, we see, befalls a woman who dies too. Her diamond ear-studs, diamond-studded waist-bands, bangles, gem-encrusted bracelets, chain-linked necklaces, nose-studs, silk saris, every other personal effect at home which were inseparable from her when alive, and the money that had been gifted to her by her fathers, or the money given to her by her doting husband ... none of these things will go with the lady along with her dead body; it matters little what might have been bequeathed to her in any deed of will!

None knows really when the spirit departed from the body, nor in what manner.... nor whereto does it go! What we see is only the lifeless, still body and when it is finally carried away from the house, every material possession of the deceased is stripped off and gets left behind at home.

A few relatives and friends accompany the dead body to the funeral grounds. After the body is consigned to flames and is incinerated, they too immediately scurry back home.

We quite often witness in the world a devoted wife tells her spouse, *"I cannot imagine my living even for an instant without you by my side!"* Likewise, we see a husband tell his beloved wife, *"Without you I cannot ever imagine living in this world for even half a moment!"* But then haven't we all seen wives, after the death of their husbands, continue to lead quite happy and leisurely lives? Likewise, haven't we all also seen a man, after the death of his first wife, take a second one, and live happily with her, showering her in fact with more love and more gifts of expensive clothes and jewelry than ever had been bought for the departed first wife?!

Thus, both a bereaved wife and husband, in the very end, as we see, does have to walk away from the funeral of their spouses, and walk, of course, they do! It's the same situation for *Acharya* or *Sishya* (preceptor and disciple), either son or daughter, lender or borrower... not one will ever remain in the spot once the funeral pyre is lit....

***

During a lifetime man can be said to have acquired through dint of work and toil, two things: one, a **manacle made of gold** and the other, **a shackle made of iron**.

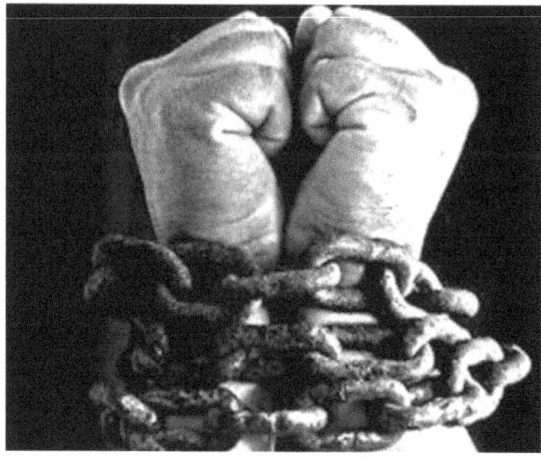

These two manacles are things that simply cannot be kept safe inside any vault or steel box. The man lives all his life under the impression that the two manacles are always in his very own possession. That is not however true. The fact is that as and when the man during his lifetime acquires them, **Bhagavaan**, who is ever resident and inhered within his spirit, promptly takes custody of the two shackles and then keeps periodically updating a record of their inventory, adds them to accumulating stock.

Thereafter, at the time of the man's death, when the agents of **Yama** (the god of Death) and agents of **Indra** (the god of the heavenly celestials) arrive to take his soul into their custody, *Bhagavaan* hands over to the former the stock of *iron manacles* and the stock of *golden manacles* to the latter. After the handing over, *Bhagavaan* instructs the agents of *Yama* and *Indra* to regard the iron and golden manacles as a sort of court-warrant issued for summons to a trial. Accordingly, thus, the soul is taken away bound and handcuffed either in iron or golden shackle to the respective courts of justice to face trial and sentencing. The upshot of all this therefore is that the only two things are inseparable from a man both in this world and beyond; the ***iron and golden manacles***.

***

To the question *"What is meant by "iron manacle" and "golden manacle"?"* our wise ancestors say that Virtuous deeds (***punnyam***) are *"golden manacles"* and Sinful deeds (***paapam***) are *"iron manacles"*. In his (Sanskrit work of poetry) *"Varadaraaja Panchaasatha"*, our Acharya, Sri Vedanta Desika has described Virtue as ***"kaaraagruha kanakasrunkalayaapi bandha"*** --- *i.e., a manacle made of gold, yes, but which yet ties one all up in bondage.*

Bhagavaan becomes generally pleased with a man, who with much of the wealth earned by him through a lifetime of toil and honest work, performs many good and socially agreeable deeds too. *Bhagavaan* thus bestows upon the man due rewards that are commensurate with such Virtue. On the contrary, *Bhagavaan* becomes wrathful towards a man who goes about in life doing evil and, in every conceivable manner, sinning against society, or against the *devatas* (gods) or against the norms and strictures of *saastra* (Vedic scripture). To such a sinful man, *Bhagavaan* delivers his just and due desserts at the appropriate time. The retribution for the sins is handed down to such a man as well-deserved justice both in this world and the one beyond, known as Hell (*yamaloka*). And as a reward for a man's virtuous deeds (*punnyam*), *Bhagavaan* bestows upon him due rewards both in this world and in the world beyond, known as *"svargaloka"* (heavenly sphere), where all manner of pleasurable and joyful experiences is to be had and enjoyed.

In view of everything explained above, the wisdom of our ancestors can establish the fact of life that both **Virtue** and **Sin** (*punnyam* and *paapam*) render the soul (*jeevaatma*) into ineluctable bondage only. The retribution meted out to the soul for all its *"paapam"* manifests in several forms of painful punishments in the hellish realms of *Yama*, the god of death. Thus, *"paapam"* can be said to condemn the *jeevaatma* to miserable bondage in hell. It is quite apt therefore to metaphorically refer to it as a terrible *"iron manacle"*.

On the contrary, in the delightful realms of *"svargaloka"*, where the *jeevaatma* gets to enjoy all kinds of pleasurable and marvelous experiences as reward for the virtuous deeds standing to its credit, there is, of course, no question of any bondage at all!

***

A question arises here whether the metaphor of a *"golden manacle"* is really apt. It is a good question indeed and I will try to answer it. Listen to me now starting with this aphorism:

"naabhuktham ksheeyathe karma kalpakoti-shathairapi..."

It is said above that any man who has committed deeds of virtue *or* sin – or, deeds of virtue *and* sin -- can never escape experiencing the resulting rewards or retribution accruing to them, and no matter how many countless births and rebirths his soul endures. The Vedic *"saastraas"* clearly reveal that no matter how many years pass by with the man not having fully experienced the rewards for his deeds of *punnyam*, nor having been fully punished yet for his deeds of *paapam*, the accumulated stock of such unexpired *punnyam* and *paapam* does not by itself ever lapse.

So long as *paapam* remains and a *jeevaatma* is yet to face punishment for it, effectively such *paapam* obstructs and prevents the soul from ascending to the supreme state of *"moksha"* in the realm of *Bhagavaan* called **"parama-padam"** which is the final destination, the *summum-bonum* of all beings. So long as the soul remains so obstructed and frustrated from progressing to the state of *"moksha"*, so long does it remain in a state of bondage and firmly held down by *"paapam"*. It is for this very reason of bondage, that a man's stock of unexpired sins is metaphorically called **"iron manacle"**.

Likewise, in very much the same way, unexpired *"punnyam"* too is an obstructive roadblock to a *jeevaatma*--- i.e., when the soul is yet to experience to the fullest measure all the pleasurable rewards due to and deserved by it by virtue of its deeds of *"punnyam"*, the unexhausted stock of Virtue effectively drags the soul down and forcibly holds it in bondage within the realms of *"svargaloka"*. It thus bars the soul from ascending to the supreme state of *"moksha"*. It is for this reason, therefore, that our ancestors, in their insightful wisdom, chose to metaphorically describe *"punnyam"* too as a **shackle**, albeit a **"golden"** one.

***

If attaining *moksha* (liberation) as explained above is going to be impossible so long as the effects of one's *"paapam"* and *"punnyam"* remain unexhausted, then how is it going to be ever possible to break free from these two **iron and golden manacles** that keep us in a perennial state of bondage? Such a question will surely arise in your minds. Listen then to our reply:

The taint of *"paapam"* gets removed if the right expiation for it is performed (*"praayaschittham"*). But there is no such thing as atoning for *"punnyam"* which too is a shackle. But then there is, of course, one way to break free from even that manacle… *What is the way?* Going about frequently gloating to one and all about all the virtuous deeds (*punnyam*) one has done in life is a sure way to extinguish the merit attendant upon or accruing such virtue completely. A scriptural epigram confirms it as follows:

"punnya: ksharathi keerthanaath…"

i.e., the merit of one's virtuous deeds keeps slowly but surely diminishing as one keeps boasting about them constantly!"

***

Now, I am going to let you all in on a secret:

Consider this: There is no denying the fact that *"paapam"* and *"punnyam"* are accumulated by us in the course of countless number of previous lifetimes (*janmaa*-s). It is possible to atone for such accumulated *"paapam"* only if it is also possible to recollect all those sins. Likewise, it is possible to go about boasting over one's virtuous deeds, *"punnyam"*, only if it is possible to, firstly, recollect them all. Under the circumstance, if one has no recollection of one's past sins and virtue at all, how is it possible to get rid of both Virtue and Sin? I will explain below.

The practice of **Bhakthi Yoga** is the most efficacious way to atone for one's *"paapam"*.

If a man were to daily practice *Bhakthi-yoga* steadfastly, it would be possible for him to break free from the manacles of *"paapam"* and *"punnyam"*. Once freed, the man no longer is subject, either in this world or in the world beyond, to the consequences of either *"paapa"* or *"punnya"*. There can be no doubt at that such a liberated man will ascend to the everlasting state of *"moksha"* (salvation) in the realm of *"parama-padam"*.

Bhakti-yoga as practiced by great souls such as Rishi-s **Vasishta, Kaashyapa** or **Paraashara** is beyond the capacity of ordinary soul. But then they otherwise can choose the alternative way shown by **Sri Krishna** --- vide his *Gita-shloka*, **"maamekam sharanam vraja…."** i.e., the way of performing, in prescribed manner, the rite of *"saranaagathi"* (self-surrender or *"prapatthi"*) unto the feet of **Sriman Naaryaayana**. That is the only way of atoning for all *"paapam"* and getting rid of it. By doing so, all taint of sin and virtue, the cause of all bondage, wither away from one's spirit instantly. Both **Bhakthi-yoga** and **Prapatthi-rite** are very lofty doctrines of Dharma indeed.

***

Be that all as it may, let us now consider the matter more closely in the context of today's world and times. In the present times, to the best of our knowledge, there is hardly anyone seen or known in the world practicing *"Bhakthi-yoga"*. You might say, *"Oh, but don't we see so many "bhakth-s" amongst the peoples around us? How can it be then said that "bhakthi-yoga" is not being practiced?!"* Of course, it cannot be denied that they are all indeed *"bhakth-s"*. But what they are practicing is certainly not *"bhakthi-yoga"*.

It is only if and when one is able to sit alone in a spot, draw in all one's senses, concentrate the mind single-pointedly and meditate ceaselessly upon the nature of **Sriman Naaraayana** and his infinite and wondrous attributes (**"kalyaana guna"**) that one can be said to be practicing *"bhakthi-yoga"*. Such intense meditation must be performed until one's very last breath in life and only then can it truly qualify to be called *"bhakthi-yoga"*. To the best of my knowledge, there is none in the world of the present times who is engaged in the practice of such true *"bhakthi-yoga"*. Perhaps in some remote corner of the land, up somewhere in the high mountains, some anonymous heir to the great rishis of the past, might be still practicing it, but then let me confess I am not aware of any such person.

***

Sriman Naaraayana can be likened to the **"kalpaka-vruksha"** – **the tree of inexhaustible superabundance** – which can yield for Man, and fulfill his every kind of desires, easily and very generously. But this **"kalpaka vruksha"** yields the fruit of **"moksha"** to the seeker of salvation only when he or she becomes like a tender sapling that attaches itself to the tree, like a creeper-plant which does so for support, sustenance and growth.

What do we do to make a creeper-plant to grow forth and flower? We water it daily without fail, don't we? In much the same way, it is only by performing the daily rite of "**sandhyavandanam**" can we expect the creeper of "*bhakthi*" to begin growing. It is only through other spiritual practices such as "*yaaga-daana*" – i.e., sacrificial rites, rituals and charitable deeds -- that the creeper or sapling of *Bhakti* can grow. It is only through due, scrupulous performance of rites such as "*tarpanam*" and "*shraadham*" (propitiatory rituals in ancestor-worship) that the creeper called *Bhakthi* grows. Again, the creeper of *Bhakti* grows only when the observances of fasting on days enjoined by "*saastra*" are duly strictly followed. Chanting at least a few Vedic passages every day without fail is what too will make the creeper of *Bhakthi* grow tall as it winds its way up the tree-trunk, and begin flowering and blossoming even as it adorns the radiant "*kalpaka-vruksha*" called "*Lakshmi-kaantha*".

When the creeper blooms thus in the fullness of *Bhakti*, at that very moment, the *Divine Couple, Sriman Naaraayana and Sri Mahaalakshmi*, begin to show their utmost love for the *Bhaktha* (the true devotee). It is a flow of love that is of ineffable purity and intensity. In that very exact moment, all the "*paapam*" and "*punnyam*" that hang like a millstone around the neck of the *bhaktha*, obstructing and retarding his journey to "*moksha*", all simply fall away!

Proceeding further along the same journey, the "*bhaktha*" begins to increasingly shed all his petty and evanescent mortal desires *("**sirru-inbam**")*. Instead, he starts pursuing the loftiest and permanent goal of blissful salvation (***pEr-inbam***") awaiting him as a uniquely blissful spiritual experience in **Sri Vaikuntam**. When the final moment then arrives for him to depart from the temporal world, his soul is enabled to travel forthwith through the trans-cosmic celestial route called "***archiraadi maarga***" that leads directly to "**Sri Vaikuntam**", the eternal abode of ***Sriman Naaraayana***!

For those who do not possess the requisite capacity to perform *Bhakthi-yoga* as explained above, there is no other alternative path to attain "moksha" other than **"saranaagath**i". This doctrine of "saranaagathi" is of immeasurable value to mankind. There is no absolute guarantee for anyone who is pursuing the path of "bhakthi-yoga" that, within one's present lifetime itself, *Bhagavaan* will grant salvation. Even if a man were to consummate "bhakti-yoga" in the present lifetime, there will still nonetheless, remain that residue of all "paapam" and "punnyam" carried forward from his previous lifetimes ("purva-janma") which were what, in the first place, caused the present lifetime. The joys and sorrows that result from such residual *karma*, will have to be perforce experienced in perhaps one or several more future "janmaa-s" (lifetimes) and have to get exhausted entirely before *Bhagavaan* confers, at the very end of the last all such "janmaa-s", the ultimate state of "moksha" upon him.

The uncertainty of outcome of "bhakti-yoga" is revealed too by a scriptural adage: **"bhogena tu itharey kshapayitvaa atha sampadhyatey..."** It is only those Vedic adepts who are steeped in and dedicated to the practice of "vedadhyaayana" and "vedaanta-adhyaayana" (Vedic discipline/austerity and Vedantic contemplation) who are qualified to venture into the path of "bhakti-yoga". True "bhakthi-yoga" is not performed through mere ritual sacrifices – such as those different kinds of Vedic *yagnya*-s through the conduct of which one may hope to realize or satiate several different kinds of earthly desires. A man can be said to be a true practitioner of "bhakti-yoga" only when he performs all sacramental sacrifices with the sole and exclusive aim of pleasing *Bhagavaan* and none else *("bhagavath preetyartham")*.

Men and women who, on the other hand, are wholly incapable of practicing strict "bhakti-yoga" in the above mentioned manner, but who yet possess perhaps at least an iota of desire to attain "moksha" (and that too thanks only to a fleeting acquaintance with some scriptural tale or *puraanic* fable that they had through happenstance heard sometime in life), are however fully qualified to embrace and perform the act of "saranaagathi", either on their very own or with the aid and guidance of an Acharya.

No credentials of any sort are required of those who wish to perform "saranaagathi", whoever they may be --- *irrespective of caste, creed, gender, family-lineage; it does not matter whether a person is learned or illiterate, deaf or dumb, lame or blind, virtuous or sinful, wealthy or poor, a social victim or oppressor, a believer or a non-believer…*

The act of *"saranaagathi"* gets done through only a single sacrament. It is conducted very quickly within a day and without any fuss of elaborate ritual or paraphernalia involving *"homam"* or rites. All that is required is that the man or woman abides by certain observances and injunctions that the Acharya lays down as protocol for the day. At the end of his or present lifetime, the person who has thus performed *"saranaagathi"* obtains salvation, and its everlasting joys, by the grace of Sriman Naaraayana!

There is no difference whatsoever in the degree of eternal bliss experienced in *Sri Vaikuntam* by a soul that has obtained salvation through a lifetime of arduous practice of *"bhakthi-yoga"* on earth and the soul that has attained it almost effortlessly on earth through the short and simple deed of *"saranaagathi"*.

※※※

For those who neither practice *"bhakti-yoga"* nor perform *"saranaagathi"*, the way of spiritual release at the time of death through the **cranial gateway** --- i.e., **"thalai vaasal"** --- does not get revealed.

What is this *cranial gateway?*

At the center of the human heart is to be found a tiny but very dense concentration of several hundreds of synaptic-networked nerves. One such nerve travels from the heart straight through the cranial cavity right into a tiny, imperceptible **aperture** found at the crown of the human skull. A *jeevaatma* that is bound for *"moksha"* departs from its body through the **gateway** of this very cranial **crown-aperture.**

From out of this hub of dense neural-concentrations, and situated in the very center of the heart, are to be found several more nerves that travel to other parts of the body. It is through these other neural-networks that *"jeevaatma*-s" headed towards spiritual destinations other than *"moksha"*, such as *"svargaloka"* etc., make their final exit from their mortal coils. At the time of physical death, *Bhagavaan*, through the power of his immanent presence within the human heart, shuts down all the neural-synaptic connections emanating from the core of this neural-hub except for the one neural-line that travels from the heart to the crown of the skull. This specific nerve, *Bhagavaan* is said to illuminate it with a blinding swathe of bright light enveloped in a beautiful hue. This illumination is for the sake of the *jeevaatma* that prepares to begin its extra-terrestrial, trans-cosmic spiritual journey. It is this neural flight-path that is called **"moordhanya-naadi"** and it travels right through what is called **"thalai vaasal"** – the *gateway of the cranial crown-aperture*.

For those who have not performed "*saranagaathi*", this neural flight-path is not revealed to them by *Bhagavaan*. Without travelling through this flight-path, the destination called "*moksha*" cannot be reached. Hence, it is only for those souls that have either practiced "*bhakthi-yoga*" or performed "*saranaagathi*" that the great gateway of **"thalai-vaasal"** opens up. The state of "*moksha*" is denied to all others…. **"na dishati mukundo nijapadam…"** Thus, indeed, have spoken our great *Achaaryas* in this regard.

***

A question arises: "*Saranagaathi*" can also be considered to be a "*punnyam*". Can it be said therefore that it gets attached to the *jeevaatma* and travels goes along with it in its onward journey to the world beyond… much in the manner described in the scriptural phrase, **"gacchantham anugacchathi…"?**

The answer is *No!*

The function of "*bhakthi-yoga*" and the function of the rite of "*prapatthi*" through which "*saranaagathi*" is performed is primarily to dissolve and destroy all inimical forces and elements in the temporal world, i.e., all "*punnyam*" and "*paapam*" that obstruct and impede the *jeevaatma* from progressing to the highest state of "*moksha*". Once all such inimical obstructions are extinguished, the *jeevaatma* gets freed from the "**manacles of bondage**" – as mentioned in the scriptural expression: **"muktha: svayam sukrutha-dushkrutassrunkalaapyam…."**, and once it has ascended to the state of "*moksha*", the yoga of "**bhakthi**" or "**prapatthi**" as yogic-pathways, having served their purpose, remain back in the realm of *Bhagavaan*. They do not return to the mortal world --- as is the case of friends or kin of a deceased on earth who, after accompanying a man in his final journey in life to the funeral-pyre, must quietly return to their homes once it is lit.

As for the soul itself, freed of the *manacles of all bondage*, it enjoys everlasting bliss in *Sri Vaikuntam* in its true and original state of eternal servitude to *Bhagavaan Sriman Naaryaayana!*

***

Living life even while journeying through this temporal world with an attitude of humble servitude to Sriman Naaraayana paves the way to overcome all obstacles in the way that may manifest themselves as *"paapam"* or *"punnyam"*. Such an attitude of servitude will finally lead to *Sri Vaikuntam*.

If a man were to build a nice big home, he ought to do it with an attitude, *"This mansion I build is for Bhagavaan"*. If he were to then fill the house with rich paraphernalia and accoutrements like expensive vessels and utensils, let him think, *"All this is for Bhagavaan only"*. If he were to acquire costly jewelry, let him do so by mentally dedicating them all to Mother *Goddess Mahaalakshmi*.

Even when the man faithfully performs daily rites of religious worship (*anushtaanam*) -- all enjoined as per the letter and spirit of the Vedic *"saastra*-s" -- he must ensure that he offers them all in the end only in the spirit of complete renunciation to *Bhagavaan*. The attitude behind all such acts should be: *"Every act of mine in life, O Lord, please accept them all as having been carried out by me as your humble slave –* **"daasa bhuthan"** *-- only for your sake alone, for your will and pleasure, and that nothing that may be the outcome of these acts, whether for good or for bad, shall ever be for my own sake or for my selfish ends. To that purpose, please you must yourself render all these acts of mine as fulfilment of the purpose of my own existence which is nothing but to serve you eternally!"*

Such is the mental attitude that Bhagavaan *Sri Krishna* in his sermon of the **Bhagavath-Gita** advised *Arjuna* to also adopt and cultivate. These are his words:

> **"Yat karoshi yad ashnaasi yaj-juhoshi dadaasi yat**
> **Yat tapasyasi Kaunteya tat kurushva mad arpanam"**

"Whatever you do, whatever you eat, whatever you offer, whatever you give as charity and whatever austerities you perform, do that, O son of Kunti, as an offering to me".

Even the obligations you carry out and fulfill in faithful compliance with the many injunctions of Vedic *"saastra"* – such as for instance, *consuming only food prescribed by the "saastra" and abjuring those it prohibits, performing rites with the sacred fire such as "homam-s" etc., using only those sacramental accoutrements as prescribed by the "saastra", observing fasting on the days like "ekaadasi"* – even all such pious and virtuous deeds, dedicate them all to me as offering in the spirit of "**Sri Krishnaarpanam**".... Thus spoke, *Bhagavaan* in the *Bhagavath-Gita*.

If one were to live out one's lifetime in accordance with all the principles and guidelines laid down above, then one's aspiration to attain *"moksha"* will gradually start growing of its own accord. If one were then to at once perform *"saranaagathi"*, then *Bhagavaan* is sure to confer *"moksha"* on its seeker. *Bhagavaan*, in fact, looks forward eagerly to the day when even ordinary souls like us -- who have surrendered in *"saranaagathi"* to him out of perhaps only the faintest desire for salvation -- shall be ready to discard at last the **shackles of our mortal bondage** and receive from him the everlasting **Grace of Liberation -- Moksha**.

***

-5-
A Session of Questions & Answers

Synopsis: The most well-read and scholarly among serious students of Visistadvaita philosophy and the most ardent practitioner of Sri Vaishnava "sampradaaya" are often beset with severe doubts and confusion over the basic principles, concepts, tenets and doctrines of "Sri Ramanuja siddhaantha". Such doubts and confusions can usually get clarified more effectively by engaging with one's Acharya in candid but humble dialogue. Both students and spiritual seekers here ask Mukkur Swamy several questions during the course of a Q&A session and are amply rewarded by listening to his most illuminating answers.

Question (Q1): How intense can the experience of bliss be for a man?

Answer (**A**): It can be as intense as that which *Srimann Naaraayana* along with his Consort, goddess Lakshmi, himself experiences Bliss in his divine abode in *Sri Vaikuntam*.

Q2: To experience such bliss, where forth should a man seek to go?

A: In the realms of what is known as *"Nithya Vibhuthi"* in *Sri Vaikuntam*, one can enjoy the same and equal bliss as *Srimann Naaraayana* does, and it has been attested to by the scriptural revelation ... ***"paramam saamyamupaithi"***.

Q3: Is it possible for a man, with mortal body, to reach the realm of *Sri Vaikuntam*?

A: There is not an iota of a chance, ever.

Q4: From the accounts of the *puraanaas*, we come to learn of human beings, such as *Dasaratha*, *Dharmaputra* and others, for example, who were able to visit *"svarga**"* (heaven) and other such celestial worlds even with their bodily form. Why must Sri Vaikuntam alone then happen to be an exception?

A: Earthly or celestial realms spoken about in the *"puraanaas"* happen to be within the boundaries of *"Brahmmaandam"* i.e., the domains that are under the sway, protection or jurisdiction of **Brahmma** (the primordial Creator). The *saastras* reveal many kinds of requisite *'tapas'* (arduous penance) which, if performed successfully, enable one to attain these celestial worlds and to be able to even frequent them with one's own mortal or bodily form. Sage Narada and a few other rishis like him who were the equals of *'devas'* (celestial beings), by virtue of the *'tapas'* they performed, could thus easily visit, to and fro and at will, celestial abodes and other higher heavenly realms. However, mere mortals with bodily form, cannot ever aspire to emulate them in reaching Sri Vaikuntam, since it is situated well beyond the frontiers of *"brahmmaandam"*, and no being that is tainted by *"paapam"* (sin) can enter there.

Q5: **If a man were to be unsullied by any sin, would he then be able to enter *Sri Vaikuntam* with his mortal body?**

A: Having taken human birth, it is impossible not to become guilty of sin even if they are only as few in number --- as few, in fact, as a mere handful of sesame seeds. If you were to ask why, it is because the present birth of a man follows crores and crores of previous births. Even if a man had committed only a tiny number of sins in those past births, they would all simply add up and then accumulate into very large, in fact, inestimable amounts in the present lifetime.

Now, those innumerable sins would have to be first redeemed completely before one can aspire to attain *Sri Vaikuntam*. And even if we assume that did happen, it would still be impossible to get there with one's mortal body because the very existence of the body is evidence of present and unexpired sin. Therefore, the body which, in fact, is really instrumental to all sin and sinning, will have to be first eliminated before one can even conceive a sinless state of being. This is borne out by the *"sruti vaakya"* (the word of the Veda):

"***tasya thaavadeva chiram…***", meaning:

As long as the body, which was created through sin in the first place, continues to exist, so long does "*moksha*", salvation, remain beyond one's reach. Once the body dissolves, "*moksha*" becomes reachable. Therefore, under no circumstances is it ever possible to attain Sri Vaikuntam with one's mortal body.

Furthermore, as the '*saastra*-s" say, as long as one's body remains in bondage to "*karma*", so long does one remain in thrall of "*sukha-dukkha*", the conditions of mundane vicissitudes of "*joy and grief*". In the realm of Sri Vaikuntam, sastra-s have revealed to us, souls assume many other beautiful forms that are of infinitely more wondrous essence and nature than the moribund body that we possess here on earth. With such supernatural body forms, they indeed revel in while eternally serving **Bhagavaan**, the Almighty who resides there in his abode. When such being the case, if a person were to as much as even entertain mere wishful thought that one can ascend to Sri Vaikuntam with one's own mortal, sin-ridden body, then such a person can only be regarded as someone who is mired already in the grip of grievous sin.

Q6: But that is not exactly what or how I am thinking! I realize how much suffering I undergo in life, and I know the cause for it all is my own body. I am asking these questions not because I harbor even as much as an iota of desire to continue surviving eternally in this body of mine, but only because I wish to know what the "*saastra-s*" have to say in the matter. My inquiry, therefore, is only for the sake of dispelling genuine doubts. And that is also why I ask now the next question: We see how when grain is harvested and kept stored for unduly long periods of time, it begins to rot, decay and finally gets destroyed. By the same token, would it not be possible to argue that our own stock of sins, accumulated from countless past lives, also might, by sheer efflux of time, completely self-destruct?

A: Such ingenious analogies will not work here since the scripture says "**naabukhtham ksheeyathe karma**" .... In other words, one's deeds as "*karma*" can never be shaken off or get erased in time, even across eons or eras, and hence, there is no escaping at all from having to experience their consequences.

Q7: You stated that one's previous births are countless in number. Now, in each of those previous incarnations, is it not possible that one might already be done atoning for sins committed therein? Would it not be fair then to say, one has been able to attain the present lifetime only to work off and exhaust the consequences of one's "*paapam*" and "*punnyam*" (evil and good deeds) arising in and from the present birth? That would thus make this birth the very last one too, wouldn't it? And if one were to live this lifetime unimpeachably, would that not by itself, in the end then, pave the way directly to "*moksham*"?

A: Your question is certainly very pertinent and hence I must elaborate an answer for it so that it registers well in your mind.

Imagine for a moment a man is in the habit of daily taking some money out of his cash-vault and giving it away in charity to the poor.

Now, if he goes on doing the same every day, surely it would surprise no one if the cash eventually gets all depleted and the money-box emptied. But then let us imagine the same man, one day, takes out five hundred rupees and gives it away in charity to a poor man for, let's just say, conducting the latter's daughter's wedding. And let it be imagined too that on the following day, when the man opens his cash-vault he discovers that the stock of money since the day before has somehow increased by one thousand rupees! And if that were to happen every day, would the money-box ever get emptied at all then?! Would not the stock of money in the vault only keep growing exponentially?

Now, similarly, if one takes birth in this lifetime to atone for, say, four or five sins of past lives, then invariably and simultaneously – and within this same lifetime too – many more sets of *four or five of the same sins* get committed, and which then simply multiply to outnumber the original *set of four or five sins*. Furthermore, other varieties of sins also get unavoidably committed in the same lifetime. Under such circumstances, one must deeply ponder over the whole matter: *Having taken this birth, and atoned for a few past sins, does not diminish the ever-increasing net-stock of sins constantly replenished by newer ones we concurrently commit.*

Q8: **How then are we to be rid of sins permanently?!**

A: By resolving to abjure committing any sin henceforth. And by expiation of sins already committed.

Q9: **Do you mean "*sethu snaanam*"? ... I.e. The ritual bathing in the sea (at Rameshwaram) ... will it be able to wash off sins? Would it suffice as expiation?**

A: Even if you kept yourself indefinitely submerged under the seas at "*sethu*", I am afraid that will just not do.

Q10: **But then is it not believed that a ritual dip at "*sethu*" rids one of even such a heinous sin as "*brahma-hathyam*" (homicide of a Brahmin)? Why won't it then cleanse us of all sins?**

A: Out of the infinite of sins committed by us, we may expect that perhaps only a few hundred thousand of them will get atoned for through such ritual "*snaanam*". But then can we deny that we are, or that we are going to be in all likelihood, guilty of crores and crores more of sins?

Q11: **Atoning through ritual bathing in such holy rivers such as River Ganga... won't that exterminate all our sins?**

A: Even if a man were to bathe in the sacred waters of River Ganga that flows in the heavenly world, he will not be able to atone fully for all the sins he is guilty of. If you ask why, this is the reason:

The scripture says "***kruthaathyaye anushayavaan ...***"

i.e., having earned the requisite "*punnyam*" – i.e., the benefit accruing to him from good deeds – that renders him deserving of the rewards of '*svarga*' (paradise), he travels there to duly enjoy and delight in them to his heart's content. But eventually thereafter, to reap the enjoyment of other "*punnyam*" which he may deserve still, and as well as to atone for sins that yet remain outstanding for him to account for, he is destined perforce to return to earthly realms again. Now, is it not perfectly reasonable to assume that during his sojourn through the delightful realms of "*svarga*", he most certainly would have availed the opportunity to take a ritual dip in the sacred waters of the river Ganga flowing there?

And therefrom, from the long and short of the tale, does it not become patently clear to us that, even in spite of his *"ganga-snaanam"* in the heavenly spheres, upon returning to earth, there still remains a residual stock of sins, both yet to be unaccounted for and un-expiated by him?

Q12: If a man, throughout his lifetime, were to faithfully conduct himself, and perform all his duties (*dharma*) without a fault, and strictly in accordance with the "*varnaashrama*" into which he has taken birth… would that by itself not enable him to permanently expiate all his sins?

A: There are *sins of omissions* as well as *sins of commission*; in trying to lead a life by abjuring all sins, one might possibly be able to avert some sins but not all of them, especially if those of the former's nature are the ones that might probably lead, at some time in the future, to grievous lapses.

Q13. Do you mean then to say that sins cannot be extinguished even through acts of service to God and fellow-devotees of God? (i.e., '*bhagavath-sevai*' and '*bhaagavatha-sevai*')

A: *Definitely yes!* The power of such good deeds to remove one's sins is rather limited and can be effective only against certain numbers of them. The power of water to douse fire is undeniable, no doubt, but then can you expect to tame a raging inferno with only a tumbler full of water? It is the same case with our sins, our *paapam*, which can be likened to an irrepressible, great forest-blaze that cannot be expected to be extinguished even by the occasional downpour of our good deeds, our acts of *"punnyam"*.

Q14. If there is then really no way in the world in which a man can hope to redeem himself of his sins, does it mean "*moksham*" is simply unattainable?

A: *Nobody has ever said there is no way at all!* In the Bhagavath-Gita, haven't we heard Lord Krishna say, *"sarva paappebhyo moksha-ishyaami…"*? **I shall deliver you from all your sins!**

Q15: How is it possible that He can absolve us of all our sins?

A: If one faithfully abides by his commands, there is no doubt he can and he will cancel all our sins.

Q16: What then has *Bhagavaan* commanded us to abide by?

A: *Bhagavaan* has spoken thus:

Residing within the mortal body is none else other than a being known as 'jeevaatma'. He is imperishable. He uses his body as instruments of both good and evil deeds and thus it is he alone who reaps the consequent "sukha-dukha", rewards and retributions for deeds committed.

Sin does not relate to the body. If a man wields a dagger and kills another one with it, for both the guilt and the ensuing punishment for such a crime, who is to be held responsible? Surely, it is the man and not the dagger, is it not? Likewise, the responsibility for all the sins of man is to be borne by the 'jeevaatma' only and not by its body which, after all, inevitably does perish.

Knowing this truth well, a man should not wittingly commit sin. He should instead engage only in good deeds and that too must be done in a spirit of disinterest without expectation of reward. It should be done in a spirit of renunciation for sole sake of "bhagavath-preethi" – i.e., the pleasure of **Bhagavaan**. *When good deeds are performed in that spirit of renunciation, then it engenders within oneself an attitude in the feeling,* **"I am the deathless soul"** *and a recognition of one's true identity too, in the feeling,* **"I am but a liege to the Paramaatma, the supreme soul"**. *With such attitude, even more pious contemplation and pious deeds are naturally enabled in a man (such as for example, frequenting temples and holy shrines and offering worship there by regularly circumambulating their environs and their sacred ponds etc.)*

"Do not steal. Do not speak untruth. See no evil. Never betray the trust of others nor that even within oneself. Place your constant trust in Me alone. Train your mind to contemplate on Me always. Evolve and remain ever as my **"bhaktha"**. *Offer unto Me alone, all your loving worship and salutations, but then again, without expectation of any rewards. I shall then give you absolution and redemption from all your sins.* **Do not ever worry about it at all!***

Q17: Can you please explain to me in a manner I can easily comprehend what I have been told by some that it is possible in life that even without my engaging by volition in any act, good or bad, I can still get tainted by sin?

A: This is profound question of Vedantic theosophy but, nevertheless, I shall explain it to you.

A very pious man, having expiated all his sons, and aspiring to *"moksham"* (salvation), approached great and knowledgeable exponents of Vedanta, and after seeking from them proper instructions on how to tread the pathway of *"bhakthi yoga"* (the way to Godhead through devotion), he began the journey of **Bhakthi**. He was steadfast in his yogic practice and quest right until the imminent end of his life.

Now, we must know that, when such a man dies eventually, *Bhagavaan* distributes all of the man's *"punnyam"*, the cumulative accrued rewards of good deeds, amongst his dear friends in the same way that *Bhagavaan* also distributes the man's accrued *"paapam"*, his cumulative sins, amongst all persons who were his sworn enemies while he lived.

Such divine distribution takes place much like how a deceased man's estate of property is inherited by his heirs and offspring; a truly pious man's *"punnyam"*, on his demise, gets inherited by his beloved friends, while his *"paapam"* devolves upon all those who were inimical to him when alive. This is what the Upanishad reveals to us. It is what our wise ancestors too have explained as precisely how one – even without direct personal engagement in any deed, either good or evil in life – can unwittingly yet inherit *"punnyam"* or *"paapam"* … effortlessly or involuntarily, as it were.

It is for this reason, therefore, that we should be extremely careful in life not to become the cause of any kind of hurt, pain, slight or grief, at any time, to a man of piety and righteousness, lest we should inherit his stock of accumulated sins upon his demise. On the other hand, if we are kindly and well-disposed towards such pious souls, we may well become, when they depart from this world, the beneficial heirs to a rich legacy of *"punnyam"* that Bhagavaan will bequeath to us, and surely, with his very own blessings added too.

In much the same way, we should also be very careful never to offend in any way – through thought, word or deed --- the pious ones who we know have performed the rite or sacrament of **Saranaagathi** (absolute Self-Surrender unto God). Upon their demise, their "*paapam*" is inherited by their antagonists and their "*punnyam*" is inherited by their good friends.

The "*bhakthi-yogin-s*" and the "*prapannaa-*s" (those who have renounced themselves in Saranaagathi) have both indeed been hailed by the "*sastra*" as being venerable "*brahma-viths*" (i.e., those who have realized the Supreme Brahman: "**thrasya brahmavidhaakasa:**").

In view of the aforesaid, thus, it can be stated with all certainty, that in line with the words of Bhagavaan when he said "**saranam vraja, sarvapaappebhyo mokshayishyaami**", it is only through surrender unto his sacred feet that one can rid oneself of all sins. We will then be able to shed our mortal coils and commence our journey through the celestial route called "**archiradi maarga**" that leads to *Sri Vaikuntam*.

Once we ascend there, we will be able to join the assembly of our forebears, who having long before us become liberated souls, began ceaselessly enjoying, in a measure equal to that which *Bhagavaan* himself enjoys, eternal heavenly bliss. We too then can equally enjoy such extraordinary, unsurpassed bliss without its least diminution. The many distinctions of caste, upbringing, creed or status that are all caused or occasioned by the operation of "*karma*" in life upon earth, find no place at all in the heavenly realm of *Sri Vaikuntam*. And whichever form that we may desire our spirits to assume in those realms, we can easily don such forms indeed and proceed to revel in the supreme delight that accompanies eternal servitude to *Bhagavaan* in the joyous company of divine archangels (*nityasuris*, such as *Anantha, Garuda* and others) and other liberated souls (*muktha-atma-*s) who are also in attendance there. All *sastra*-s rousingly attest to such a state of eternal bliss being attainable by everyone, and beyond any shadow of doubt. That presents a glorious spiritual opportunity for us, which we must never lose or let slip.

***

-6-
The essence of the 13th Chapter of Srimadh Bhagavath Gita

*Synopsis: The thirteenth chapter of the Bhagavad Gita delineates the subtle theological doctrine of "**Ksetra Ksetrajna Vibhaaga Yoga**". The word "kshetra" means the **field**, and the "kshetrajna" means the **knower of the field**. We can think of our material body as the field and our immortal soul as the knower of the field. While explaining to Arjuna, the concept of this Yoga, Krishna discriminates between the physical body and the immortal soul. He explains that the physical body is temporary and perishable whereas the soul is permanent and eternal. The physical body can be destroyed but the soul can never be destroyed. The chapter then describes God, who is the Supreme Soul. All the individual souls have originated from the Supreme Soul. One who clearly understands the difference between the body, the Soul and the Supreme Soul attains the realization of Brahman.*

Most students of Vedanta and spiritual seekers (aasthikas) generally find it difficult to understand the subtle, rather esoteric truths embedded in this Gita Chapter. Mukkur Swamy, however, in this brilliant epistle, with the aid of telling real-life examples and illustrations decodes this Yoga, step-by-step, for the benefit of his "sishyas".

I shall now explain to you the essence of the thirteenth of the eighteen chapters of the Bhagavath Gita that Sri Krishna as Acharya imparted as Vedantic sermon to his beloved disciple Arjuna.

इदं शरीरं कौन्तेय क्षेत्रमित्यमिधीयते |
एतद्यो वेमि तंप्राहु: क्षेत्रज्ञ इमत तमिद: || 2 ||

*śrī-bhagavān uvācha idaṁ śharīraṁ kaunteya kṣhetram ity abhidhīyate
etad yo vetti taṁ prāhuḥ kṣhetra-jña iti tad-vidaḥ*

(Courtesy: R.Chithralekha)

"Arjuna, tell me what the nature of the Body is --- your body, that of all the armies you command, of the armies arrayed in the enemy ranks on the battlefield of Kurukshetra, or of everything that is embodied in fact and that which is visible to the naked eye here?

"Let me tell you all that which is visible to us as Bodies is called "kshetram" – a Dynamic Field. And the intelligent entity within the Body which is fully conscious of this Dynamic Field is known as "kshetragnyan" – the "Knower of the Field." And if you ask what is that intelligent entity is which is able to comprehend "kshetra" as a dynamic Field, the answer is Jeevaatma, the individual soul. This soul possessed of fulsome intelligence which is conscious of this dynamic Field is called "kshetragnyan"".

Sri Krishna then continued, "Every intelligent jeevaatma embodies itself in flesh and blood… i.e., it obtains as just desserts in accordance with all its past deeds of virtue and sin… And it is I who has willed it to be thus!

"In a way, therefore, you might say that I too who, possessing this body that as I do, happen to be Master "kshetragnyan!"

"Now, you might mistakenly think that it is alright to call this body of mine too as a "kshetra" – i.e., a dynamic field like all other human Bodies? But that would be folly and to know why you must first let me explain to you the real nature of this great Dynamic Field called "kshetram." So, please listen to me carefully."

***

This Body, the "kshetram" or the dynamic field, is constituted by twenty-four ontological principles – the five elements (*pancha-bhoot*a), matter (*prakruti*), primordial matter (*mahat*), the consciousness of "**I-ness**" or the Ego (*ahankaaram*), the physical and sense organs numbering eleven and the five organic faculties.

These twenty-four principles are verily the dynamic determinants of all physical, phenomenal Existence (*prakruti*). However, these twenty four principles do not have any bearing at all on what constitutes the divine nature of Sri Krishna's own Body (*tirumeni*). Hence, whatever Krishna himself explains as "kshetra", it must never be construed as being in any way related to his own. The dynamic field over which the twentyfour principles prevail, and is conceptualized as "kshetra", refers thus to only those Bodies (*sarira*) whose nature is physical and phenomenal and it pertains to the very same existential domain (i.e., *prakruti*).

The reason Sri Krishna emphasized the above matter for the sake of Arjuna's understanding is that the Scriptures contain many expositions of this extremely subtle (Vedantic) concept and it was Krishna's wish that Arjuna be enlightened specifically on the correct interpretation.

What are the different connotations of the word "kshetra" denoting a dynamic field?

Three metaphors are often used to refer to it and they are as follows:

- The earth, soil, a **farmer's field**

- A prominent **place of pilgrimage** or worship e.g., don't we all know the famous holy places of *'sathyavrata kshetra,' "Sri ranga kshetram'*?

- A **collection of twelve 'saalagraama'** (sacred pebbles) our wise elders also refer to as a "kshetra."

***

"kshetra" and "kshetragyna" – The metaphor of the Farmer's Field

Let us first examine the concept of "kshetra" in the sense in which it is compared with a farmer's field.

It is needless to recount all the strenuous efforts that a farmer will expend to till, seed, and cultivate his farm fields to make their yields plentiful. Without proper ploughing and seeding, strong rooting is not possible. Without weeding the saplings will not grow. If not properly fertilized, the plantings will not grow robustly, and yields would be poor. If not copiously irrigated at the right time, the soil would become infertile. If not securely protected, the growing crops would be raided by roaming stray cattle like goats and cows. If left unsecured or secured inadequately, paddy growing in the fields awaiting harvest, could also get stolen by thieves.

If a farmer were however to properly tend to his field otherwise than in the careless manner described above, then with the bounteous harvest crops brought home, he, and his entire family could indeed surely be able to live comfortably with heartfelt thanks given unto Bhagavan, the Almighty (*tiruvaaraadanam*) for blessings received!

Now, the Body (*sarira*) we possess too must be likened to such a kshetram called the farmer's field and we too must diligently work upon it as if it were truly one. The tilling and ploughing of the soil may be compared to one taking a daily bath and cleansing oneself by uttering appropriate mantras, donning fresh, clean clothes, habitually applying the sacred (Sri Vaishnava) symbols of the Lord's feet (*tirumann kaappu*) on one's forehead, neck, chest, arms and back, together with the holy mark of *sri choornam* (vermilion paste) too. All such acts would be tantamount to purifying our Body (*sarira*) in the way a farmer clears, ploughs, and tills his "kshetram", his agricultural field.

Furthermore, just as the farmer tends his field by carefully and continually removing unwanted weeds from it, the "kshetra" of our *sarira* too must be rid of unwanted natural elements that try to constantly encroach upon it. Such elements are three and they are called "sattva," "rajas" and "tamas".

Out of the three, it is only the first element, *sattva*, which, sown and seeded into the bodily "kshetra", must be carefully cultivated as crop. Once this *sattva* element takes root in the field, and is tended to with tender loving care i.e., in accord with the will of Bhagavan, it grows abundantly and yields a cornucopia of goodness, gain and benefits in life for us.

What impedes if not obstructs the cultivation of this element called '*sattva*' in the human 'kshetra *sarira*' are the other two elements or *guna* called "*rajas*" and "*tamas.*" Just as the farmer regularly weeds out unwanted growth encroaching upon the crops cultivated in his field, so too must we keep removing the weeds of "*rajas*" and "*tamas*" that constantly try to invade and infest our bodily "kshetra." That de-weeding, we can accomplish through unfailing observance of the daily regimen of *karmaanushtaanam*" as prescribed in the scriptural '*saastras*'. The significance of this spiritual 'de-weeding' or, in other words, self-purification, has been attested to in the Vyaasa-sutra text in a phrase **"anabhi bhavam cha darshayati."**

The Field that our Body, the "*sarira*" is, needs frequent fertilization. What is that fertilizer or manure? It is nothing but clean, nutritious food prescribed variously in the "*sastra*" as food grain, fruit, vegetable, milk, yoghurt, curd which the Body or "kshetra" needs for its sustenance and growth. All such Food should however first have been offered by us as oblation to Bhagavan.

Quite like the farmer's field, our '*sarira*' too needs copious irrigation in a timely manner. That water is the holy water that one sips as "*aachamanam teertham*" while performing the daily ritual procedures of *Gaayatri Sandhyaavandanam, Maadhyaahnikam*; during the *Nithya Bhagavath Tiruvaaraadanam* rite at home; during the funerary annual "*shraadham*" rites conducted for spirits of the departed ancestors when *Sri Paada teertham* is sipped; and on the 12th day of the lunar fortnights when (after the previous day of fasting) the rite of "*dwaadasi*" is observed when the holy "*Sri Paduka teertham*" is ritually sipped.

Besides all these acts, the irrigation of the "kshetra" i.e., the Field which is called our "*sarira*", is also affected when we worship inside the sanctum of a temple and receive there the sacred "*perumaal teertham*", or when we take a holy dip in the cool waters of the temple pond (*pushkarani*); and even when we go to **Sethu** (the great temple on the seashore of *Tirupullani*) for a dip in the ocean there... and equally so too when we bathe in the waters of the River Ganga.

All the waters described above, when ingested by us, have the effect indeed of increasing the potency of "*sattva guna*" in our Body, the *guna* which we ought to cultivate... And so, in the same manner as good irrigation enriches the good nutrients present in the soil of the farmer's field, these waters enrich the "*sattva guna*" present in us.

Just as crops cultivated in the farmer's field must be carefully husbanded and secured, so is it also especially important to protect and preserve what is cultivated within ourselves in our body as "*sattva guna*".

Such protection we can give ourselves through the following ways viz. constantly seeking the company of men of piety and spiritual wisdom, frequently seeking audience with *Acharyas*, and obtaining from them their grace by having all our mental and spiritual doubts clarified and dispelled, learning valuable lessons from wise men discoursing upon spiritual matters pertaining to divine knowledge (*bhagavath bhaagavatha charithram*) etc. Such activity indeed helps preserve the carefully cultivated "*sattva guna*" in our '*sarira*' just as any farmer would take pains to ensure protection of his field from the devastation that stray cattle grazing upon it can easily cause. The danger posed to growing crops on a farmer's field by stray, grazing cattle is the same as the danger posed to our '*sarira*' by wicked objects as well as wicked thoughts, ideas, urges and feelings of the world that may prey upon and pollute our sense organs.

Just as the farmer labors to ensure that the growing crops do not get stolen by felons, so too must we ensure that *'sattva guna'*, which is really the valuable crop under cultivation in life, does not get stolen from us under any circumstance. Now, after all the effort, in the end what is exactly the bounteous harvest that we may expect reap from this *"sattva guna"*? The answer is **"sattvaath sanjaayatE gnyaanam"** – clear and luminous Knowledge that we will surely gain in life.

The sum and substance of everything that our venerable *purvaaacharyas* impart to us, we will eventually imbibe through such knowledge. Like glittering gems encrusted in pure gold, the *Almighty Bhagavan Sriman Naaraayaana*, who is verily the abode of all auspiciousness and felicitous qualities, together with his divine consort, *Sri Mahalakshmi*, will in fact embed himself in such Knowledge we gain. And once such Knowledge grows, matures, and slowly ripens in life, it will consummate itself in the realization of Sriman Naaraayana Himself!

Even at that time of consummation, when *"gnyaana"* is at the very verge of realizing Bhagavan, one must beware of thieves stealing it away just as full-grown crops, even after harvest and lying-in storage, robbers might easily loot. If you ask who such thieves of Knowledge are, the answer is it is the *Devata-s*, the demigods and lesser gods of the world who will do everything within their powers to obstruct and despoil *"saatvic"* Knowledge obtained; and they will do their utmost to distract it away from its goal of consummation in Godhood.

Hence one should constantly beware of falling into traps, allurements and treacherous designs that may have been laid for us by the *devata-s*; and this is what is meant by the saying: **"tridashah: paripanthinah:"**

To sum up all the above, what is thus really meant by the Body or *"sarira"* being called "kshetra", and the *"jeevaatma"* being called "kshetragnyan", is only this:

Like a farmer tending his field with such extreme care to reap a rich harvest, the *jeevaatma*, the kshetragnyan too shall have to till and cultivate his body, the kshetra, irrigate it, de-weed it, add fertilizers and rich nutrients to it to make it grow, protect it from vandals and thieves… And in the end, the rich harvest the *jeevaatma* reaps will surely be received as yield from the great Master of all "kshetragynan-s", the Almighty Bhagavan himself. It is he who will then grant each *jeevaatma* all kinds of goodness, why salvation even (*mukthi*), but only as just desserts truly deserved in accordance with the stock of its own accumulated karma i.e., the many virtues and sins it has committed.

***

"kshetra" and "kshetragyna" – The metaphor of the "brahmapuram"

Now let me explain why a few knowledgeable people within our fold have opined that the words "kshetra" and "kshetragnya" in the Bhagavath Gita, as used by Sri Krishna, serve as brilliant metaphors for places of pilgrimage called *"divya kshetra"* which we all know dot the length and breadth of our vast country. Please listen keenly.

What is a *"divya desam"*? It is a place of pilgrimage where a great, imposing temple will stand; there would be a temple pond (*pushkarani*); the temple would be presided over by a Deity. The Deity would have dedicated temple-servitors (*archakas* and *aaradhakaars*); and they would perform rituals (*tiruvaaradana*) to the Deity, such as *"tirumanjanam"* (ritual purificatory bath); they would dress the Deity in fine silk and rich brocaded finery; they would adorn the Deity with precious gem-studded jewelry; they would also beautify the idol of the Deity with colorful, fragrant flowers and garlands. Then they would also chant litanies in praise of the Deity to please Him. Thereafter they would offer the Deity food-oblations (*thaligai*) as token of sacrificial worship (*neivedhyam*).

Next, ritually they would light up the sanctum by waving of lamps and lights (*deepa-haarathi, karpoora-neeraajanam*) before the idol of the Deity. And finally, after what is known as *"mangala-haaraathi"* (the waving of auspicious flames from a lamp), the Deity would be offered the joyous consummatory chants of the *"saatrumarai"* --- a ringing litany of holy benedictions showered upon him in worship.

Soon after, the gathered congregation of devotees would receive holy *"perumal teertham"* (holy water) to sip and be blessed with the *"sattaari"* (the placing of the symbol of the Perumal's Feet (*paaduka*) lightly on the heads of the devotees) …

We all have of course witnessed such scenes as above, haven't we, in many *divya-kshetrams* we have had occasion to visit on pilgrimages through this country? If any of you have not yet witnessed such scenes inside a temple or experienced the joy therein, then I urge you to please tarry no further! Get thee at once to a *divya-kshetram* and get to behold such glorious scenes inside the temple there! The very sight will ensure for you the Almighty's benevolent blessings without you even asking for it! And a pilgrimage to such places of worship is not really going to cost you all that much…

That this *sarira* of ours, the human body, is verily a *"brahmapuram"* – or *divya kshetra* – stands attested to by the Veda itself.

We know from human anatomy, that inside the chest there lies a lotus-bud shaped organ called *"hrudaya,"* the heart. This heart symbolizes the temple that the Almighty God has built for his very own purpose and pleasure inside the kshetra of our Body. Reducing himself in size so that he can reside in this tiny temple or *"divya-kshetra,"* situated deep inside the coronary crevice of the human body, *Sriman Naaraayana*, accompanied by his divine consort, *Mahalakshmi*, and bearing all his divine weapons, like '*sankha, chakra, gadhaa*' etc. presides over it in all majesty, glory, and splendor. In close contact with, and within the same heart and in the precincts of the Almighty's presence, lives a servitor, called the *jeevaatma*, whose duty it is to serve the presiding deity. That jeevaatma is the 'kshetragnyan.'

The jeevaatma who is kshetragnyan, by dint of faithful service and rendering constant worship unto the *Lord Maadhava* resident inside the temple of its body, i.e., the kshetra, succeeds in ridding itself of all its accumulated sins. It then ultimately attains everlasting spiritual bliss. Such is indeed the meaning that is sought to be conveyed through this metaphor of the *"place of pilgrimage."*

Now, how the "kshetragnyan" goes about his duties as servitor inside the temple of his '*sarira*' or "kshetra," offering worship (i.e., *tiruvaaraadanam*) to the Deity presiding there, has been described eloquently and variously by the holy saints, the Azhwaars in their Tamizh *"divya prabhandham"* verses.

Sri Peria Azhwaar has affirmed clearly that the human heart is indeed the temple inside the "kshetra" of the human body and the dedication and devotion – *shraddhai* – shown by the jeevaatma is indeed what symbolically floral offerings to the Almighty become: *"maarvam enbadhor kovil amaitthu, maadhavan ennum deivattai naatti, aarvam enbadhor poovida vallaarkku, arava thandatthil uyyallaamey!"*

What is *"shraddha"*?

If one takes himself to a secluded and clean spot, seats himself there and then with a pure mind, begins to concentrate on the Deity enshrined within his own heart, then by that very act of intense contemplation, he is deemed to have secured all the requisite sacred waters needed to be drawn from a temple-pond or some other holy river for the due performance of the outward ritual of *tiruvaaraadanam*.

A pure mind serves the same purpose as pristine water in the worship of God. And such a pure mind regarded as riverine sacred water is what aids in the ceremonial act of offering *"paadyam," "aachamaniyam"* and *"tirumanjanam"* – purificatory oblations – which are worshipfully rendered unto the Deity of Madhava.

Even a moment of steady meditation upon the Lord Madhava's form assumes the form of silk raiment offered to him as his vestment. If that moment of meditation lingers for yet another moment, then it must be deemed to have assumed the form of fragrant sandal paste *Chandana kaappu)* that is ceremonially smeared upon the divine figure of the Deity. And again, if we worship Madhavan humbly with folded arms and joined palms even once, then that act must be held to be equivalent to the act of bejeweling the Deity and clothing him with splendid raiment. If that Bhagavan then is praised in word and thought through solemn chants of hymnal poesy (*stotra*), then that deed assumes the form of offering floral adorations to Him as jasmine, marigold, lily, hibiscus etc. and vibrant garlands too made of the same.

The very same sentiment and symbolism expressed above has been voiced too by **Nammaazhwar** in his *"paasuram"* (verse) that runs as follows:

poosam saandhum en nenjamey punayam enadh-udaiya vasagam sey maalayE vaan pattaadaiyyum agathey desamaana anigalanum enn kaikoopa seyygaiyE eesan gnyaanam-mundamizhndha endhai eka moorthikkE!

Furthermore, we must understand that the five golden chalices (or *"vattil"* used while performing the holy rite of *tiruvaaraadanam*) represent our five physical and facultative sense organs; and the water collected inside them represents what the *saastra* describes as primordial Matter in terms of Form (*roopam*), Substance and Essence (*rasam*). The little ladle (*uddharani*) used in the same ritual symbolizes our Mind (*manas*) with which we reverentially make the motions of offering the Deity '*arghyam*' and other sacraments. The offering of ceremonial *dhoopam* and *deepam* (fragrant smoke and lighted lamp) to the Deity, is nothing but a symbolic way in which we convey our act of contemplation upon the various glorious incidents in the life of the divine avatars undertaken by Bhagavan when He descended upon the earth as the savior of his devotees.

What is *"nivedanam"* or offering of sanctified food offering to Bhagavan is but a symbolic representation of our deep awareness that there is nothing in the material world that exists which can ever be said to be our possession, as our very own or as belonging inseparably to us ... for, all that we are and all that we have... is truly all His and His very own.

What is the symbolism of the final act of offering *"mangala haarathi"* and reciting the litanies of *"saatrumarai"*? It lies in presenting to the Deity varieties of delicious food offerings (*paayasam* etc.) lovingly prepared in the household-kitchen (*anna jaatam*) and, thereafter, in the prostrations (*saashtaanga sevitthal*) made before the Almighty while uttering the prayer:

"kadhaa punah sankha rathaanga kalpaka dvajaaravindhaankusa vajralaanchanam..."

Thus, from all that has been said above, what finally must be understood to be the central message of Sri Krishna's words spoken in the Gita is verily this and it is also the opinion of many wise preceptors of our tradition:

We as *"jeevaatma kshetragnya"*, by regarding our *'sarira'*, the body, as *"brahmapuram"* or *"kshetra"*, and by worshipping the resident Bhagavan present within our heart, attain in time the high spiritual status and bliss that Sri Krishna himself confers upon us.

***

"kshetra" and "kshetragyna" – The metaphor of the twelve *"saalagraama-s"*

It is well-known belief that a collection of 12 or more sacred *"saalagraama"* --- the hard, dark pebbles found on the bed and banks of the River Gandaki, Nepal --- have the same and equal sanctity as a temple in a *"divya-kshetram"*; and therefore, if the human *'sarira'*, the Body, as already explained above, is a veritable "kshetra", then by the same token, it is to be regarded as the equal of 12 or more sacred *"saalagraama"* too.

If we ask what the reasoning behind such a belief is, the answer lies in the significance of that scriptural aphorism uttered when one gives away in charity a precious gift of *"saalagraama"* to another: *"saalagramashila chakre bhuvanaani chaturdasha...."*

The *"saalagraama"* pebble has a surface that is naturally etched by several small whorls of the image of the *"chakra,"* the wheel or discuss of Vishnu. Those tiny whorls of the *"chakra"* represent fourteen different worlds or planes of existence. So, when a donor makes a gift of the *"saalagrama"* to anyone, he is deemed to donate every goodness and value that may be found in fourteen different worlds! And so, the prayer above of the donor, while making the gift, must be understood as meaning to convey that whatever blessing might be accruing to a person making gifts of 14 worlds to anyone, should also be bestowed equally upon the donor of the *"saalagraama"*. The human *"sarira'* is fit indeed to be compared with a sacred *"salagraama"* stone.

The reason why is clear:

As the 3 sacred mantras (i.e., *ashtaakshara, dvaya* and *charama-shloka*) convey their esoteric meaning to us, Sriman Naarayana, as *Lakshmi-kaanthan*, who even while residing in his eternal abode in *Sri Vaikuntam*, high and beyond the highest of heavens, does however ensure that his divine presence manifests itself still upon earth; and his divine will and purpose (*sath-kaaryangal*) too are realized here upon earth. This, the Almighty effects through his devotees, the "*bhaagavataas,*" who are great bodies of his own proxies and agency. And it is they who, wherever they go and through whatever they accomplish, verily constitute the great wonders of the world we see in the world -- whether they appear as great rivers like the Ganga or Kaveri, or great mountains like the Himalayas, the vast oceans, or holy cities like Kanchipuram that grant even salvation or the highest state of heaven, "*svarga loka*" to one and all. It is to this significant aspect of how "*bhaagavatha sarira*" serves the Will of the Almighty that Swami Vedanta Desikan alludes to in his famous poetic lines: **"theynaar kamala tirumagal naathan"** and **"tattak-shata tapovanam".**

It is therefore to be understood that the *saastra* itself attests to the fact that he who lives life as a devout *bhaagavatha* possesses indeed a body that is equal in sanctity to twelve or more sacred "*saalagraama*". That is what Sri Krishna in the Bhagavath Gita implies.

***

Now, after describing the nature of the human 'sarira' as the metaphoric "kshetra" and that of the "jeevaatma" as the indwelling "kshetragnyan", Sri Krishna next proceeds to detail the qualities that the soul of a true "*bhaagavatha*", who destined to attain the supreme state of grace from which there is no question of he ever returning to the mortal world, possesses.

Such a "kshetragnyan" is seen to be free of ego and arrogance; is non-violent, patient and forbearing; follows the path of rectitude and is ever deferential towards his preceptors and implicitly abides by their instructions; maintains purity and dignity of self in everything he does; who is unwavering in his faith in God; whose mind is absolutely self-controlled; who desires nothing material in the world except "*moksha*", salvation; who in spite of possessing great riches still shuns feelings of any self-importance; who remains ever mindful of the state to which all human life must ultimately reduce itself to – death, rebirth, degeneration, disease and decay; who maintains detached attitude in relationships with spouse, progeny, home and pelf; who is free of lustful desire and avarice; is free from anxiety over whatever good or ill the future may bring; cultivates feelings of constant *Bhakti* towards Me; longs to retire to a state of seclusion away from the madding crowds of the world; remains fixed in contemplation of his own *Atman* and in the knowledge of My form and nature; remains steadily meditating upon spiritual principles and *tattva*-s....

All the above qualities, thus, are those that a *jeevaatma* who is "kshetragnyan", will cultivate and desire to seek high spiritual status in life. By honestly examining our own selves, we too will be able to discover which of the above qualities may be lacking in us. We should thus thereafter be enabled to proceed immediately to redress such inadequacies in ourselves by seeking the guidance of men of wisdom and spiritual luster.

***

Having detailed all the qualities a "kshetragnyan" must cultivate and possess in life, Sri Krishna next proceeds in this chapter of the Bhagavath Gita to portray the typical character-profile of such a jeevaatma.

This is what he says:

"That jeevaatma knows no beginning and knows no end; it is fundamentally different from mere Matter or other insentient beings; it cannot be said to perish even at the time of cosmic dissolution. After shedding its mortal body in the state of attaining "mukthi" or salvation, it can still act with volition; but while living in the mortal world, it can act with volition with the aid of the body or sarira only; it assumes manifold corporeal forms of life in accordance with the effects of its innumerable previous karmic deeds; it remains untainted and unaffected by the infirmities that its own 'sarira' suffers; it is a monad and there is none more atomic in size and nature than itself; it experiences all the joys and sorrows in life that its own body undergoes; it is self-luminous gnosis in its essential nature; it resides within the throbbing heart of all living beings; it lives within each bodily form that it comes to assume in accordance with whatever karmic legacy it inherited; it

possesses the potential to submit to the will of the Bhagavan and thereby free itself of all sin and thereby enjoy everlasting, unceasing bliss; it knows no death or change by itself although through successive series of birth, death and re-births, its body undergoes manifold transformations; it's reality and true nature is never realized by the mass of unregenerate humanity; it's true form and nature can be realized only through Vedantic knowledge; although its body may grow in form from small to big, and may also shrink from big to smaller forms, the jeevaatma itself neither ever grows or shrinks in size; It remains in a permanent same state of blissful self-consciousness.

"Arjuna, firstly I explained to you what is "sarira". Then I explained to you the various qualities or "guna" that a jeevaatma must cultivate. I also then described to you the typical character profile of the jeevaatma. "So long as the jeevaatma must live in this mortal realm, it can never do without the sarira. Even the greatest of Vedantins will have to lead earthly life with this body only and will be subjected hence to experiencing mortal joy and sorrow. There is no escaping the clutches of mundanity. All that the jeevaatma can do under the circumstances is only to strive to do whatever is necessary to cease forthwith the operation of the relentless cycle of karma that leads to repeated rebirths in the mortal realm. The soul can free itself forever from mortal rebirths only by ridding itself of its self-replenishing stock of sins accumulating over countless earthly incarnations.

✻✻✻

To rid itself of its countless sins, the *jeevaatma* must cultivate within itself the needed qualities of *sattva* with which it will become possible for it to pursue the path of **Yoga** – i.e., *karma yoga, gnyaana yoga* and *bhakthi yoga*. Attainment of the realm of Sri Vaikuntam will then become possible and with that state of eternal attained, there will be no more rebirths in bodily forms conditioned by sin and/or virtue. Eternal and ultimate bliss will follow, and it can then be enjoyed in the glorious presence of Bhagavan.

It is possible for a man to attain that eternal state of spiritual bliss only with the aid of his *'sarira'*. If a man were to purchase a pair of bullocks, bring them home and were to begin caring for them by daily feeding them both with copious amounts of silage, fodder, water, hay etc. he would succeed certainly in fattening them. But then, to what real purpose is such fattening? At the end, the well fattened bullocks would certainly die, wouldn't they? All the care and food given to the animals would then be worth naught unless he had also put those creatures to any practical use and productive work, isn't it so? Otherwise, people would only look upon the man as being an utter fool engaged in the futile occupation of fattening beasts for senseless purpose.

In the same analogous way, this *jeevaatma* too must be seen to have acquired the human *'sarira'* as though it were a pair of bullocks. In like manner too, the soul too after having obtained its bodily form begins to tend to the *'sarira'* by feeding and sustaining it well lifelong – i.e., by keeping it clean, clothing it, beautifying it in all sorts of manner etc.

However, if this *jeevaatma* fails to extract real, purposeful work from its own *'sarira'* to meet its own true goals in life (*purushaartha*), then that would be no different than fattening bullocks with no thought of putting them to work. Such a *jeevaatma* then would qualify to be crowned the regal preceptor to motley fools.

Therefore Arjuna, think deeply over everything that I have told you so far and after doing so, you must resolve accordingly to proceed on the most suitable path for you to attain *Sri Vaikuntam*.

Thus did Sri Krishna conclude his sermon to Arjuna in **13th Chapter of the Bhagavath Gita** and thus has its very essence been summed up here.

***

-7-
Nuggets of Vedanta

Synopsis: The philosophy of Vedanta cannot be understood properly without a thorough grasp of some of its fundamental concepts and doctrines, many of which to the layman might seem rather dense or inscrutable. Here, the Pontiff's exposition of Vedantic fundamentals makes the philosophy quite understandable even to an unschooled mind.

There are many indeed in the world who go about expounding at great length so much about the subject of Vedanta. But let me proceed to explain the very essence of it as can be found in priceless nuggets of gems mined from out of the very depths of the vast sea called Vedanta and offer it here below as finely refined concepts and truths

Naayam devo na marthyo vaa na thiryak sthaavaropi vaa I

Gnyaanandamayasthvaatmaa seshohi paramaathamana: II

The soul -- or *jeevatma* -- that enlivens this body is of the nature of Pure Knowledge (*gnyaana*), Absolute Bliss (*Ananda*) and is Monadic in form (*anu*). It is a property of the *Paramatma* i.e., a chattel of Bhagavan.

This *Atma* is unlike other celestial entities or *devatas* like *Brahmma*. Even *devatas* like *Brahmma*, *Indra*, *Rudra* and others that are either seen or conceived by us as possessing some kinds of form, are mere bodily appearances only. However, that which inheres such bodily forms as an intelligent entity is the *jeevatma*. That entity does not carry any such name such as a *"deva"*. It is indeed that entity called *jeevatma* which Bhagavan himself endows with a bodily identity --

such as *Brahmma*, *Indra* etc. -- and which, in fact, arises as a result of its manifold acts of virtue and goodness (*punyam*).

All such bodily manifestations however are subject to decay and dissolution in course of time. But that which is the *Atma*, inhering within all such bodily forms, is indestructible and everlasting. No matter how big or otherwise the bodily form, the inherent *Atma* is always of the same atomic size and monadic form. The *Atma's* own form is neither dependent upon nor determined in any way by the bodily form it assumes as a devata or as any other celestial entity. Within the bodies of all entities, celestial or heavenly, the form of the *jeevatma* remains ever one and the same.

Similarly, *"na marthyo vaa"* ...

The form of the *jeevatma* bears no relationship or resemblance whatsoever to the manifold bodily forms in which humanity appears. Lameness, blindness, dwarfishness etc... all these are attributes of the body only, not of the soul. In fact, the appellation, *Man (or Woman)*, relates to the body only and not to the *Atma*.

One cannot obtain a measure of the *Atma* in the same way as one gets a measure of a man's body (or a woman's). In other words, we cannot describe the *Atma* in the same manner in which we characterize the human body as possessing limbs, head etc. No matter how big the size of the bodily frame of the human being, the *Atma* resides unseen as an atomic entity inside an unknown space within the beating heart known as *"hrudaya"*. Within the beating hearts of all humans on earth, the *jeevatma* resides as the one and same entity, of same form and nature, and goes by the same description.

"na thiryak" ... The *jeevatma* also cannot be said to be defined by or to possess the same bodily forms as any of the myriad creatures seen in the animal kingdom --- such as the elephant, horse, tiger, lion, or, birds such as the eagle, ravens etc. or reptiles such as serpents, scorpions, mongoose, lizards etc. Neither the size nor the shape of all these creatures – big or small -- can ever be attributed to the *Atma*. They are only attributes of the body of such creatures. Within all such creatures inheres their *Atma* which is of the same nature, same form and description.

Then there are other living beings in the world that are stationary or immobile – "*sthaavara varga*" – which take innumerable bodily forms such as trees, plants, creepers etc. Those myriad varieties of forms too cannot be ascribed to the *jeevatma* that resides within each of them as an inhering spirit that assumed such particular bodily form and bodily nature (*anugunam*) by reason of its past "*karma*" i.e., sins and virtues (*paapa, punyam*).

The innumerable resident-souls within the vast plant kingdoms too are imperishable, they possess cognition (*gnyaana*), they are monadic and are one and the same in nature and description. This has been revealed to us by Maharishi Parashara.

Now you may wonder why the Maharishi did not exactly specify the actual dimensions of the atomic size of the *jeevatma*? The Maharishi has clarified the matter in yet another scriptural work of his where he has said this – "*sarirakruthibhedaasthu bhoopa ethae karmayonaya:*" … i.e., *It is only by reason of countless past paapam and punnyam that a jeevatma gets endowed with a bodily form that it deserves or is fated to assume.* Accordingly, the bodily form it begets can be manifold --- perhaps as an elephant, a mosquito or even as a human or a *devata* too!

One must therefore rightly dwell on this question: If the *jeevatma* within the body of an elephant were to be of the same physical size as that of an elephant, how could it then in a succeeding life, when it must take on the bodily form of a mosquito, ever be able to morph into such a tiny creature? It therefore stands to reason that it is only because of its monadic size and nature that the *jeevatma* is enabled to assume any and all varieties of bodily forms in those successive manifestations in which it appears in life as pre-destined by its many past acts of *paapam* and *punyam*. It is thus then that the question about the actual dimensions of the size of the *jeevatma* gets answered. It is also thus why in Vedanta it is said, "*Esheranu: atma…*" which means that the soul that inheres the body is a monad. Nothing exists anywhere which can be said to be smaller than the *jeevatma*. Such is the atomic nature of the soul.

Maharishi Vyasa also affirmed the atomic size of the *Atma* through an aphorism (*sutra*): "*svasapthonmaanaapyaamcha…*".

There is thus nothing extant which is more atomic or subtle than the *jeevatma*. The soul is neither male, female nor transgender; it is neither plant nor human; neither a celestial nor a bird. As per the scriptural utterance – *"nithyo nithyaanaam…"* and *"na jaayathe mruthyathe vaa…"* – the soul is neither born nor does it die. The soul exists everlastingly (*nithyamaan*) in Pure Knowledge (*gnyaanasvarupan*) and in Absolute Bliss (*anandamayan*).

Infinite are the numbers of such *jeevatmas* that exist eternally. By virtue, and as consequence of the respective deeds of *"paapam"* and *"punya"*, each *jeevatma* gets endowed with a certain pre-destined bodily form (*sarira*) and lives as creatures of nature in the vast universe. They are reborn again and again in similar fashion through ceaseless time. Unable to extricate themselves from out of this endless cycle of birth and rebirth, the *jeevatmas* continue to flounder and remain mired in the myriad bodies to which they are consigned by destiny. It is in that pathetic state that we as human souls too undergo all manner of mundane pain and sorrow, while being guilty in life of numerous acts of grievous commission and omissions. Either out of negligence or complacence, or both, our lives only end up wasting away in nescience.

Thus, what is the very first thing to know about ourselves is this: What we are accustomed to referring as *"I"*, *"me"* and *"mine"* is not be associated with flesh and blood, or *'sarira'*. It is rather the indwelling *Atma* residing within the body that is the real *"I"*. This Vedantic truth must be well and firmly grasped and understood at the very outset.

***

"adhya me saphalam janma jeevitam cha sujeevitam I

Gopuram ranganaathasya sampoornam pashyatho mama II"

In continuation of what was earlier explained above, it must be noted that this concept of *"atma svaroopa gnyaanam"* has been expounded in the **Brahma Sutras** itself by *Maharishi Vyasa* in a *sutra* titled *"palamatha: upapatthe: …"*.

In his Tamil hymn in 1.9 of **Periya Thirumozhi**, this subject has also been spoken of (by *Sri Tirumangai Azhwar*) in the *"paasuram"* –

"*piRarkkE uzhaitthu yEzhai aanEn* (meaning, "*All my life I have only been working for others and have become poor by frittering away all my wealth....*"). The Tamizh word "*piRar*" in the literal sense means "*others*" but in the context in which the Azhwar employs it, it means the Body, or '*sarira*'. In other words, the Azhwar rues over this fact thus: "*Alas, I have mistaken myself to be one and the same as this body of mine; having identified myself with it completely all my life, I have slaved for its sake and benefit. I see now that I have only ended up wasting my life serving this wretched, decaying, impermanent 'sarira'! When I look back, I see that there now is nothing left of life in me which could have been otherwise devoted for the sake of the Atma, my soul, and to take it beyond, safely and securely, to the yonder shore of life! Thus, have I have made myself utterly destitute ("yEzhai aanEn")!*"

Thus, what the Azhwar's "*paasuram*" emphasizes is that the Body or '*sarira*' is "*piRar*" i.e., *others*; and it is the *Atma* or soul which is the "I". Thus, it stands to reason that all human relationships in which one as the "I" is involved – *father, mother, son, sibling, spouse et al*... they all relate to the "*sarira*" only. Between one *Atma* and another, in reality there exists no relationship of kinship at all, such as father, mother, child, sibling etc. Such relationships arise only as a result of *kaarmic* bondage pertaining to the "*sarira*" only. To illustrate this truth, the '*purana*' tells a tale.

There once lived a great and virtuous king. For many years he had no offspring. To beget an heir, he performed many holy rituals of propitiation. Finally, he was blessed with the birth of a son. The king doted on his son as he grew up, showering the child with great love and care. However, suddenly, at the age of five, the son died. The king was plunged into an abyss of grief and denial. He cradled the dead son on his lap and remained so deeply distressed for many days, while even starving himself. Since the king was a very virtuous man, the sage Narada, out of compassion for the monarch's plight, decided to come down to earth to not only console him but also impart some lessons in spiritual wisdom.

After commiserating with the grieving king, Narada asked him, "What do you want?"

"I want my dead son here to be restored to life again!", said the king.

"Alright, if that is what you want, move that dead body of your son from you lap and lay it on the ground", Narada said.

The king did as he was told. He laid the lifeless body of his son on the ground. The sage Narada then invoked his great yogic power to revive the prince by beckoning back the life breath that had taken leave of the boy to return to him and restored the child thus back to life!

The king could not contain his joy! He took hold of the son brought back from death and embraced him tightly.

The boy however recoiled and turned to ask the father, "Why do you smother me in your embrace like this?!"

The king replied, "My dear son, you were dead but now you are alive again and have returned to me! My joy knows no bounds! Hence, I embrace you, my son!"

The little boy however sharply retorted:

"Oh, you fool! Let go of me now! What kinship do you and I have? It was only as consequence of some past karmic deed operating as *"punyam"* that had brought you and I, as father and son, together in life. That bond of kinship was however timebound. Once its time was up, the kinship too ended. That was the reason why I exited from this body. My Atma has no relationship with you, none whatsoever. This body alone is related to yours. This body has constantly undergone decay. I must therefore now shed it and take leave of it to go to yet another place to where I am destined to go."

Looking then at the boy, Sage Narada asked, "Where will you go now?" To which the boy replied calmly:

"As a consequence of my past deeds, I am destined to be reborn as a dog's puppy. So, I am now destined to go there".

Narada the posed another question to the boy, "If I were to erase your past deed that predestines you to be born as a puppy, would you wish to be reborn instead as the princeling of this king, your father, again?"

The child replied to Sage Narada with these words:

"This king is a man who possesses no Vivekam, spiritual Wisdom. He has no knowledge of Vedanta. I do not wish to be reborn to him".

Saying so, the boy's spirit took leave of both the king and Sage Narada.

The sudden turn of events brought the king to his senses. He became utterly ashamed of himself for his lack of wisdom. He realized his folly and ignorance; he entreated Sage Narada to begin imparting to him the wisdom of Vedanta and lessons thereof with which he could then refashion his life, live purposefully and realize the true goals to which he knew his soul must aspire. Thus ended the story of the *"purana"*.

Therefore, one can conclusively say that one *jeevatma* is not the offspring of another *jeevatma* --- either as father or mother. The only true and everlasting kinship a *jeevatma* has is its inseverable bond with the *paramatma*. This truth about *Atma* is precisely what is the very core of Vedanta as has been conveyed in a nutshell to us by Bhagavadh Ramanujacharya as *"upadesa"*, his central precept.

***

Now, let us proceed to present in a nutshell the conception of *"paramatma"*, otherwise known as *"kadavull"*, *"Bhagavan"* or God.

Paramatma is all-pervading. Unlike the *jeevatma*, the *paramatma* does not possess any physical form such as limbs, head, eyes, ears, nose etc. Just as the expanse of the sky (*'Akaasa'*) overarches over everything in this world as limitless, unseen space looming over us as vast universal awning – over moving vehicles, mankind, railways, aircrafts, birds. This overarching *"Akaasa"* although it pervades everything universally, still it does in no way obstruct or impede the state or condition of any living object in the world from going hither and thither. In the same way, the unseen, immeasurable form of Bhagavan (*bhagavath svaroopam*) too pervades everything universally without causing in any way any sort of obstruction or impediment to such living entities. The form, presence and the reality of *paramatma* can be experienced or apprehended as pure Knowledge, *"gnyaana"*, i.e., as an ethereal medium surrounding Bhagavan like a great halo of omniscience (*prabhai*). Such Knowledge neither waxes nor wanes in time. It forever remains pure and absolute. This gnostic nature and all-pervading form of Bhagavan constitutes also Absolute Bliss – *"Ananda"*.

The nature of Paramatma, being both Absolute Knowledge and Absolute Bliss, also possesses other aspects of the same such as qualities of Compassion (*kaarunyam*), Solicitude (*vaatsalyam*) and other innumerable attributes of excellence, auspiciousness and infinite perfections (*anantha kalyana guna*) e.g., strength (*balam*), resourcefulness (*aiswaryam*), valour (*veeryam*), power (*shakthi*), effulgence (*tejas*). It is all these qualities of infinite perfections (*kalyana guna*) that constitute, as it were, a veritable treasure-chest of precious gems that are divinely cut and used by Bhagavan from time to time as and when he deigns to give protection and care to any being that yearns for his grace.

None can ever perceive the form or grasp the presence of "*paramatma svaroopam*". It has no shape or bodily feature. The Upanishads reveal to us that all of Creation owes its very existence to this *paramatma*. But much like the *jeevatma's* own nature, this too is neither male, female or transgender. While however the *jeevatma* is destined to assume bodily gender through and according to its deeds of karma, the *paramatma* assumes whatever gender, specie or form it deems appropriate, out of its own will and pleasure, only to realize its own purpose viz. to confer protection and salvation for all Creation. It is such forms of the *paramatma* that have come to be called and known as "Rama", "Krishna", "Vamana", "Narasingha". The Bhagavan who in his primordial abode of Sri Vaikuntam possesses a divine form that is absolutely unlike any that is conceivably mortal. However, he descends to the mortal realms taking form as *Rama, Narasimha* etc. only for the sake of realizing the sole purpose of his avatar viz. to protect his devotees (*bhakthas*) and grant them salvation while at the same time destroying evil and their enemies.

There is yet another deeper significance and purpose to Bhagavan's avatar which is described in effect to be his wilful descent of his own accord from the realms of Sri Vaikuntam to the mortal worlds.

Jeevatmas are reborn in the mortal worlds, repeatedly, in manifold bodily forms according to their respective karmic deeds. Inside all such bodily forms, one will find a spot in the region of the upper chest region, and situated above the umbilical cleft, a small lump of muscular tissue shaped like a beautiful, inverted lotus-bud. It is the organ called the heart (*hrudaya*). It is inside this fleshy nesting place called "*hrudaya*" that Bhagavan instals the "*jeevatma*". Once made resident inside this nesting place, the "*jeevatma*" by itself cannot hope to exit it. Along with the "*jeevatma*" inside the "hrudaya" also reside its inner sensory faculties such as the Mind, Sight, Hearing, Taste, Touch etc. These faculties each get invoked from time to time to be employed in various physical tasks that the body must accomplish such as "seeing", "feeling", "hearing", "tasting" etc. Thus, the "*hrudaya*" and the Mind (and its faculties) are not to be identified as one and the same. Rather the "*hrudaya*" must be regarded as the small cavity inside the bodily form of the *jeevatma* wherein the *paramatma* too co-resides as the former's custodian, controller and protector. This avatar -- in which Bhagavan co-resides within the mortal realm along with the *jeevatma* -- is known as "*antaryaami*". It is as this "*antaryami*" verily that Bhagavan created the vast universe and gave it its manifold forms --- right from the devatas and gods such as Brahmma, humans, plant and animal kingdoms, the hills, oceans, lions, bears, the winged creatures et al…. His own nature and form however, as "*antaryami*", forever remain unchanged.

***

Bhagavan's own nature as well as his bodily form or substance *i.e.*, his "*sarira*" as "*antaryami*" or the immanence of all creation, is eternally existent. It is Matter known as "*moola-prakruti*" which is the primordial and causal substance of all things palpable in the universe. At the same time, it is also the "*subtle substance*" i.e., the "*sookshma sarira*" in which every "*jeevatma*" is clothed when born into its present mortal state or condition. That is the reason why Bhagavan is often described as "*sookshma-chethanaachethana visishta Bhagavan*". He is posited thus to be the ultimate cause of all Creation as well as its dissolution.

Furthermore, Bhagavan is also described by men of truth to be the *Protector of all Creation* by means of his own divine Will (*sankalpa*) and by means of his Pleasure (*icchai*), both of which are manifested in any bodily or substantial form that he chooses to take. It is that Bhagavan who has been eternally protecting countless numbers of his creations;

and it is he alone who continues even today protecting countless numbers of his proteges in this universe.

Exactly like Bhagavan, the *"paramathma"*, who is the ontological acme of every conceivable perfection and consummate virtue *("anantha kalyaana guna ganaan"),* there is yet another such *"paramathma".* If you ask, who that could be, the answer is it is his feminine counterpart called *Mahalakshmi.*

Bhagavan and Mahalakshmi are conceived as inseparable *Groom and Bride.* The former is the paragon of all perfections of masculine quality while the latter epitomises the absolute sublimities of femininity. The two absolute entities operate together in tandem to protect and nurture all Creation.

It is generally said (in theological discourse) that Bhagavan rules the universe from his celestial kingdom of *Sri Vaikuntam* in the same manner as that of a young Crown Prince, wielding a royal sceptre *("sengkol"),* might preside over and rule his empire as a sovereign would.

Some people might ask: How can a scion of a regal dynasty, a callow youth bearing the royal sceptre *(sengkol),* be regarded as the sovereign ruler of the land? how would it be apt to call him a *Crown Prince?* Isn't it only when such a youthful prince succeeds his parent, either Emperor or Empress, who have bequeathed the throne and *sengkol* to him, that he can be called the Sovereign? Until then, he remains perhaps only a *Crown Prince,* an underling of the Ruler but not the Ruler himself, doesn't he?

By the same logic, if Bhagavan were to be called a *Crown Prince,* won't it beg the question, *"Who is the Emperor or Empress still holding sway over the Crown Prince?"* The answer is quite simply this: *Mahalakshmi is the Empress*!

However, some might immediately protest, *"What?! But how can that be?!"* It is indeed nonetheless so!

As has been explained in the scripture: *"yasya veekshya mukham tadhingitha paraadheeno vidhathe'khilam...",* Bhagavan's acts of universal creation, protection, his generosity, caring attitude and the nurturing of his devotees *(aasritas),* his solicitude for them and his act of bestowing upon them redemption and final salvation --- all such divine acts are indeed urged and motivated by only one predominant cause: *Mahalakshmi's bidding*! It is by simply looking at her face (*'mukham'*) and by gleaning the meaning and the intent of her graceful glances – and not even by virtue of any spoken word or other utterance of any sort of hers -- that Bhagavan goes ahead to do her bidding and which become his divine deeds and exploits. Thus, since he acts in accordance with her wishes and desires, it is not inapt to say (as theologians do) that Bhagavan acts thus like a *Crown Prince* at the behest and pleasure of Mahalakshmi, who is the *Empress* -- indeed the silent mover and shaker, the ever-present consort of Bhagavan who is ever beside him but, in the background, or in his shadow.

Bhagavan's Universal Creation is called *"leela vibhuthi"* – a vast, immeasurable expanse of different cosmic worlds, collectively known as the *"14 heavenly spheres"*. All such worlds operate in their own respective domains overseen, controlled and regulated by celestial functionaries known as *"devatas"*, and at head of whose hierarchic order presides *Brahmma*, the progenitor. All such powerful *devatas* too are but creations of Bhagavan for it is he who endows each of them with their respective status, station and office – but then, to each *'devata'* only according to its own just desserts.

The divine will of Bhagavan is indomitable. Once he resolves to grant grace to protégés, no power on earth or in the heavens can either resist or stop him. There are innumerable instances and episodes to illustrate the fact. Here are a few of them:

***

- In the Ramayana, Sri Rama vowed to protect the *maharishis* of the Dandakaranya forests from the rampaging *Rakshasa* hordes in spite of Sita *piraatti* cautioned and restrained him from going all out on a campaign of vigilantism.
- In Lanka, when Vibheeshana came seeking his refuge and protection from Ravana's ire, Rama granted him safe haven, ignoring the vehement advice given by Jambavan, Sugreeva and many others in the *Vanara* camp who were against giving the *Rakshasa* asylum.

- The mighty and fearsome army of Ravana, and the most valorous of his warriors, could not stop Sri Rama from vanquishing them all.

- We have all also heard, haven't we, about how Sri Krishna overpowered into abject submission, the terrible 1000-armed *Asura* Banasura in spite of he being a protégé of Lord Shiva? The *Asura* had 998 of his shoulders all severed by Krishna!

- We all also know how one elephant (Gajendra) was saved by Bhagavan. We also know about another elephant, *Kuvalayapidam*, the tyrant Kamsa's own terrifying mastodon, that was subdued by Krishna. Similarly, Krishna granted the great serpent *Kaaliyan* reprieve while he slew the other terrible serpent, *Ajakaram*. Rama granted absolution to one lady, *Ahalya* while he destroyed another woman of the forests, *Tataka*. Again, he dealt death to one king (Vali) of the simian tribes while he rehabilitated yet another one (Sugreeva). He broke asunder the great bow of Lord Shiva but nonchalantly bent the bow of the terrible Parashurama!

The above exploits of course belong to past ages. But then, even in the present age, Bhagavan residing as *"archa murthy"* (consecrated idol) in various *"divya desams"* (terrestrial sanctums) such as in Sri Rangam temple and others, continues to grant protection and succour to millions of souls in this world. As the Deity presiding in the great hill-temple of Tirumalai today he continues to provide relief to millions of people from their earthly miseries and afflictions.

Likewise, Bhagavan presides over the lofty hills of Ahobilam as *"nava narasimha"* (nine forms of the Narasimha avatar) and grants protection to all his devotees. The nine glorious *archa* forms are *jwaala, ahobila, maalola, kroda, kaaranja, bhaargava, yogaananda, chattravata* and *paavana*. The Deity who presides over the Sri Ahobila Muttam is that *archa* of Bhagavan who is named *"Maalola"*. There can be none in the world who are unaware of the glory and power of Sri Lakshmi-Nrisimhan...

Then there is also Bhagavan presiding as Deity in the temple of Tiruvallur (near Chennai) as *Sri Veeraraghavan Perumal* who cures his devotees of all afflicted by all and any kind of physical and mental illnesses.

***

When we dwell upon the subject of Bhagavan's many avatars it is likely that a certain doubt may arise in our minds: If Bhagavan assumes a certain bodily form (*tirumeni*), would the rigidity of such form – i.e., its morphological structure -- impose any kind of constraints upon him?

The answer is that since Bhagavan's form is infinitely expansive and all-pervasive, all Matter and all Beings existent remain subsumed into his avatar form, both internally or externally. In other words, his immanent presence dwells universally in all Matter and all *jeevatmas* in turn too are inhered into the very core of Bhagavan's heart (*sarira hrudaya*), as it were. In that one specific respect, the *jeevatma* and *paramatma* are co-extensive and that condition prevails both in the phenomenal universe as it does equally in the meta-celestial heavens of *Sri Vaikuntam*. The theological conclusion to be made from all this reasoning is thus exactly what the wise and knowledgeable Vedantins tell us: That there is no inch of space in all this vast cosmos, or even in the conceivable beyond, where the immanence and pervasiveness of Bhagavan is absent; just as all physical (or physiological *sariras*) are inhered by the *jeevatma*, likewise so does the *paramatma* inhere in all existent beings as verily their life-force or principle.

***

There are also a few instances where Bhagavan's one avatar has occurred along with yet another one almost simultaneously or else contemporaneously. For example, he appeared as the midget-sized brahmin boy-mendicant who went to beg for alms from Emperor *Bali Chakravarthy*. When King Bali granted him his wish for land admeasuring the length of no more than the extent of merely three strides of his leg, Bhagavan transformed himself from the midget *Vamana* into the humongous form of *Trivikrama*, the awesome colossal avatar that rose into the skies above to stride the three cosmic worlds with just one step! Such was the glory of the *Vamana-Trivikrama avatar*!

Similarly, the *Sage Narada-muni* also witnessed the multiple avatars of Sri Krishna who multiplied himself into eleven thousand versions of himself simultaneously, with each impersonated self being seen with each of the eleven thousand *gopa-sthrees* (his devoted *gopikas* of *Gokulam*) that were besotted with intense *bhakthi* for Bhagavan and had made them all his paramours.

It is impossible however for any being to impersonate Bhagavan; and should that be even attempted, the result would only turn out as ridiculous as fashioning a replica of Garuda with wooden material and claiming it to be the original *"Pakshirajan"* or *"Garutman"*, the majestic *"vaahana"* or vehicle of the Almighty!

There is a tale that is often told in connection with this matter, and many of you might already know it. I am sure you also know the fate of all those beings who puffed up their chests with self-conceit and strutted about claiming *"I am God myself!"*; it turned out eventually that they had their chests torn apart. There was also once a time when even "devas" and gods like the powerful Indra ventured to defy Bhagavan but, in the end, when they faced existential threats and all utterly humbled, they fell at the feet of Bhagavan and sought his protection. Also, you might all heard how men of this world who, at one time, went about denouncing Bhagavan and his very existence, in the end however, after being struck down by some deadly disease or affliction, scamper in desperation to the nearest *Pillaiyaar* temple with offerings of coconuts to the deity as token of their contrition and atonement.

On an occasion, I once told a doctor, "You are god since you save and protect so many people from pain and suffering" to which he replied, "However never to be forgotten is the fact that there is another God above me who grants me the same protection".

"What do you mean?", I asked him.

"There was a time in my life when I was felled by a mysterious pulmonary illness *('vaayu vaata')* and became bedridden, unable to move my limbs and even speak. My mind plunged into depression. It was impossible for me to even direct anyone to go to my medicine-chest and fetch from it the medication I knew was good for me. It was because I was simply able to neither utter a word out of my mouth or even use my hands to scribble the name of the medicine! I was in deep despair and wept silently over my pathetic condition... There was absolutely nothing in the world that I possibly could do to rescue myself from my abject, pitiable state...

"It was then in that utterly destitute moment when suddenly my thought began dwelling upon how Bhagavan had rescued and protected Gajendran. Within myself I cried out, *"O saviour of Gajendra! O my guardian!"*

"In the next instant, I saw my wife rush towards me with something in her hands and say to me as I lay paralyzed on my bed,

"My dear, isn't this the medicine that you always prescribe for the affliction you're now suffering yourself? Here, let me administer it to you now", she said.

"She then gently fed the potion into my mouth and I consumed it".

"About half an hour later, I found I was able to slowly lift myself up from bed and be seated. I then beckoned my wife and asked her, "Tell me now from whom did you obtain the medicine that you just gave me? How did you get it?"

"My wife then told me this:

"At the temple, the man who is the temple elephant's mahout accosted me suddenly and told me "Your husband at home is now desperately clinging to the great elephant mahout and imploring him to rush to go to his aid. I am the mahout for the elephant in this temple. I am giving you now this medicine. Take it now and hasten forthwith home to your husband and give it to him at once. And so that's what I did now..." she said. And then she also told me this: *"The mahout at the temple was dark-complexioned and he also held a giant falcon ("garuda kodi") which had perched itself on his hand"*.

"On hearing that, I was struck with wonder!

"I heaved myself out of bed with difficulty and plodded my way to the doorway hoping to catch a glimpse of the elephant-mahout who had just visited us! But *alas, he was nowhere to be seen... he had vanished!* I sat down rueing my ill-luck as a sinner who had just had a miraculous opportunity to see Divinity but it had by then passed by in fleeting moments".

The doctor finally told me, "When I beseeched him for succour in my direst moment of crisis (as Gajendra had done), Bhagavan showed himself to save me. And that is the reason why I tell you that even though as a doctor people may say I am godlike because I sometimes save lives, there is yet Bhagavan, the greater God above me who alone is my only protector…"

There is one more thing the good doctor then told me:

"From the day I recovered from my near fatal illness, the medicines I now administer to patients who come to me with their illnesses is called *"yaanai marundhu"* – elephant medicine! And to prove to me that what he had resolved was indeed true, the doctor took me aside to show me the medicine chests in his clinic. All of them, I saw the, had the sign *"yaanai marundhu"* painted clearly and neatly on them!

What the doctor showed me that day put me to shame since I felt that the intense *"bhakti"* for Bhagavan the doctor cherished in his heart, made mine own even seem pale in comparison….

***

In summing up, therefore, it should be our firm conviction that *paramatma* is *"sarva rakshakan"* (the universal protector), *"Apathbandhu"* (the universal lifeguard), *"anaatha rakshakan"* (the saviour of the forsaken) and that it is he who alone who bestows his protection upon every *jeevatma* according to its just deserts of *punnya* and *paapa* karma. He is the all-pervading and immanent principle of all existence (*param porul*). He is omniscient. As and when his presence becomes incumbent on earth, he assumes various bodily forms to descend into mortal realms to realise his divine purpose.

Today, the Deity of the great temple in the city of Kanchipuram (*Perumal Kovil*), presides as Lord *Varadan* or *Peraarulan*, and rides the festive procession on his magnificent chariot (*tiruther*) along with his consort, *Perundevi*, showering bliss and grace along the way upon the thronging devotees. He indeed is that *paramatma*.

***

-8-
The Questions of Yaksha and The Answers of Dharmaputhra

Synopsis: The **Yaksha Prashna** *is the story of a question-and-answer dialogue between* **Yudhishthira** *and a* **Yaksha** *in the great epic* **Mahabharata.** *It appears in the* **"Vana Parva"** *part of the epic, and the story is set as the Pandava princes end their twelve years of exile in the forest. This dialogue between* **Yudhishthira** *and the* **Yaksha** *is also known as the* **"Dharma-Baka Upakhyana"**, *or the "Legend of the Virtuous Crane". The Yaksha Prashna legend is narrated in the epic in the format of a grave and tense dialogue between a ghoul of the forest and Yudhishtara. On the pain of death, if the right answer is not given, the Yaksha poses one hundred and twenty-three searching questions to Yudhishtira. The questions pertain to a wide, bewildering variety of subject matters – philosophy, ethics, human virtue and folly, dharma and adharma, the meaning of life and death....*

The Yaksha Prashna in the Mahabharatha is narrated in Sanskrit. Mukkur Swamy translates it in this epistle of his into Tamil in his elegant and inimitable way. It gets translated into English as follows.

The Pandavas were very dear to Sri Krishna. They had reposed their utmost faith in him after he had come forward in the nick of time to save all of them, and their spouse Draupadi, from dishonor and distress (in the royal court of Hastinapur) and thus did they come to be Krishna's protégés during the twelve long years they had had to perforce remain banished in exile in the forests.

Sometime during the twelfth year of their banishment, an indigent Brahmin, greatly perturbed, came running one day to the Pandavas and cried plaintively, *"My lord, O Dharmaputhra, while I was preparing to perform the sacred fire-ritual, a vagrant deer came into my dwelling, grabbed the wooden pestle and flint-stone mortar with which the holy spark of fire for my rite is ignited, and ran away into the forests with them. I ran in pursuit but the deer vanished ... Without the pestle and mortar, I cannot kindle the sacred fire needed to commence my ritual and complete it. I am greatly distressed! Please I beseech you, royal princes, to go forthwith in search of the delinquent creature, retrieve my ritual tools and restore them to me again, please!"*

Dharmaputhra, heeding the Brahmin's cry for help, then went forthwith to scour the forests along with his four siblings, trying to look for the errant deer. Despite strenuous efforts, they failed to apprehend the creature. Utterly exhausted from their long search, they at last came to rest a while in a forest-clearing. They began looking for water to quench their thirst. To their consternation they could find no water body easily anywhere in the vicinity. However, the youngest of the Pandavas, Nakulan, told them he remembered having recently come across a pond not too far away from where they stood. Then, at Dharmaputhra's instance, Nakulan set out alone to locate the pond and fetch water.

A little while later, Nakulan did come upon the pond he was looking for and gladdened to find water at last, he decided he would proceed to first drink the cool water and quench his own burning thirst before beckoning his brothers to the spot. Just as he was about to gather and cup the water in his hands, he suddenly saw and heard a stork that stood nearby on the banks speak clearly to him:

"Before you touch the water, know this that I shall have to put to you a few questions to answer. If you fail to respond or if your responses are unsatisfactory, then you shall certainly die here".

Nakulan chose to simply ignore the stork and proceeded to drink water from the pond. Instantly, he fell to the ground and died.

Back in the forest-clearing where the Pandava brothers awaited Nakulan's return, Dharmaputhra, grew concerned and hence sent Sahadeva to find out what was delaying Nakulan. Sahadeva too reached the same spot as Nakulan, was accosted again in the same way by the stork and likewise, ignoring the bird's dire warning, proceeded to drink water from the pond to quench thirst… and dropped dead.

Disconcerted again by Sahadeva too not returning, Dharmaputhra next asked Arjuna to go in search of the two younger siblings. Arriving at the pond, Arjuna too immediately sought to quench his thirst by dipping into the waters when he heard the magical stork again speak the same words of dire warning to him. Arjuna haughtily replied to the bird, *"Oh you are a mere stork giving out warnings from the safety of your hideout! If you are brave show yourself to me… I'll send you packing at once to hell!"* Paying no heed to the stork, Arjuna too tried to drink water from the pond, collapsed instantly and died.

With Arjuna not returning, the exasperated Dharmaputhra then dispatched Bhima to go find the siblings. When the mighty mace-carrying Bhima arrived at the pond, he was shocked to find his dead brothers there and flew into a rage and looked around for the assassin. A strange disembodied voice from nowhere then called out to him, warning him of the same fate awaiting him if he behaved in the same way his fallen brothers had done before him. The ebullient Bhima ignored the warning, and proceeded to drink water from the pond. Instantly he too died.

At last, unable to bear his burning thirst, Dharmaputhra himself went looking for his brothers. When he came upon the waters of the pond, he saw his siblings all dead. Deeply distressed but then sensing that he could do nothing really for his dead brothers, Yudhishtira decided to save his own life from desperate thirst. He descended into the waters to gather water. It was then that a gigantic, hideous creature appeared in sight from the woods of the forest and, leaning nonchalantly upon the trunk of a great tree, spoke to him in a deep, stentorian voice:

*"I am no mere stork… I am a **Yaksha**… a ghoul of these forests. Your brothers did not heed my warnings and hence had to die at my hands. If you answer to my satisfaction all the questions I shall pose to you now, you may drink water from the pond safely. But if you too decide to disobey me as your brothers did before you, then you too shall suffer their fate".*

Dharmaputhra, unlike his brothers, immediately responded tamely to the Yaksha, *"Please go ahead and put to me the questions you wish to be answered by me. I shall answer to the best of my knowledge and ability!"*

Thus, commenced the **Dialogue between the Yaksha and Dharmaputhra** (*Yaksha Prashna*) wherein to the former's pointed questions, the latter provided fitting answers that were all in true consonance with the most profound of scriptural authority. I shall now narrate to you that dialogue as it happened which you may please follow closely:

Question 1. What power makes the sun rise and journey across the skies?

Answer: The sun rises on the eastern horizon and is able to traverse across the high firmament thanks to the libation of water poured solemnly by good Brahmins as oblations to the sun-God even as they, at the same time, chant the **"gaayatri mantra"** *(in the daily rite of "sandhyaavandanam").*

Q.2. When he journeys across the skies, the sun-God is accompanied by whom?

*A: The nine planets (**navagraha-s**) are the fellow-travelers of the sun-God on his journey.*

Q.3. By what power does the sun set at dusk into the horizon?

*A: By the power of the sacrificial rites (**yaagaa**-s) conducted by sages and men of piety (**dharma**) does the sun set at dusk.*

Q.4. In deference to what law or order, does the sun-god journey forth every day without ever veering off his ordained course?

*A: As pronounced in the Upanishads, **"lokah sathyE pratishtithah:"**, it is in deference to the Will of the Supreme Almighty (**bhagavath-sankalpa**), that the sun-God does travel without ever veering off course.*

Q.5. By what means does a Brahmin evolve into a 'srotriya' or a "man of spiritual wisdom" i.e., a "brahma-gynaani" (knower of God)?

A. By means of the knowledge attained from the Vedas and Vedanta does a Brahmin mature into a "srotriya" ... a knower of the Supreme "Brahman"

Q.6. Through what deeds does a Brahmin ennoble himself?

*Answer: The Brahmin ennobles himself through constant observance of austerities, penance and contemplation (**tapas**).*

Q.7. What is it that binds a man to all the things of this world?

A: What binds a man to the things and beings of this world is revealed in the scriptures and through means by which a man is able to gain the strength to bind those others to himself too.

Q.8. How does an ordinary man become a man of wisdom?

*A: A man gains wisdom by associating with men of wisdom – they who have acquired true knowledge by dint of their study of both spiritual and secular subjects found in the "**saastra**" (scriptures).*

Q.9. What bestows upon Brahmins the mark or stature of divinity?

A: It is through the long study and arduous practice of Vedas under the tutelage of a qualified Acharya and by following his guidance faithfully that a Brahmin is able to attain divine stature.

Q.10. What is the dharma practiced by the Brahmin that gives him strength of character?

*A: Performing constant "**tapas**" or austerities alone is the dharma that gives the Brahmin his strength of character.*

Q.11. What makes a Brahmin (*endowed with marks of divinity*) **make him still a human?**

A: The inevitability of death makes him human.

Q.12. When does a Brahmin fall from grace and behave wickedly?

A: A Brahmin falls from grace and becomes wicked when he goes about in life berating men steeped in the learning of Vedas and Vedanta and belittling too other virtuous people of the world.

Q.13. What bestows upon a "*Kshatriya*" (*caste of warriors and rulers*) **the mark or stature of divinity?**

A: His weaponry, and his prowess in the art of war with it, bestows divine stature upon the Kshatriya.

Q.14. What is the dharma practiced by a *kshatriya* that gives him strength of character?

*A: The dharma of performing great "**yaaga**-s" …. sacrifices for the welfare of the commonweal… gives him strength of character.*

Q.15. What makes a "*Kshatriya*" (*with the marks of divinity*) **human?**

A: His punctiliousness towards his ordained duties makes a "Kshatriya" a human by nature.

Q.16. What is moral failure in a "*Kshatriya*"?

A: Refusing to do his duty to go forward to fight in a righteous war is moral failing in a "Kshatriya".

Q.17. What does the *Saama Veda* signify to the conduct of a great "*yaaga*" (ritual sacrifice)?

A: The lifeblood of a "yaaga" is the Saama Veda.

Q.18. What does the *Yajur Veda* signify to the conduct of a great "*yaaga*"?

A: The Yajur Veda is to the "yaaga" what the mind (manas) is to man.

Q.19. What gives a great "*yaaga*" its true form and structure?

*A: It is the **Rk Veda** that gives the "yaaga" its true form and structure.*

Q.20. What is most indispensable for the conduct of a great *"yaaga"*?

A: A great "yaaga" can never be embarked upon without the Rk Veda. It is the most indispensable.

Q.21. What is that substance which promotes growth, provides nourishment and sustains all beings?

A: Rain is that substance that provides growth and sustainability for all creations on earth.

Q.22. Amongst the several varieties of grains that exist, which one is the most productive in yield and for which it is worthwhile expending great cultivating effort?

A: Paddy seed-grains are the most deserving of the effort of cultivation.

Q.23. What is that being that is most worthy of domesticating and nurturing at home?

A: The husbandry of cows at home is extremely worthy of domestic effort.

Q.24. What is the most valuable of human productive effort?

A: Ensuring an unbroken line of progeny is the most valuable of human productive effort.

Q.25. When does a man who enjoys all kinds of abundant means and material resources in life, who possesses keen intelligence, who commands the respects of his peers in society and who is even-tempered and just in all his dealings with fellowmen ... when is even such a well-endowed man considered to be nothing but a *dead man walking*?

*A: The man who, in spite of being endowed in life with all manner of abundant material endowments, fails yet to please the gods (**devata**-s), honor house-guests, and treat house-servants well and venerate his departed ancestors.... such a man, even though he might walk upon this earth, is nonetheless to be regarded as a dead man walking ... a walking corpse verily.*

Q.26. In the mortal world what may be regarded as being ever more precious than the earth?

A: One's mother may be regarded as being more precious than the earth.

Q.27. Who in the world may be regarded as being higher than the overarching skies?

A: To a son, his father is to be regarded as a being higher than the overarching skies.

Q.28. What is faster than the wind?

A: The mind travels faster than the wind… It can travel to as far as even Kaashi (Varanasi) within the blink of an eye.

Q.29. What is it which is more innumerable than wild weeds or grass?

A: Mental worries or perturbations (**chinthaa**) outnumber even wild weeds or grass.

Q.30. What beings even while fast asleep do not ever close their eyelids?

A: The eyelids of fish do not close even when the creatures are asleep.

Q.31. The seed of which creatures in the world cannot be re-planted or grown again?

A. The egg of the duck, the hen and other such similar creatures cannot be made fecund seed again (after they are hatched).

Q.32. What is utterly heartless in the world?

A: A cold stone is the most heartless of all things on earth.

Q.33. What is that which thrives upon swiftness?

A: The flowing river-waters thrive most on swiftness.

Q.34. What provides comfort of companionship for the highway traveler?

A: The highway traveler finds comfort of companionship in humans' groups or clusters.

Q.35. What provides comfort of companionship for a homebound man?

A: For the homebound man, comfort of companionship is provided by the spouse.

Q.36. For the man ailing from disease, what gives comfort of companionship?

A: For a man ailing in sickness, comfort of companionship is provided by his attendant doctor.

Q.37. What is it in the world that is received as a most welcome guest by all creatures?

A: The fire (that gives warmth to everyone) – **Agni the fire-God** *-- is the guest welcomed most by all creatures on earth.*

Q.38. What is eternal, or "*sanaatana*" **Dharma**?

A: That Dharma which enables one to seek Bhagavaan, the Almighty, who is undying and eternal, and the same Dharma which is spoken about in the Vedas, and that which is faithfully followed and practiced by seekers.... that is verily Sanaatana Dharma, the perennial philosophy.

Q.39. What can be said to be elixir of life on earth ("*amrutham*")?

*A: The spirit manifested as the Moon (***Chandran***), which bestows upon every linctus in the world with its respective curative essences and properties... that is indeed the elixir of life ("amrutham").*

Q.40. What is that which may be regarded as the most valuable worldwide?

A: Of all things existent, the Air that pervades the atmosphere is the most valuable to all creations worldwide.

Q.41. Who may be said to be the ever-solitary traveler?

A: The ever-solitary traveler is the sun-God **Suryan**.

Q.42. What created thing vanishes only to be yet re-created?

A: The moon-god **Chandran** *appears, disappears and then again re-appears.*

Q.43. What may be said to be the antidote for the dark fog of mistiness?

A: The glow of a blazing fire is the best antidote to remove the misty darkness of fog.

Q.44. Of all places in the universe which is the one that is the most conducive for the act of Creation --- of humans and of all other beings?

A: This Earth is the most ideally suited place indeed for all Creation, human and otherwise.

Q.45. Which is the Dharma that is universally uniform and constant?

A: Showing due courtesy (*"**daakhshinyam**"*) to one and all is the universally constant and uniform Dharma.

Q.46. What deed does bring renown instantly to one even when done just once?

A: Even a single act of Charity (***daanam***) done in the proper manner unto good souls can indeed bestow instant renown upon one.

Q.47. Which deed is that when done even once, secures for one the reward of heavenly paradise (*svarga*)?

A: When a man speaks the Truth exactly as revealed by scriptures (***saastra***), done even just once, surely secures a place for him in heavenly paradise.

Q.48. What is that which unfailingly bestows Happiness upon us?

A: It is good-naturedness that unfailingly bestows Happiness upon us.

Q.49. What is regarded by a man to be verily his soul (*Atma*)?

A. A man regards a son born to him to be verily his soul.

Q.50. Who is the divinely appointed confidante of Man?

A: A man's spouse is indeed the God-appointed confidante of Man.

Q.51. What is the most essential requisite for human survival?

A: The most essential requisite for human survival is copious rain-bearing clouds.

Q.52. Which deed must the human soul habitually do every day?

A: The human soul must daily offer ritual libation of water (*"**arghyam**"*) as oblation to the gods, he must chant the Vedas and he must engage in other such acts of piety regularly....

Q.53. To what reason might a man attribute his good fortune in life and which would enable him to claim, "*I am privileged indeed!*"?

A: *He can claim so if in the execution of all his good deeds in life he is able to display both competence and enterprise (**saamarthyam**).*

Q.54. What is the greatest of wealth amongst all the riches of this world?

A: *For the Brahmin, the greatest of all wealth in this world is* **the Veda.**

Q.55. Of all the gains that may be secured in life, which one is the most profitable?

A: *Robust Health is the most profitable of all gains in life.*

Q.56. Amongt all the pleasures meant to be enjoyed in life, which is the foremost one?

A: *To remain wholly content with whatever enjoyment is afforded by all that one happens to possess in life --- that is indeed the greatest pleasure.*

Q.57. What is that Dharma that leads to Perfection (*uthkrishta*)?

A: *The Dharma involving compassion (**kaarunyam**) being shown to all Life in this world (**bhutha**) leads to perfection.*

Q.58. Which Dharma yields benefits perennially?

A: *The Dharma-s prescribed in the Vedas, if practiced faithfully, yield perennially all manner of benefits.*

Q.59. By subduing which may one avoid all sorrow?

A: *By subduing the Mind one may avoid all sorrow.*

Q.60. Which amongst all kinds of human relationships is the most enduring?

A: *The relationship with peace-loving souls (**saadhu**-s) is the most enduring of all human kinship.*

Q.61. By jettisoning what does a man become agreeable to one and all in life?

A: *By jettisoning his egocentricity (**ahankaaram**), a man becomes agreeable to one and all in life.*

Q.62. By jettisoning what does a man avoid despair?

A: By jettisoning Rage within himself does a man avoid Despair.

Q.63. By jettisoning what might a man realize the true ends of his life?

A: By jettisoning all unworthy desires in life can a man attain the true ends of life.

Q.64. By jettisoning what might a man gain Happiness?

A: By jettisoning Greed does a man gain Happiness.

Q.65. Why must one be charitable towards Brahmins?

A: Charity to Brahmins generally induces both cause and affirmation of Dharma.... That is why charity is done unto the Brahmin.

Q.66. Why is it important to liberally remunerate artistic people like dancers (and other *aesthetes*) **etc.?**

A: By remunerating artists and aesthetes well, society at large attains worldly distinction and acclaim.

Q.67. Why is it important to remunerate the servant-classes well?

A: They are to be well remunerated to ensure their lasting wellbeing and protection.

Q.68. Why are rulers of state to be endowed with great wealth and resources?

A: So that the wealth and resources of rulers of state can be employed for the sake of larger public security, welfare and interest.

Q.69. What enshrouds this world?

A: This world is shrouded by a great veil called enveloping Nescience.

Q.70. What is it that renders things to remain obscured from the world?

A: Darkness and Nescience makes them remain obscure.

Q.71. What makes a man cast aside his good friends?

A: Rapaciousness makes a man to cast his good friends away.

Q.72. What makes heavenly paradise unattainable for a man?

A: His bondage to things unworthy and wicked in this world makes heavenly paradise unattainable.

Q.73. What makes a living man no better than a corpse?

A: A man utterly lacking in any learning – i.e., knowledge of the **veda, saastra** or **puraana** – and the man utterly devoid of wealth or property are both regarded in this world as being no better than a corpse.

Q.74. When does the State start becoming moribund?

A: A State wherein Justice neither prevails nor is respected soon becomes moribund.

Q.75. How is the annual rite of offering oblations to ancestors ("*shraadham*") wasted or rendered futile?

A: When men of loose morals, or else atheists, are invited to preside at the "**shraadham**" rite in their capacity of "brahmins" who must ceremoniously consume the sacramental victuals --- that ritual becomes utterly infructuous.

Q.76. Why do the sacred sacrifices – "yagaa" and "yagnya" – become infructuous?

A: They become infructuous because the oblations prescribed by the scripture are either not offered at all, or offered as insufficient benefactions, to the manes.

Q.77. What defines sense of all direction?

A. It is Strength that defines all sense of directions.

Q.78. What contains the Waters?

A: Space contains the Waters.

Q.79. What bears Food?

A: The cow bears Food.

Q.80. What is toxic social pollutant?

A: Destitution is toxic social pollutant.

Q.81. What is the time apposite for performing the holy rite of "*shraadham*"?

A: Anytime when a noble Brahmin arrives home is time apposite for the "**shraadha**" ceremony.

Q.82. What is the hallmark of penance (*tapas*)?

A: To be diligent and steadfast in performing one's ordained duty is the hallmark of "**tapas**".

Q.83. What makes Perfection (*tamam*)?

A: Control of the Mind makes Perfection.

Q.84. What is Forbearance?

A: To remain equanimous in facing or accepting both joy and sorrow, gain and loss, triumph and defeat, honor and ignominy is Forbearance.

Q.85. What causes one to be ashamed of oneself (*lajja*)?

A: To fall prey to doing evil causes one to be ashamed of oneself (**lajja**).

Q.86. What is that knowledge that aids attainment of salvation (*moksham*)?

A: The knowledge that results in intuitive realization of the true nature of "**jeevaatma**" (individual soul), of "**paramaatma**" (universal soul) and such other truths is knowledge indeed which leads to salvation.

Q.87. What is equanimity?

A: Tranquility of the Mind is equanimity.

Q.88. What is compassion?

A: To wish always for the wellbeing of all others is Compassion.

Q.89. What is forthrightness (*aarjavam*)?

A: To look upon all things and all beings as though they were divinized and to treat them all equally as such ... that is "**aarjavam**".

Q.90. Who may be that enemy of man who cannot be vanquished?

A: Anger is the enemy of the man who cannot be vanquished so easily.

Q.91. What is the most chronic disease afflicting man?

A: Coveting desires that are way beyond one's means is the most chronic disease man suffers from most.

Q.92. Who is he that one may regard as "*saadhu*" ... a saintly one?

A: The saintly man is he who strives as hard as possible to achieve the welfare and betterment of every living being in the world.

Q.93. Who is the unsaintly man?

A: The unsaintly man is he who is utterly devoid of compassion.

Q.94. What is delusion?

A: Delusion is the inability to discriminate between what is righteous and what is not.

Q.95. What is self-consciousness?

A: The mistaken self-belief that the Body is no different from the Soul.

Q.96. What is lethargy?

A: To keep putting off doing good deeds which ought never to be procrastinated.

Q.97. What is the cause of Despair?

A: Ignorance is the cause of all Despair.

Q.98. What is that which the great sages (*rishi-s*) keep affirming is Constancy?

A: Fidelity to Dhaarmic duty is what the sages affirm is constancy.

Q.99. What is true courage?

A: True courage lies in the conquest of the senses.

Q.100. What is self-purification?

A: Self-purification lies in getting rid of the defilements of the mind.

Q.101. What is philanthropy?

A: Philanthropy means protecting the welfare of all beings in the world.

Q.102. Who is to be regarded as a man of erudition?

A: The erudite man is he whose erudition has endowed upon him knowledge of true Dharma.

Q.103. What is one to generally make of an atheist.

A: The Atheist is generally regarded as eminent fool.

Q.104. Who is the unintelligent man?

A: *The atheist is regarded as a man of low intelligence.*

Q.105. What is the nature of lust?

A: *It is the cause of birth and death.*

Q.106. What is the nature of Envy (maatsaryam)?

A: *Envy is that feeling which is aroused in the heart which covets wicked or forbidden desires.*

Q.107. What is the nature of self-conceitedness or "ahankaaram"?

A: *Self-conceit arises out of Delusion.*

Q.108. What is arrogance?

A: *Arrogance is to go around publicly proclaiming all the good deeds one has done in life… It is an attitude of self-adulation.*

Q.109. What may be regarded as a man's *guardian angel?*

A: *All the charity that a man has done in life indeed stands by him as his* **guardian angel.**

Q.110. What best describes violent behavior?

A: *Violent behavior is in being abusive and irreverent towards one's elders.*

Q.111. Is it possible that one's pursuit of the three ends of life, Dharma, Artha and Kaama *(righteousness, material wealth, and sensory pleasure)* **might turn inimical to one's wellbeing and advancement?**

A: *If a man's mind pursues both* **Dharma** *and* **Bhakthi** *(god-devotion) together, then none of the three ends of life can ever turn inimical to one's advancement in life.*

Q.112. Can you tell me, in pith and substance, what is that misdeed which can instantly land a man in the state of hell for the longest tenure?

A: *If a man were to invite a poor Brahmin into his home, and after promising him gifts that the poor man might desire, only to later deny him any such gift and to send him away empty-handed…. such a man surely makes a travesty of the* **Vedas**, *the* **saastra**-*s indeed, and he, in fact, insults the Brahmin and Kshatriya caste, and he slights the gods and the manes too… Therefore, such* *a man instantly stands condemned to hell and suffers the horrors there for the longest possible tenure.*

Q.113. Now tell me quickly, what is that which typifies a Brahmin and bestows upon him his identity? Is it ancestral lineage, his Vedic learning, his study of the scriptures or his innate good-naturedness?

A: What determines a Brahmin's identity is his good conduct and his fidelity towards carrying out the ordained duties of his station in life.

Q.114. What does a sweet-tongued man desire most in life?

A: The sweet-tongued man's greatest desire in life is to please everyone and make everyone be pleased with him.

Q.115. What does the man of deliberative thought desire most in life?

A: Such a man desires maximum results from minimum effort.

Q.116. What good does the man with a very wide circle of friends attain?

A: Such a man enjoys great delights in life.

Q.117. What does the man of constant virtue attain in the end?

A: Such a man attains felicity in the highest of eternal worlds.

Q.118. Who is the man of this world said to be self-contained?

A: A man may be said to be self-contained if he is free of debt obligations and who needs to serve none as either servant or minion.... Such a man even if he is able to gather daily alms no more than is probably adequate to offer as sacred oblation to the Almighty Bhagavaan before he consumes it himself to keep body and soul together .... That man is indeed one who is self-contained.

Q.119. What is to be marveled most in life?

A: Everyday people watch the dead ones depart to the realms of Yama, the god of death. But while they watch their dear and near ones so depart, inwardly they all nonetheless think that their own moment of departure will never arrive! Is there anything in this world to be marveled at more than that?!

Q.120. What is the best pathway to take in life?

A. *All mental reasoning at the end is mere quibbling; it serves no enduring purpose; the ways of the wise sages (**rishis**) are so many; the scriptures are far too many; each one of them offers us so many pathways; true dharma remains mystery. In life, therefore, we must choose our path wisely. The most prudent choice for us is to tread the same path upon which we find the footsteps of our venerable elders. That is the best possible course to take.*

Q.121. What is to be generally said of the universal human condition?

A: *What may be said of the universal human condition is this: The Great One who may be called Time (**Kaala**)… he holds all Creation captive in a gargantuan iron cauldron kept boiling over a great big Fire (**Agni**) fueled by the great sun-God, **Surya**, ceaselessly stirring it too, as it were, again and yet again with giant ladles, all through numberless days and nights, fortnights and through the endless cycles of seasons… stirring and stirring while all creation grinds its way towards death.*

Q.122. Who is the Maker of all this that exists (*Purushan*)?

A: *Whose beneficent Writ is the one and only one that runs large everywhere both in this world and beyond… such an Almighty One is the "**purushan**".*

Q.123. Now answer this one too, finally: Who is He who is the most munificent (*sarvadhani*)?

A: *He in whom all of the most auspicious and most effulgent qualities reside and shine forth eternally …. He is the most munificent one, the most supreme of all!*

The Yaksha, the ghoul of the forest, then spoke thus to Yudishtira:

O King! You have acquitted yourself well by giving apt answers to all questions I posed to you! I am extremely gratified! Here lie your four sibling brothers, all dead. As a mark of my appreciation of your having passed the test of my questioning, I offer to bring back to life again one amongst the four of your dead brothers. Choose one now and I shall revive him instantly to life for you!"

Dharmaputhra said: *Let then my brother Nakulan be resurrected from the dead.*

Yaksha: Your choice is surprising! You choose Nakulan over even the other two great heroic brothers, Bhima and Arjuna, of yours? Why? Tell me the reason!

Dharmaputhra: *O Yaksha-raja! We are four siblings but we are born of two mothers who were wedded to my deceased father... I was born to my mother Kunti-Devi. I shall now live. But I wish that at least one son of the other mother's womb, Maadiri's, should also live. And he is none other than Nakulan. So, amongst the other siblings to be given life back, I seek from you his very own.*

Yaksha: Dharmaputhra! I am so touched by your nobility! Let me tell you now that I am no ghoul of this forest. I shall reveal myself to you now! I am in truth your father... I am the **Dharmaraja** myself --- *the god of Righteousness*! It was my intention that through this dialogue I have had with you, the world should be enlightened upon the verities of true Dharma. This little playacting, I did with you was for that purpose only. *I shall now revive all four of your brothers to life!*

All four Pandava princes were then instantly revived to life. Dharmaraja showered them all with blessings. Yama-dharma raja, the god of death appeared on the scene too, and being equally pleased with the Pandava brothers, he restored to Yudhishtira the ritual instruments --- i.e., *the wooden pestle and flint-stone mortar* that had been lost by the poor Brahmin and at whose behest the brothers had set out to search for them in the forests. On returning to the forest-clearing, Yudhishtira handed them all back to the Brahmin who went away very pleased. The Pandava princes lived thereafter very happily in the forests during the rest of the period of their exile from the Kingdom of Hastinapur.

Those who with utmost faith study or narrate this **Yaksha Prashna** (appearing in the great *ithihaasa* of **Mahaabhaaratham**) they indeed earn all manner of grace and blessings in life.

***

-9-
"Praise the High-Souled"

Synopsis: *Srimadh Mukkur Azhagiyasingar in this epistle affirms in no uncertain terms that it is only men possessing "**brahmagnyana**" – the higher or greater intelligence by which Man can secure clear knowledge of Truth and Divinity -- who deserve to be regarded as truly superior humans amongst us and are worthy of our veneration.*

All universe is but the Creation of Sriman Narayana and is the habitat of all forms of life, be it plant, creeper herb or insect.

Amongst these life-forms there are some specie that possess the faculty of Intelligence and some do not. Some life-forms are rooted or stationary; some others are peripatetic. Amongst those life-forms that locomote, some are earth-bound while some others are sky-borne. Amongst species that live on land, there are some that are bipeds or quadrupeds while others move around by crawling.

Most of the life-forms described above possess little Intelligence. There are other life-forms that however possess greater degrees of Intelligence. Examples of species that possess no Intelligence at all are trees, plants, creepers, grass, herbs etc. The only reason that could be cited to explain why at all such species have come to assume certain unintelligent forms of life in their present existential condition on earth is that the soul (*jivatma*) inhered in each of them, as a result of sins (*papam*) in past lives, was predestined to take precisely such life-forms in the current one. The Vedic "sastra" contextualizes this fact by saying, *".... **yaathi sthaavarathaam naraha...**"*

The Veda says that every earthling that possesses Form and Name is indeed inhered by a *jivatma*, a monadic soul. Thus, even an inert piece of rock or stone is indeed inhered by a soul. A doubt may arise as to how a soul that is said to inhere an inert stony life-form can ever possess Intelligence? The answer is that (by operation of the law of *karma*) as a result of past deeds of *"papam"* or sin, a soul inhering even inert matter is indeed possessed of a modicum of Intelligence commensurate with such a lowly life-form. As for other higher life-forms – such as species that walk on earth, fly in the sky or crawl about – we are able to witness the natural Intelligence that they all clearly exhibit. For example, we all see how even such lowly insects such as the house-fly, the tiny ant and other such insects live intelligently too by foraging for food here and there all the time.

In such a vast world filled with a fascinating diversity of life-forms, each possessing varying degrees of superiority of Intelligence, it should really be of no real surprise at all that *Homo sapiens* -- the species called Man who is endowed by nature with a great degree of Intelligence -- should regard itself as the highest of all existent mortal life-forms.

Now, amongst this most intelligent specie called Mankind there are some who succeed in realizing for themselves a life of ease and general wellbeing; socially, they are regarded as highly accomplished individuals. Superior to them are those others amongst mankind who led lives in accordance with the high values, beliefs and ethical standards laid down in time-honored *sastra* i.e., the canons and dictums found in the wisdom of scripture. Then there are some others who are even more superior: they are the ones who consider themselves in all true modesty to be far less in worth – i.e. in terms of knowledge, wisdom and spiritual advancement – than the high-souled *"sadacharya"*, the wise and noble preceptor whom they try to seek out and venerate, so that they can then learn great verities and lessons of life after having cultivated an abiding relationship with him.

The Intelligence that the common run of mankind possesses and puts to use in life to acquire Knowledge is often rather vainglorious… To express it metaphorically, Man uses the gift of his natural Intelligence to *fly the skies* (on fantastically designed and engineered aircrafts!) and then gloats over the accomplishment as though it were verily his crowning glory! But ultimately it turns out however that all Knowledge (*arivu* in Tamizh) is mere resource (in the modern world it is called *intellectual capital*) ... or plain raw-material being ingeniously transformed into material wealth. Again, if one were to put it metaphorically, Intelligence is used to convert Knowledge into ways and means of simply satiating and pleasing the belly! If you contemplate upon the matter seriously and honestly, you will indeed find yourself asking *"What else is the ultimate purpose to which all human knowledge is being put to use? Is it not merely to achieve low-end selfish, and mundane ends?!"*

In the past, our wise elders in fact have held that this kind of low-end use of Intelligence to enrich mankind in mundane terms to the exclusion of every other kind of knowledge is really nothing but agnyana – Ignorance masquerading as Intelligence. In both nature and purpose it is inferior to a greater, more evolved Knowledge that Man can gain, if only he were to become predisposed towards it. Such predisposition would mean Man willingly setting apart at least a small part of a lifetime to pursuing opportunities for imbibing the teachings and the wisdom of the high-souled-ones, our Acharyas....

As the scripture says, "...**nareshu brahmavaadinah shreshtaa:**", it is only men possessing *brahmagnyana* – that higher or greater intelligence by which Man can secure clear knowledge of Truth and Divinity -- who can be regarded as superior ones amongst us. A man can, of course, heroically strive to acquire and master mundane knowledge with the aim of soaring to empyrean heights of even outer space and beyond and try conquering it. But nonetheless, he will still have to return to this mortal earth ultimately. Whereas the man who by dint of *brahmagnyanam* has scaled spiritual heights will find himself soaring to the very zenith of all celestial heights, and there having ascended the very summit of Vaikuntam, will eternally enjoy bliss.

***

Brahmagnyanam is two-fold. One way to acquire it is through *kalapshepam* received humbly at the feet of an Acharya i.e. by undergoing a formal course of rigorous learning wherein certain cardinal truths of Vedanta are imparted to the disciple such as... "Brahman is none other than Sriman Narayana"; that "all other gods and deities are *"angaan-nyanyaan devataaha"* i.e. merely organic adjuncts or bodily limbs of his, so to say"; that "He is the cause of all creation; that his form is all-pervading; that of his own divine will (sankalpa), he reveals himself from time to time to mere mortals like us, leaving us in awe and delighting in his many facets and exploits." To grasp, intuit and realize all such truths also constitutes *brahmagnyanam*.

Furthermore, there is another way to *brahmagnyanam* which is to realize the truths revealed in the scriptures that say that although it is impossible to conceive Brahman in its absolute and infinitely perfect state of being (*anantha-kalyaana-gunaan*), it is possible nevertheless to get in some small measure a conception of his true nature. That is possible through acts of worship, or *upaasana*, directed towards at least a few of the attributes of perfection and excellence that describe Sriman Narayana. Knowledge gained through such upasana constitutes *brahmagnyana* too.

Such upaasana is also indeed part of what is called **Bhakthi Yoga** and, thus, it is the bhakti-yogis too who are often referred to in various scriptures as brahma-gnyanis or brahma-viths. Such brahma-gnyanis are indeed high-souled ones of a very superior order in the world. Even amongst such high-souled ones there are some whose sole aspiration in life is the attainment of moksham or Salvation. In their practice of bhakti-yoga they in fact seek nothing else.

Lastly, there are amongst high-souled ones those few who, notwithstanding their abiding faith in the scriptures, in Bhagavan and in the ideal of salvation, are resolved to advance towards the ultimate goal of moksham simply by performing the act of saranagathi, the act of absolute, unconditional surrender of a soul unto the feet of Sriman Narayana.

"Naarhanthi saranastasya kalaam kotitha-meemabhi..."... There are yet other high-souled ones of the world too who are deserving of veneration. They are (i) the ones who have gained consummate realization of the three absolute principles of metaphysical reality (Tattva-traya) viz. Sriman Narayana (whom all the sastras without exception glorify as the supreme One (Isvara)), sentient beings (cit) and all insentient entities (acit); (ii) the most ardent and faithful disciples of a sadacharya (iii) those who have purified themselves through absolution of sins (papam) in and through the act of

saranagathi and (iv) those who in their capacity and role as Acharyas, steeped in knowledge of matters spiritual and esoteric, impart it to their dearest disciples.... All such men of the world too must be regarded as the high-souled ones.

***

We witness in the present times many disturbing and telltale signs of all round human decadence... We see many kinds of lapses and laxity in upholding even basic religious disciplines (anushtaana) -- snana-sandhi and upanayanam for instance. Such egregious laxity and apathy cause one to fear that the tiny seed of spiritualism in Man, before it can have a chance to begin even sprouting, will have its life washed away by the deluge of un-virtue!

As for adherence to moral injunctions of sastra in matters of matrimony these days... well... the less said the better! Scant is the respect given to family lineage or ancestry (jathi pazhakkam) ... and more and more weddings are getting solemnized in the Office of the Registrars of Marriages than at the altar of Vedic traditions. All kinds of unwholesome Food are being consumed indiscriminately – inside seedy restaurants in unkempt surroundings – without due observance of hygiene or purification mantras prescribed by our sastra such as pariseshanam and pranahuthi. Today, we see also that the young in our families showing least respect to the elderly, and often even treat them in fact with disdain and ridicule.

Observing such a sorry state of affairs prevailing all around us in society, one cannot but rue the fact that it is impossible to pursue the path of Karma Yoga... let alone Gnyana Yoga! And if neither path is possible to tread then how on earth is it possible to attain atmavalokanam? Just as the soul, the jivatma, can be perceived by and through the subtle inward eye (*kanngal*), so is the subtle landscape of inward mentality perceived by the Mind (manas) known as atmavalokanam. Without it, we may all just as well bid goodbye to Bhakthi-Yoga and prepare ourselves to end up finally in a predicament of dark despair... a deep, unfathomable pall of burden. It is awareness of the pall of heavy burden hanging over one's soul which (in the terminology of the doctrine of Saranagathi) is called "bhara". At some point or other in a lifetime such awareness gives rise eventually to an intense desire in us to get shuffle off and get rid of the pall of burden, once and for all times… That riddance is what is known as bhara-samarpanam…. Now if you wish to know more on what bhara-samarpanam is and what is needed to realize it, please seek guidance and comfort from the high-souled ones of the world.

***

Let me finally affirm this: There are no souls in the world who are higher or nobler than those who, through both precept and exemplarity, illuminate the path to redemption for us who must be held guilty on account of a variety of flagrant, omnibus lapses in life such as the following:

a. Failing to do duties that ought to have been done; but continuing to do so many other deeds that ought never to be done.

b. Failing to have spoken when it was duty to speak up; but then to have spoken on many an occasion, out of turn or when one ought not to have spoken at all.

c. Failing to listen to what ought to have been paid close attention to; but to have paid instead attention to so many other things that ought to have remained unheard.

d. Failing to visit places that deserved to be visited but then to have instead gone on frequenting places that ought to have been shunned outright.

e. Turning away from witnessing what ought to be beheld; instead, continuing to set gaze upon that which never ought to have been set eyes upon.

f. Not eating what is wholesome but instead consuming indiscriminately what ought to be abjured.

g. Failing to expend effort in studying what is essential but instead avidly reading what is unworthy and lapping up the unsavory.

h. Not spending time in contemplation of matters of life that ought to be contemplated upon; instead frittering away time obsessing on matters undeserving of any thought.

i. Failing to offer praise to the praiseworthy; and instead bowing and scraping to those undeserving of praise.

j. Being generous in charity for unworthy causes; and instead, being uncharitable towards truly worthy ones.

It is thanks to such high-souled ones – and thanks also to the blessings of our dear ancestors who wish us always nothing but the very best in life – that despite all the above-mentioned lapses, our *sadacharyas* are actually still able to instill in our minds the spark of an urge and desire to seek union with Bhagavan Sriman Narayana! It does happen rarely but it certainly does happen at some opportune point of time in our lives!

Truly blessed are those places on earth wherever such high-souled *sadacharyas* dwell and they come forward to lovingly tend to the spiritual wellbeing of their band of disciples and faithful followers!

Now, if you ask in wonder if it is possible at all to come across anywhere today such high-souled persons, I say, yes, it is possible to meet them… If you ask in wonderment if it is possible that you could ever mingle with such men and listen to them in discourse, I say, yes, you can. It is possible if we are ready and willing to offer such high-souled ones, according to our modest means, even as little as mere tokens of our deep veneration, affection and solicitude for them (*sambhavanai*).

If you ask me now "Why don't such high-souled ones appear before us? Or else, where and how can we meet them?" my answer to you is simply this: Seek them out sincerely and you will find them, for there are truly many high-souled ones that walk and live amongst us! If look around earnestly for them, they will surely appear before us! Recognizing them by name and praising them in person, we can indeed rid our souls of the taint of all sin.

***

-10-
"The 9-Stepped Stairway to *Parama-Padam* Sri Desikan Built"

Synopsis: *In this epistle Srimadh Mukkur Azhagiyasingar delivers a brilliant exposition of one of the most celebrated and authentic works of soteriology that can be found in the annals of Sri Vaishnava "sampradaaya". It is Sri Vedanta Desika's "rahasya grantha" (esoteric work on doctrine) written in Manipravalam language,* **"Paramapada Sopaanam"** *("The Ladder to Salvation")*

"Viveka nirveda virakthi bheethaya:
Prasaadahetu uthkramana archiraadikaa: I
Prakrutthyathikraantapadaadhirohanam
Paraapthi: ithi: athra tu parvanaam krama:" II

By reason of being born in this world, every man and woman is obliged to do a certain important duty in life. What is that duty? The simple answer: it is the duty to sit alone in a spot and silently engage oneself in thought.

You might retort, "Sir, already in life we find ourselves being preoccupied always with one thought or the other... So, what other thought do you wish us now to dwell upon?"

So let me tell you this: I am not talking about the various other preoccupations of yours that relate to all your personal ambitions all of which you find yourself striving to realize in life through ceaseless work, day and night, but, alas, which often perhaps only end up being utterly frustrated. What I am going to tell you is different. Please pay heed to it with a little patience. If you devote deep thought to what I am about to tell you, it will surely fetch you all manner of wellbeing and felicity.

I urge you to sit alone quietly in spot for at least five minutes focusing your mind to dwell deeply upon a question: *"What is the purpose of human birth? What deeds in life can help realize that purpose? What good will accrue from them?"*

At the end of your deep contemplation, you will most probably arrive at this conclusion: "Everything in the world witnessed, everything heard, everything felt, and every sensation or impression of pleasure or delight experienced in life is but as momentary as a lightning streak and as evanescent as froth floating on a stream. Sooner or later, within the blink of an eye, they all vanish. But so long as they last, it is quite common to see they are cause for much strife, tribulation and distress in life. Many families and homes, even those that are very affluent or belonging to high social status, we often see are afflicted by them.

Thinking thus, you will at last come to the conclusion: All that has been described above can never constitute the true goal of life. If you then asked yourself what is the true goal of human life, you will come up with no more convincing an answer as that it can only be one thing viz. securing an eternal state of being wherein there is no prospect anymore of mortal births, none whatsoever. One's present lifetime can be truly meaningful only if it ensures cessation forever of all future ones…which is exactly what the Azhwar (Tondaradipodi) too exactly meant when he said, *"aadhalaal piravi vane-dane…"* As the "sastra" too attests, when Bhagavan bestowed the rare and wonderful gift of earthly existence upon Man, it was in the hope and expectation that it would be directed singularly towards realizing that ultimate goal.

***

Five minutes of such deep thought should indeed be enough for you to conclude that the purpose of your life is to strive to never be born again in mortal realms. That maybe will however at once make you sit up and anxiously ask yourself: "But how is one to put an end to all rebirth forever?!" Now I say, there is no need for any such anxiety at all when **Kavitarkika Simham, Sri Vedanta Desikan** of Thoopul, in a scripture-based treatise of his titled "***Parama Pada Sopaanam***", has shown us a clear and well-illuminated path leading us out of it. I will relate to you in summary the crux of what is to be found in the treatise. Please listen to me carefully. If you follow the exhortations of Sri Desikan, you can be sure that at the end of your lifetime there will be none that ever follows. All trials and tribulations shall cease at the end of this lifetime. Perennial joy will ensue. Consummate bliss will be experienced in Sri Vaikuntam in the company of Bhagavan along with the assembly of his heavenly servitors there.

Our final resting place, the spiritual home where we truly belong, is indeed Sri Vaikuntam. We live only as tenants here in these mortal realms that extend from earth right up to the frontiers of *brahmalokam*. But yonder in Sri Vaikuntam, we live as permanent and liberated citizens. Everyone knows only too well the constrictive conditions of life for a tenant. It is in stark contrast to the joyous freedom of a full citizen's life, is it not?

Parama Padam is Sri Vaikuntam. It is situated way beyond and outside the sphere of brahmalokam (and about which in the past, in the columns of the "*Nrisimha Priya*" magazine, I have already written describing it greater detail). To a place so high and deep beyond the heavenly spheres in infinite space, where Sri Vaikuntam is situated, there is a stairway that has been built by Swami Desikan with no more than nine steps, none too steep nor difficult to ascend.

(Courtesy: R. Chithralekha)

In that staircase the very first step has been named as **Vivekam**. The second is **Nirvedam**, with the third being **Virakthi**.

Thereafter, there are the fourth, fifth, and sixth steps named respectively as **Bheethi**, **Prasadahetu** and **Uthkramanam**.

The seventh step is **Archiraadi** while the eighth known to be transcending *Prakruthimandala* is **Suddhasattva-prapthi**.

The ninth step culminates directly in the presence of Bhagavan and is known as **Prapthi**.

If these nine steps, with such beautiful-sounding names given to them by Sri Desikan, are ascended by us, one by one right up to the top, then it is certain there shall be no more rebirths for us.

It is not enough for you to merely know these nine steps by name. It is more important you should also understand what each step signifies or conveys by way of philosophical truth. I shall now explain it to you. Please pay attention carefully.

***

VIVEKAM is the name of the first of the nine steps. What it presupposes is that any person who is a seeker of mukthi or liberation from rebirth must first cultivate discriminative knowledge. In other words, the person should first develop true awareness of self. That self is the jivatma, the soul within. It is an indestructible entity. It is monadic. Its essential nature is that of pure Cognition (gnyana). As a spiritual entity it is property belonging to Bhagavan. The beginning of Vivekam is in knowing and being able to mentally internalize fully the fact that the jivatma -- after having journeyed through countless past incarnations and experiencing life in various bodily forms consequent upon countless deeds of paapam (sin) -- has attained at last the human state and condition in its present lifetime.

The second aspect of discriminative knowledge is to know and be able to intuit the nature of Bhagavan i.e. to be able to comprehend that he is an omnipresent entity; that he is absolute, universal principle (param porul); he is the parent of all creation; his nature is innately compassionate (daya murthi); he is omnipotent (sarveshwaran); he is inseparable from his consort Mahalakshmi (lakshmisamethan); and that it is he who metes out universal justice in the form of due reward and punishment (i.e. as sukha and dukham respectively) to all beings as may be commensurate with their individual deeds of Virtue or Sin (punnyam or paapam). It should also be comprehended that Bhagavan is the Supreme One who presides in Sri Vaikuntam, his eternal abode; that he is verily the fountainhead of ineffable spiritual Bliss; and also, that all beings that ascend it, reside there eternally, immersed in such bliss.

The third aspect of Vivekam or discriminative knowledge lies in the realization that the cause of human birth and all human bondage (prakruthi sambhandham) is but the result and operation of Karma. The means to liberate oneself from the mundane bonds of Karma lie in learning from the wisdom and precepts of the lineage of our Acharyas as well as in treading the paths in life that have been proven by our ancestors to lead to a state of supreme bliss.

To sum up, if a person is able to gain as much as possible of the basic knowledge described above, and understood it well too, it can be said then that he has indeed successfully climbed the very first step of Vivekam.

NIRVEDAM, the second step, is best described as a profound sense of regret that overcomes a person in life. Regret over what and why? The explanation is that the person feeling Nirvedam typically looks back at his past and says to himself:

"Sriman Narayan is mother and father to me and I am his child really. If I unite with him then an eternity of pure bliss awaits me. Yet, in this lifetime of mine as in perhaps countless past lives too, I have done nothing at all that one might say makes me worthy of receiving the grace of bliss which he, in fact, is ever so eager to bestow upon me!

"Alas, I have wasted away my life foolishly! I made no effort at all to seek out the company of learned men of Vedantic wisdom and learn from them. I have committed innumerable acts of sin and only degraded myself lower and lower! All habits of noble behavior have I abandoned! So wretched and horrific in various form have I experienced that were indeed the wages of sins I committed! So fraud and deceit am I guilty of! I have mindlessly frittered away so many a lifetime! Embracing so many false notions of unbelief, I have only misled myself into the rot of atheism! Scoffing insolently at all the sastras (scriptures) as being nothing but fantastic superstition, I took to so many wanton and wicked ways! If only I had had better sense in the earliest years of my life and had I embraced Bhagavan, perhaps, I would not be in sorry plight I find myself in today! Who knows, possibly I might have even attained salvation (mukthi) long before now! But what am I to do now! Can I ever hope for redemption? At least sometime before the end of this lifetime? ***Aiyo!*** What shall I do?! Who will save my soul?! At whose feet shall I now go and fall and seek solace? Is there any kind and high-souled one who would deign perhaps to ferry me across these dark seas safely to shore?"

Now, if a person were to be filled with such intense feelings of remorse, genuine contrition and regret, then surely it can be said that he or she has ascended the second step of Nirvedam.

VIRAKTHI is the third step. It is also called Vairagyam. What it means is that once a person is seized of the overwhelming longing to unite with Bhagavan and to experience eternal bliss in Sri Vaikuntam, attachment to mundane existence and all its pleasures appears trivial. It gradually begins waning.

We see that even gods, right from Brahmma down to other lesser devatas, are all as prone to remain in thrall of all kinds of mundane, temporal pleasures as Man is. We see how they consequently come to suffer great woes. From the earliest time of the *kruta-yuga* down to the present day, we know again of so many great emperors who had been sovereign lords of fabulous wealth and the unbounded delights it afforded but then who, at the same time, came to terrible, even deathly grief on account of them. So many powerful personages in history too are they who, we have heard, did suffer so grievously when their vaulting worldly ambitions came to naught in a trice! Amongst even the wealthiest of the world we see some who, despite acquiring billions in hard-earned money, are unable still to enjoy the fruits of their labor for many an unfortunate reason... such as for example, bitter dissension, distrust or disharmony within family members or, maybe onset of sudden severe, chronic or incurable disease.

If one's mind dwells deeply on the above infirmities and conditions of misery in life, would one still remain in thrall of the many pleasures of this mundane world or even those that lesser gods in svargam are said to enjoy? Certainly No! ... One would have to come to accept sooner or later that "all this is only lowly and worthless in nature!" And thus, for a Man of Vivekam what true Vairagyam or Virakthi entails is the complete uprooting of all his petty desires arising out of enchantment with mundanity. If a person were to do that in life, then he is said to have ascended to the third of the 9-stepped stairway of "parama pada sopanam".

BHEETHI next is the fourth step. It means Fear. Once this steep step of Fear is successfully climbed, then the ascent becomes thereafter relatively easy. What is this Fear? I shall explain it now to you and so please listen carefully with keen minds.

Now, let us consider this: We are born now as human beings. This present human incarnation of ours has been attained after journeying through countless other previous ones. Who knows really how those past lives were lived? Maybe as ants, worms, insect, serpent, an ass, a bear, dog, cow, elephant, fox or lion? In those previous incarnations, we might have endured countless sorts of pain, suffering and nameless plights... again who knows?!

However, one thing that is quite clear is that it was thanks to some randomly fortunate act or series of good or virtuous deeds (punnya phalan) on our part that we eventually somehow evolved into our present human incarnation and that too with excellent faculties of intelligence (buddhi) bestowed upon us. For a moment imagine that our present life as human being is the penultimate ninety-ninth mile in an evolutionary journey of a hundred. So where then do we go from here?

If thus, we were to ask ourselves whereto we go from here... or rather, in what different form we would probably be incarnating as in lives ensuing in the future, there is no doubt we will be filled with sheer mortal dread! The reason for such terrible fear is that we know only too well how or in what life-form we might incarnate again is going to be solely determined by the quality of virtue in present deeds in life. Our ledger-balance of virtuous deeds in this life (punnyam), we might have to confess to ourselves, shows virtually zero. So, it should not surprise us at all if we start to shudder in sheer terror as we give in to imagining the fate probably awaiting us in a future life. Mortal anxiety seizes us as we start wondering clueless whether we will not perhaps be born again -- as an ass, a horse, a worm or an insect. In such a dreadful moment, it would seem to us that all sins committed by us in a lifetime (paapam) are but logs of firewood getting added to the already raging flames of hellish retribution that awaits us.

Even the prospect of yet another rebirth as a human being in the next life will only petrify a man of ripened wisdom (Viveki) since he would realize that too again might well turn out to be only yet another round of miserable existential experiences -- marked as always by all kinds of infirmities such as hunger, disease and age (pini, pasi, moopu tunbam).

Such indeed is the terrifying state of Bheethi or Fear that afflicts the Viveki who in that particular state of mind can be said to have climbed over to the fourth step of the stairway of 9 steps to salvation erected by Sri Desikan for us.

PRASADAHETU is the name of the next step, the fifth.

What this celebrated step signifies is this: After having committed countless number of sins and transgressions in equally numberless past incarnations of ours in temporal existence, we end up only earning the extreme displeasure if not wrath of Bhagavan. There comes a time at last in the present lifetime when we realize the need to propitiate Bhagavan by any means to turn his displeasure into solicitude for us and our sad plight. There is no more effective means of such propitiation as the sacramental act known as **Saranagathi**. This is indeed the fifth step and if one fails to climb it, then ascent into Sri Vaikuntam becomes impossible. In his *magnum opus*, **Srimadh Rahasyatrayasaram**, Swami Desikan has written an exhaustive, most authoritative and yet so lucid a commentary on the entire doctrine of Saranagathi. Below in brief is the crux of his work:

In the ancient past, our maharishis possessed the spiritual caliber or capacity to practice the discipline of Bhakthi Yoga and become adepts in it. Unfortunately, none of us possesses such capability and hence we have no other option but to resort to the only one revealed to us by the Bhagavath-Gita as an alternative means to salvation: *"sarva dharmaam parithyajjya maamekam sharanam vraja, aham tvaa sarva paapebhyo moksha-ishyaami ma sucha:"*

In other words, through the act of Saranagathi, we affirm our absolute faith in Bhagavan by swearing a solemn oath: "Oh my Lord in whom all perfections and excellences reside (anantha kalyaana guna), I hereby swear that I shall be your loyal liege. I shall henceforth commit no transgression against you. No matter how grievously I may have sinned in the past, I am surrendering to you now in the firm faith that you will no longer be enraged with me and will grant me instead the grace of mukthi (salvation) I seek. Once I am rid of mortal coils, please bestow upon me the state of "moksha" which will save me forever from rebirth. I have no other recourse in life but to throw myself at your feet and mercy. This soul of mine, this Atma, I hereby return to you as it belongs to you alone! And I now eagerly await the prospect of rendering unto your sacred feet eternal service (kainkaryam) as a mere servitor in your abode of Sri Vaikuntam, deriving infinite bliss from doing so. Every deed of mine, whether sin or virtue, committed over infinite past lives or in the present, even if it makes me utterly undeserving of "moksha", is now being laid down at your feet! Verily it is all yours to dispose of as you deem fit!

Whatever be my fate or just desserts are also for you alone to decide and dispose!"

The soul that uttering such abject and plaintive words in absolute submission to Bhagavan, then proceeds to solemnly chant the sacred "dvaya mantra" and also recites thereafter the litany expressing total renunciation or "saatvika thyaaga". It is then that it is said that a person completes the journey of ascent to the fifth of the nine-stepped stairway of "parama pada sopanam". It should be noted here that an Acharya too comes in at this very point in the journey of the *jivaatma* and helps it constantly to advance and progress towards the next step.

UTHKRAMANAM is the name of the sixth step. The *jivaatma* that has ascended from the fifth step where it performed Saranagathi unto Bhagavan, on arriving at the sixth step is ready to shed its mortal coils. The moment of shedding the mortal body or sarira is said to be Death or "uthkramanam". Death of course is common to all mortals. So, it may be questioned why there is any need to mention it here as if it were special in any way?

Although death is indeed common to all beings, there is nonetheless an important difference between a soul dying after performing Saranagathi to Bhagavan and the death of a soul that has not done and has not ascended, in effect, to the previous fifth step of the stairway. So, "uthkramanam" of the jivatma that has performed Saranagathi is to be clearly distinguished from a jivatma facing death without performing it.

When bodily death occurs what happens is this: All the faculties (such as sight, hearing, breath, taste and touch) are all conjoined to unite with the Mind; the Mind is then united with Pranavayu (the vital air); the Pranavayu is then united with the jivatma; the jivatma is then made to inhere into another subtle body (called "sukshma sarira"), said to be an ethereal distillate of the five primordial elements (bhuthas) constituting the gross body. The jivatma now clothed in the subtle body is drawn by Bhagavan unto himself seated within the cavern of the heart (hrudaya akasa).

Up to this point in the above process of death, both the jivatma that has performed Saranagathi and the jivatma that has not performed

Saranagathi undergo the same experience. But it is in proceeding further that the two jivatmas take separate paths. And it is Bhagavan himself who causes them each to take different routes.

In the case of those jivatmas that have not performed Saranagathi and hence are not destined towards Moksha, Bhagavan Paramatma causes them (embodied in their sukshma sarira) to exit the cavern of the heart through a tortuous process of spiritual churning. However, once out, they then travel through millions of fine synaptic neural passages (*Naadis*), and emerge from noumenal space to enter once again into phenomenal space where they once again assume a gross bodily form in strict accordance with the karmic inheritance that each jivatma carries respectively within itself.

In the case of those jivatmas that have performed Saranagathi, and hence are bound for the state of Moksha, they are all caused by Paramatma himself to rise up easily from out of the cavernous space within the heart through a Naadi specially designated for the purpose and is thus readied for its onward journey. No sooner than does the jivatma embark upon such journey it already begins to experience ineffably blissful sensations.

The person who understands well the esotericism of "uthkramamam" can be said to have ascended and climbed across the sixth step of Sri Desikan's "parama pada sopanam".

ARCHIRADI next is the seventh step. It is to this step that Bhagavan summons his celestial servitors, functionaries and agents and asks them all to ensure safe conduct for the *prappannan jivatma* (i.e., the soul that has duly submitted to him in sarangathi) through the vast cosmic pathways leading to "parama padam".

Such delegates of Bhagavan are many – Agni, the fire god, the god of Daytime, the god of the ascendant fortnight (Shukla paksha devata), the god of the summer solstice (uttarayana devata), the god of the calendric cycle (samvatsara devata), the Wind God, Vayu, the Sun God, Surya, the Moon God, Chandran, the god of Lightning, Amaanavan (or "vidhyut purusha"), the Rain-God, Varuna, the chief of devatas, Indra and Brahmma, the cosmic Progenitor himself. All these celestial functionaries of Bhagavan come forward to dutifully conduct the jivatma in its onward journey in the direction of Sri

Vaikuntam. Amongst these celestial devatas, the one called Amanavan or Vidhyut Purusha is the one who personally chaperones the jivatma through the many cosmic routes and passages enroute to Sri Vaikuntam, the destination where the jivatma will finally be admitted into the glorious presence of Bhagavan. The celestial chaperones of Bhagavan are also known as *"Adivahikas"*.

A person who has understood well the significance of the journey of ascent up to this point or spot on the stairway of Swami Desikan's "parama pada sopanam" can be said to have successfully scaled its seventh step.

SHUDDHA-SATTVA-DESA-PRAPTHI: The onward last-mile phase of the jivatma's journey to the supreme abode of Sriman Narayana in Sri Vaikuntam is described as *"padadhirohanam"*.

This journey is undertaken by the jivatma along with the Vidhyuth Purusha (the god of Lightning) who shows it the way out of the outermost boundaries of the cosmos known as "brahmaandam".

Beyond the cosmic borders lies the great, celestial and pristine river of ambrosia named Viraja.

It is in a ceremonial bath in this river Viraja that the jivatma discards its subtle bodily form called "sukshma sarira".

The jivatma then reaches the yonder shore of the river and there is able to don a resplendent new spiritual form known as "deva sarira".

Thereafter, the jivatma is met by a bevy of beautiful celestial nymphs (apsara-sthri) who seat him comfortably under a decorated canopy on the sylvan banks of a lovely pond (pushkarini) and then proceed to bedeck the soul with divine "alankaram" viz. wardrobe, aromatic unguents, perfumes, luxuriant finery, jewelry and accessories.

Readied in attire thus for the great occasion, the jivatma is next led, amidst great fanfare, pomp and pageantry, in a procession, led by pipers and divine musicians, wending its way slowly past the city gates of Sri Vaikuntam and through its many magnificently festooned streets all winding away beneath grand towers and ramparts.

The jivatama then is ceremonially ushered into the great vaulted chamber (manimaamantapam), in which seated upon a dazzlingly majestic throne Sriman Narayan presides over Sri Vaikuntam! The sound of irrepressible cheering, hurrahs and shouts of unbounded joy from all quarters surround the space on the momentous occasion!

If a person were to fully comprehend the significance of the journey of ascent to "parama padam" right up to this point, then he must be regarded as having succeeded in climbing the eighth and penultimate step on the stairway built by Swami Desikan.

PRAAPTHI is the name of the ninth and last step of the journey undertaken by the jivatma.

Here, the Amanava devata known as Adivahika, finally delivers the jivatma unto the presence Bhagavan Sriman Narayana who with his divine consorts, Sri and Bhu Devi, sits enthroned upon Adisesha, the divine hydra-headed great serpent...

It is finally here then that the jivatma gets gathered up in the arms of Bhagavan in close embrace of love! The soul gets showered with the supreme grace of ineffable, infinite joy whose intensity is the very same as that which the heavenly servitors and archangels of Sri Vaikuntam -- such as "nithyasuris" and "mukthatmas" – too enjoy, and that which, in fact, constitutes Bhagavan's very nature itself! This is attested by the scriptural expression – **"svena roopenaabhinishpathyathe..."** In that very same climactic moment, the jivatma attains luminous gnyaana or omniscience i.e., the consciousness through which the soul is able to perceive and realize the all-pervasiveness and all-immanence of Sriman Narayanan. Immersed in such all-expansive knowledge, the jivatma thereafter is able to experience all-transcendent joy ("soshnutey...") – much in the same way as nithyasuris and mukthatmas of Sri Vaikuntam do – while performing unceasing, constant and ever-faithful services to the Supreme Will and Pleasure of Bhagavan.

In very brief summary above, such is the grand and full account of the ninth step in the stairway to "paramapadam" given by Sri Vedanta Desikan. The lifetime of any person who has grasped and understood in full measure the significance of this final step cannot go waste nor will it ever end up in futility. It will not be very long before such a person journeys forth to attain the supremely blissful state of Vaikuntam.

***

It is out his extraordinary compassion for all humanity, that our Acharyan, Sri Nigamantha Mahadesikan has gone to great lengths to cull out many truths from our sastras and authoritative Vedantic scriptures to erect for us the *parama pada sopanam*, his magnificent treatise. Many great souls in the past are known to have embraced all of those profound truths and thus attained the Grace of Sriman Narayana.

Many also are great souls who although lacking the ability to follow the lofty example of their more illustrious forebears, nonetheless succeeded in understanding and embracing at least the most significant of lessons contained in the paramapada sopanam up to the fifth step viz. lessons in life on how to perform Saranagathi with the aid of spiritual guidance received from a venerable Acharya and then lead life accordingly. Through the momentum so created by an Acharya's guidance, they were also able to attain the abode of Sriman Narayana. They are known as *"andhiyargal"* and are greatly celebrated in the *pasurams* of the Azhwars.

To follow in the footsteps of such *"andhiyars"* and to attain the state of *moksham* is an opportunity that is open to one and all irrespective of caste, class or station in society. Therefore, I urge all men and women not to lose such an opportunity. If they do not understand fully the significance of all the nine steps of the *paramapada sopanam* they should approach an erudite guru or a venerable Acharya for help in gaining fulsome clarity. Having gained such a clear understanding, they should also then share it amongst their larger circle of friends who too will surely and greatly benefit from the enlightenment it provides. The Grace of Nigamantha Mahadesikan will surely then be showered upon all.

***

-11-
Six Traits of the Salvation Seeker

Synopsis: *In the previous epistle while expatiating upon "Vivekam", the first step called Wisdom on the stairway to Salvation ("parama pada sopanam" of Sri.Vedanta Desikan), Mukkur Swami had broadly sketched the attribute of Wisdom or what in Vedanta is referred as "discriminative knowledge". In this epistle below, he further expands upon the theme of Vivekam by revealing six of the traits of a man of true wisdom.*

"Discriminative knowledge or real Wisdom (*vivekam*) consists of 6 traits: Renunciation (*vimokam*), Perseverance (*abhyaasam*), Diligence (*kriya*), Felicity (*kalyaanam*), Mental sanguinity (*anavasaadam*), Mental equipoise (*anuttdarsham*).

It has been established that one who possesses these 6 traits possesses "*vivekam*" and is sure to attain Salvation (*moksham*).

Wisdom or Discriminative Knowledge, "*vivekam*", is a determinant of the mortal body or the '*sarira*' which in turn is composed of 5 elements of nature viz. *earth, water, fire, wind* and *ether* which are the seat of all sensory faculties such as *sight, hearing, smell, touch* and *taste*. The mortal body is also inhered by three basis humors or "*gunas*": 1. **Sattva** 2. **Rajas** and 3. **Tamas**.

It is the first of the three *gunas* which impels Man to act virtuously in life and be rewarded beneficence accordingly.

The second "*guna*" of Rajas arouses the base or gross instincts in Man and impedes or retards his advancement towards higher spiritual or God-ward goals in life.

It is in the nature of the 3rd *guna*, Tamas, to induce in Man heretical and atheistic proclivities in life. It leads him to turn inimical towards or show irreverence to the precepts of the wise and the elderly. Such dangerous attitudes invariably lead Man to great moral peril, ultimately to the soul's perdition even.

It is therefore very important that in life one must exert oneself in cultivating strong Sattva *guna* and, do the best one can to discourage or curb the other two instinctual *gunas* of Rajas and Tamas. By constant cultivation of the Sattva *guna* one can maintain the health and purity of one's body, the *sarira*.

If one asks how to cultivate Sattva *guna* the answer is wholesome diet – i.e., what we consume as grain (rice or *annam*), milk, curd, vegetables, fruits, tubers etc. It is only through abjuring foul or improper food that one can induce the growth of the intellect and its powers of discrimination (i.e., *vivekam*).

The term *Food* denotes generally all kinds of gustation but there are some foods which ought to be totally eliminated from our diet. They are foods like onions, garlic, alcohol, bottle-gourd, artificial processed dairy produce, silage etc. Foods like rice, wheat, milk etc. are those which should not be abjured. Even generally acceptable food if improperly delivered or served should not be consumed. For example, water or milk served in iron-utensils, grains that before cooking have been threshed with human feet, or edibles stored under unhygienic conditions. Food prepared by women of low morals or by persons known to have unclean personal habits, or food that has been prepared in the proximity of dogs and other household pets should not be consumed.

It is intake of good, wholesome and pure Food alone that can promote the growth of Sattva *guna* in the *sarira* which in turn leads to the growth of the intellect (*kaayashuddi*) which is what keen discrimination or *vivekam* is really all about.

1. Let us now turn to examine what is *vimokam*.

   "Kaamanapishvangam vimokam" is the expression used by wise men to denote this quality of Renunciation.

   What is renunciation? It is renouncing the hankering after all petty or low desires of this mortal life (*duraasai*) and maintaining instead steadfastness in pursuing the overarching desire to attain

Bliss – i.e., bliss supreme, bliss undiminished, bliss indestructible, and bliss unsurpassed.

For all humanity, it is quite common to wish for such enduring quality of Bliss but it is only amongst those seekers of Salvation (*veedu*) that the desire is found to be predominant desire.

What is "*veedu*"? It is Sri Vaikuntam. It is only there that the Almighty confers upon one such supreme Bliss.

Thus, vimokam is the trait in man which makes him renounce all petty and undesirable desires in life and concentrate all his desires towards realizing one goal alone viz. attaining the supreme bliss of salvation.

2. Next, "*abhyaasam*" (Perseverance) is the trait in Man that impels him to keep his mental focus unwaveringly riveted on *Sriman Narayanan*, contemplating upon him as the primal source of supreme bliss. Such contemplation demands Man to turn away from all other alluring objects of the world that possess the power to attract, distract and bewitch him. It is therefore necessary he never lets up on persevering to gradually wean himself away from the many enchantments of the ordinary world, remaining as far as his God-given faculties enable him in contemplation on **Bhagavan** alone. This perseverance in godly contemplation is what is meant by "*abhyaasam*".

3. Then there is the trait called "*kriyai*" ….

As revealed in the phrase, "**chaaturvaranyammaya shrushtam guna karma vibhakasah**" …, in this world there are four classes of beings (*varnas*) created with each *varna* possessing certain unique properties and characteristics. Each "*varna*", at the same time, is also subjected by natural order to perform certain enjoined duties (*anushtaanam*). Duties are also enjoined upon the 4 *varnas* belonging to the particular station in life (*ashrama*) at any point in time. Realizing that such natural order of duties (i.e., "*anushtaana*" enjoined on both *varna* and *ashrama*) is verily the will and command of the Divine, one should always faithfully perform them in a spirit of loving devotion to God. While performing some of these "*anushtaanams*", it may so happen that the mantras involved therein are seen to be extolling other lesser gods and divinities (*devatas*); yet while worshipping them there should be inner realization that they are all only various manifestations of the one Supreme, all-pervading *Paramaatma*. It is only then that worship becomes fully effective means to attaining salvation. Thus, it is this constant performance of *"anushtaanam"* (such as the daily rite of *"sandhyavandanam"*, for example) that is referred to as *"kriyai"*.

4. Next, *"kalyanam"* (loosely translated as Felicity) can be defined to be... **"sathya, arjava, daya, daana, ahimsa, anabidhyah kalyanaani" i.e.,** *Sathya* means commitment to Truth, avoiding untruth, being generally genial in speech. *Arjava* means maintaining consistency and integrity of thought, word and deed. *Daya* means being empathetic to the sufferings and grief of fellow humans and being moved to lend succor to them. *Ahimsa* means never needlessly being the cause of hurt, pain or any distress to others. *Anabidhya*: means never coveting the property or possessions of others nor harboring any rapacious thoughts. All these traits together can be said to be *"kalyanam"*.

5. *"Anavasaadam"*: The word *"avasaadam"* refers to a general mental deportment of brooding surliness. It also refers to a mental state of chronic anxiety over the future, over what it might hold and what one might have to do about it... It is being in a constant state of worry and stress. To be otherwise i.e., in a state of mental sanguineness is what is known as *"anavasaadam"*. Those afflicted by the angst of *"avasaadam"* generally land themselves in all sorts of perilous situations and predicament in life. This condition is also known as *"dainyam"*.

6. *"Anuttdarsham"*: The word *"uttdarsham"* means over-exuberance, or over self-indulgence... i.e., getting over intoxicated by pleasures of the world and what such worldly pleasures are is only too well known to all of us. If such pleasures happen to be derived through unlawful or immoral means, then the fallout is bound to be hellish. Even if, on the other hand, such pleasure was to be derived through good or virtuous means, delighting over it should be tempered by self-restraint; over-indulgence in it, or

otherwise getting overly enchanted with it, should be avoided. Sobriety or mental equipoise should be maintained even in delighting. That is what *"anuttdarsham"* is.

He or she who diligently cultivates all the aforesaid 6 elemental traits of *"vivekam"* in the course of a lifetime will eventually succeed in fortifying the noble instincts of Sattva *guna* within his personality. He will then be able to rid himself of all taint and stigma of sins (*"paapam"*) committed in countless previous mortal incarnations (*purva janma*). The *vivekam* thus attained by him will then enable him to resort to means such as *"bhakti yoga"* or *"saranagathi"*, thereby qualifying himself, and rendering himself spiritually fit to ascend to the state of **Sri Vaikuntam**, and delight there ceaselessly in the consummative, ever-blissful experience of **Bhagavan**.

It is in the long lineage of our *Acharyas* and spiritual forebears that we can see truly great exemplars of all the above noble traits. It is to commemorate and celebrate their personalities that today we have deified them within our temples so that their memory will serve us as genuine role-models to be emulated.

Those who are dismissive of or fail to appreciate the value of the above 6 traits explained above, or show scant respect for their idealization, are said to be spiritually retarded or irresponsible humans. Even merely acquainting or in any way associating with such irresponsible persons brings only demerit or sin to one. That is precisely what the *sastras* say… that **Yama**, the *Lord of Death*, reserves for such people a very special place in Hell (*narakam*).

***

There is an old story usually told about such sinners.

There once lived a sinful man in a town who since birth never knew the meaning of virtue. At home were kept two sacred pebbles of *"saalagraama"* which his father had been faithfully worshipping as household icon for many years in his lifetime.

After his father died, the man fell deep into vagrant, immoral ways. He began visiting prostitutes. The habit became a steady drain on his finances and one day he thought by selling the sacred *"saalagraama"* he could raise some money.

His mother and wife protested saying that the sacred *"saalagraama"* had kept the family protected for many years.

"Even if you do not wish to offer daily worship to the "saalagraama", it's alright, but please do not take them out of our home to sell them!" they cried. *"These sacred stones bring auspiciousness unto our home. They have kept us protected against all ills and afflictions all these years!"*

The man however, bent upon selling the holy icons for money and convinced it was the best thing to do to meet his unholy purposes, ignored his mother and wife's words and went ahead with the heinous deed.

Very soon thereafter, the man then went on to sell even the holy Vedic and scriptural books like the *Ramayana* and *Bhagavatham* which had been reverently kept and cherished in the family library for many years only to raise money for his sleazy purpose.

This man was of degenerate character. He was a glutton given to savoring all sorts of food unfit for consumption. On the other hand, if his mother who worshipped daily at the temple brought home holy *'prasaadam'* to give to him, he would spurn it and feed it instead to a pet dog.

As days went by, he sank ever deeper into sin and his need for money grew so desperate that he began to resort to even thievery and brazen fraud to earn an income. And yet he would give not even a dime in charity for any good or worthy cause. He would rebuff the company of elderly, virtuous men. He would mock them for the sacred sign they wore on their foreheads (*urdhvam*). He would disdainfully scoff at all the Holy Scriptures and dismiss all *"puraana"* sermonizers as mere charlatans out to make merely a livelihood. He deferred to none in the world. He did not seem to fear even *Yama Dharmaraja*, the God of Death.

The man however did one day die at last. His family had his remains duly cremated in the funeral grounds and returned home after disposing of his body.

However, the cremated body of the sinner was so repugnant to the celestials that the Almighty himself refused it entry into his realm. The body was expelled. It was hurled back to earth. In a mutilated, half-incinerated condition it then lay on the funeral ground.

It was then that a pack of hungry foxes happened to be prowling around the cremation grounds. When they chanced upon the half-incinerated cadaver of the man sprawled on the ground, the foxes decided to make a delightful meal of it.

Amongst the pack of hungry foxes, there was an old wise old one.

The old fox asked the rest what they were intending to do when they said, *"The cadaver's hand looks to us so juicy… we shall tear it to pieces and eat half-burnt, half-done flesh to our heart's content! Yes, we are going to devour the hand first".*

The old fox replied, *"Hold on! Stop! Wait a moment! Do not do any such thing in haste! Please pause now and let me tell you something very important".*

Saying so, the old fox retired to a spot and fell into deep trancelike thought.

Moments later, within its mind the old, wise fox was able to envision this -- the sinful condition of the cadaver expelled from the realm of Yama and the soul (*Jeevan*) that had once lived within it and the terrible punishment the sinful soul was now undergoing at the hands of the Lord of Death in Hell.

The old fox then turned to the rest of the pack and told them, *"My brethren, please do not eat the hand of this cadaver. It is made of sin… this is the hand of a sinful gambler; this is the hand of a man who sold away sacred 'saalagrama'; this is the hand of a forger who committed countless frauds; this is the hand which pilfered and thieved… thus, please do not touch this cadaver's hand. It is unfit to eat".* Saying so, the old fox held back the pack from eating the hand of the cadaver.

The foxes however were very hungry. They thought to themselves that if the hand was unfit to eat, then perhaps other body-parts of the half-incinerated flesh of the cadaver might be more edible. They lurched forward to tear away the flesh of the ears of the cadaver to eat it.

Again, the old fox restrained them saying, *"No, don't eat the flesh of those ears which too are sinful! When alive those ears had only listened to the precepts of atheists and unbelievers. They had turned deaf to the entreaties of the man's good wife when she had beseeched him not to fail in his duty to provide care and protection to his aged parents!"*

The rest of the pack now turned and sniffed at the cadaver and said that the flesh of the abdomen seemed to be good to eat. But again, the old fox held them back saying, *"Stop! Do you know how the abdomen, stomach and entrails of this cadaver grew? It was fed the sin of every kind of food the 'sastras' had forbidden as unfit for human consumption. The belly here was filled with foodstuff procured from those very places and sources that the sastras had forbidden humans to procure food from. Therefore, please do not touch the flesh of the cadaver!"*

In the same way, the old fox forbade the pack to touch any part of the sinful half-burnt cadaver lying before them on the ground.

The hungry foxes were greatly disconcerted by the old one obstructing them from having a good meal. Greatly annoyed, they asked the old fox how it came to know all that it seemingly did about the cadaver. To which the old fox replied:

"I know all about this cadaver here through dint of the "tapobalam" --- great austerities practiced by which I acquired extraordinary powers in my previous lives (janma)!"

Surprised by the answer given, the foxes retorted, *"If you possess such exalted powers as a legacy from your earlier lives, how come then you were born to live as one amongst us, as lowly creature, a feral fox and suffer the same miserable plight on earth as we?"*

The old fox then narrated the story of its soul's journey in past lives:

"As a man in my earlier 'janma' I once had to visit as guest the home of a man who possessed none of the noble traits of vivekam, vimokam and such like…

In that home I happened to see a beautiful self-portrait of the man hung on the wall. It was a beautiful work of art and out of a sudden momentary impulse I coveted it for myself. I reached out and took down the portrait thinking I would secret it away… But then coming to my senses, I realized my mistake and so furtively returned the portrait to its original place.

The only sin I had committed in that moment was to have merely come in contact with, or to have simply touched the portrait of that sinful man… But that was enough to taint my soul… I became condemned to descend to earth and to lead the life of a lowly fox in the very next birth I was about to take… So, there you are, now you know why I am here amongst you in this pack!

"It is for that very reason, that I am now cautioning you all against eating the flesh of this cadaver that once belonged to a sinful man… For merely coming in contact with the portrait of a heinous sinner in a past life, I was fated to descend in this life to the lowly life-form of a fox. So, pause for just a moment to imagine what form of misery as some wretched creature you might be destined endure in some future birth on earth as retribution for consuming the cadaverous meat of the sinful soul that once had possessed this dead body!"

After listening to the words of the old fox, the rest of the pack became filled with dread. To expiate for the *"paapam"* they feared they had committed by merely sighting the sinful cadaver, the entire pack decided to observe that day a ritual fast. Following the day of fasting, the entire pack then also took a ritual bath in the pure waters of a river to sanctify themselves. Thereafter they scattered into the forests to begin hunting and foraging for food elsewhere.

***

The moral of the story is that as humans we must strive therefore to cultivate those 6 traits of *"vivekam"* that will surely fetch for us the blessings (*kataaksham*) of both the Divine and Devout – viz. *vimokam, abhyaasam, kriya, kalyanam, anavasaada, anutthdarsham* – all leading us ultimately to the everlasting bliss of salvation.

Let it be noted that all that has been explained above is based on the authority (*pramaanam*) of the chapter titled "***jignyaasa adhikarana***" in Sri Ramanujacharya's **"Sri Bhaashyam"**.

***

-12-
Six "*Bhaktha-s*" in a "*Divya-Desam*"

Synopsis: *Six tales about life-transforming events happening under six different circumstances in the lives of six different men are recounted in this sterling epistle by Sri Mukkur Azhagiyasingar in his own inimitable, simple, down-to-earth and endearing style. Very meaningful lessons of Vedantic ethics can be found to have been seamlessly woven into the narrative flow that leaves a profound impact indeed on the reader's mind.*

Once upon a time there lived in a holy temple-town – a *"divya-desam"* – six *"bhaktha-s"* (devotees of Bhagavan). It was their daily unfailing habit of worshipping the temple-deity with fresh floral offerings of many varieties duly provided to the temple-priest.

Of the six bhaktas, one was a person whose daily prayer at the temple was for divine blessings of a good education and a lucrative job-career. It was his hope that with whatever income he would then earn, he would be able to do some good for the general welfare of the community at large.

The second *bhaktha's* prayers were for divine blessings enabling him to thrive in a prosperous business venture that would yield much returns and with which he could donate generously for public philanthropy.

The third *bhaktha* was a farmer and his prayers to Divinity was to be blessed with fertile farmlands whose copious harvest-yields would enable him to provide sufficient foodgrains for hosting on the two sacred occasions of *"dvaadashi"* every fortnight, charitable feeding of at least 100 deserving guests.

The fourth *bhaktha's* prayer was for good fortune in his speculative and wagering ventures. His earnest wish was that out of the windfall gains from such ventures he would be able to spend on charitable causes such as conducting mass-weddings for young underprivileged couples and mass-*upanayanam* (Vedic rite of passage) for poor young boys.

The fifth *bhakta* prayed for enduring robust health and physique which would enable him to pursue spiritual pathways in life, of *karma yoga*, *gnyaana yoga* and *bhakthi yoga*, leading to the consummative experience of *Sriman Narayana* both here in the mortal world as well as in the celestial realm of *Sri Vaikuntam*, the abode of the Almighty.

The sixth in his worship of Divinity was motivated by his desire to earn and deserve the love and grace of *Sriman Narayana* through the act of renunciation of all worldly desires as absolute surrender (*bharannyaasam*) unto him and by selflessly serving all good causes that secure the general wellbeing of fellowmen in society.

***

The first *bhaktha*, named Venkata Krishnaswami, was blessed with very good education after having secured several academic degrees, landing a very lucrative job in life and he prospered. However, in the subject of Vedic scriptural knowledge, he scored a naught. However, given his predisposition to do good for the community, he generously supported many public charitable causes.

In good time, he also became wealthy with his personal net-worth accumulating to several hundreds of thousands of rupees. How he was able to accumulate so much money could however be left only to imagination! The accretion to his sudden surge of wealth was mainly through ill-gotten, corrupt and utterly unlawful means. Although he did of course donate money for public good and causes, at the same time he also never shied away from making money through wholly dishonest and venal ways.

One day when this *bhakta* was way from home while on a tour to his native village, a band of burglars broke into his house, stole all his stash of ill-gotten money and slipped away, never to be found. On his return when he discovered the robbery, his heart sank and he became extremely distressed by the sudden loss.

The break-in and burglary in the *bhaktha's* house somehow came to the immediate notice of the local police. The police wanted to investigate him to know the details of what items of household were stolen and their estimated value. The *bhaktha* was left then in a very difficult predicament. If he were to disclose to the police the fact that several lakhs of currency were stolen from the house, he would be expected then to also account for how such money came into his possession and its source. If the truth of the matter were then to come out in the open, and the nefarious source of all his ill-gotten money were to be uncovered, the *bhakta* knew the consequence would be that both his job and career would be in jeopardy. So, to wiggle out of his precarious situation, the *bhaktha* told the police in writing that while there had been indeed a burglary in his house, nothing however was stolen or missed whatsoever. The police treated the case then as closed forthwith and went away, quite happy there was little they needed to do in the matter.

The *bhaktha* however was left behind to rue his great loss! Utterly crestfallen, he cried to himself, *"Oh, how hard did I work to earn all that money and now it's all gone in the blink of eye! Woe unto me!"* He could not hold back shedding tears even!

It was in that moment then that the *bhaktha's* wife appeared before him and told him blandly:

"What is the point now, my dear, in bemoaning the misfortune that has befallen you? You have brought it upon yourself, haven't you?

"In the past many a time I have had unknown persons come to our home and meeting me alone; they would furtively slip into my hands hundreds of rupees. I used to be surprised and would ask them *"Why are you giving me this money?!"* They would then reply to me in whispers, *"Your husband has helped us out in certain difficult situations and cases. So, in return for such exceptional favours rendered by him, we are giving you now this money"*.

"I used to be puzzled and would ask then ask them, *"If he has done you favours willingly, why must you make these payments to us?! I don't understand!"*

They would then tell me in hushed voice: *"Ma'am, do you know what would happen to us if we didn't make these payments as desired by your husband? He would threaten to expose us all through the power his office he held which could easily falsify our books of accounts... So, just to ensure his cooperation, we are thus compelled to make these secret payments to you... These monies we often cannot really afford... but what choice do we have? So, to raise these monies we go through much pain, trouble... and even tears. We sometimes are forced to even go the extent of pledging and pawning all our family jewellery just to be able to make these payments..."*

"Thus, have I seen", said the wife to the *bhaktha*, "these pained persons come home here and secretly hand over these payments as *protection-money* to me. Virtually some of them used to have tears in their eyes..."

"The money that you have extorted from them and accumulated so far through such immoral means had a terrible price viz. the tears that they had to shed to procure it.... Now, you see that it has landed us both in the same situation where we too are fated to pay the same price! It is now our turn to shed our painful tears over the loss of all the money that was so extorted...!"

The *bhaktha's* wife then began counselling him:

"Henceforth, whatever you earn from your job as salary income of four hundred rupees, you please hand it all over to me every month. I will manage it for you and ensure there is enough savings we make out of it too. Trust me and do not feel grieved about it. Money earned through corrupt or immoral ways will only surely lead to this sort of self-destruction and perdition..."

The *bhaktha* listened intently to everything his wife said and realized the folly of his wicked ways. His mind was then made up. He firmly resolved to follow his wife's sincere and sage advice. He gave up his venal ways and stopped his extortion and bribery racket. Out of the income he earned and brought home to his wife, she was able to put away much by way of savings and which soon in time grew into a handsome, thriving fund!

The moral of the story: It is utter foolishness on the part of man to seek to amass wealth in a lifetime through any means, suspect, avaricious and immoral, simply for the sake of providing enough for future generations of his progeny. There is no need at all to be anxious about the future wellbeing of our offspring. Just as Bhagavan has given us all the protection and care needed in our lifetime, likewise, so will Bhagavan provide all that our children, grand-children and great-grand-children too will need in their own lives to live happily. He will never let us down.

***

The second *bhaktha's* name was Anantharaman. He was the proprietor of a trading business firm dealing in various grocery-goods and foodstuff. For a little while, he was running the business earning handsome profits generated through honest transactions and lawful dealings. However, in course of time and quite suddenly, he was possessed by great greed. He began associating with unscrupulous business partners and dealers. Pretty soon he discovered many different shady ways to adulterate all the foodstuff and grocery he was selling without being detected. The business began to profiteer hugely from such adulteration and in such quick time too.

Even as he was raking in ill-gotten profits from his unlawful business, he still continued donating to a few temples his adulterated grocery and merchandise without any compunction. Such adulterated food was ritually offered to Lord Krishna, the temple-deity too. Thus, as days went by, so much of adulterated foodstuff did Krishna as *"archa murthy"* (idolized deity) have to consume that it seemed as though it exceeded even the quantities of mud, grit and stones which Krishna as a playful, frolicking boy during his avatar days (*vibhava avatara*) was known to have consumed. The devotees at the temple who also partook ("bhagavath prasaada viniyoga") and consumed the adulterated foodstuff suffered severe alimentary illness.

As events however soon turned out, Bhagavan himself seemed to intervene and rendered swift justice to the sinful adulterator.

Very soon the *bhaktha* himself succumbed to the same affliction that the foodstuff he had been supplying to the temple had caused to both the Deity and devotees alike! He was brought down by a disease of the alimentary system called *"Mahodara"* ((महोदर) refers to *"combination of more than one "udararoga" which is of eight types ("diseases affecting the belly"*)) which caused excruciatingly painful abdominal inflammation and ulcers. It became impossible for him to eat. Medical treatment became imperative and critical. The doctors' bills began to mount exorbitantly as the treatment too prolonged. Little by little, all the money he had earlier made while profiteering from business of adulteration, began to vanish into hospital and medical payments. The medical treatment itself, however, did little to alleviate or cure his disease. He continued to suffer great distress even as he saw that the doctors were fleecing him steadily with ever more and higher fees and charges for medical care.

One day, after the attendant doctors had left the ward, the *bhaktha* ruefully turned to his dear wife and began to wail:

"*May woe befall these accursed doctors!* They are fleecing me with this prolonged medical treatment! So far, no cure! *My money down the drain!* They are only administering me more and more adulterated medication --- perhaps it's all nothing but plain water mixed with tonic! *The sins of these guilty doctors will not go unpunished.* Surely, they too will suffer one day this same ailment as I do now… And who knows which doctors will fleece them too then as retribution!"

The wife replied tersely to the husband: "*It is my guess that the doctors who you say may in future wreak retribution on them will be no different from the ones attending on you today…*"

The ailing *bhaktha*, rather astonished, turned to his wife and said, "*I don't understand what you are trying to tell me!*"

The wife replied calmly, "You should know that the symptoms of the ailment plaguing you are the same as those that result from food-poisoning."

When he heard his wife's remark, the man, being well acquainted with diseases caused by food-adulteration, in a sudden flash of penitent realization, understood the bitter truth of his wife's remark: Divinity always finds a way in due course of time to inflict retribution for sin; and that purveyors of adulterated food one day will certainly suffer the very same painful fate that they brought upon innocent consumers....

The *bhaktha* was now thoroughly chastened. Remorsefully, he lifted his hands high above his head and cried out loudly for divine pardon: "*O Bhagavan, I have learnt my lesson now! I shall never again resort to sinful, greedy ways of making gains! I resolve never to adulterate food henceforth in my business! I beseech your forgiveness!*"

The man then went on to undergo further medical treatment until every penny of his ill-gotten wealth was consumed by doctor's bills! But at the end, mercifully, he was fully cured. He returned to normal life and resumed his business but now desisted from resorting to old sharp, sinful and unlawful practices. Gradually, his fortunes turned for the good again. He lived then happily ever after, finding fulfilment in the kind of charity work he had been always predisposed towards in the first place.

***

The third *bhaktha* was named Dhanarajan. This man was a wealthy landlord who had inherited vast farmlands of about 1300 acres from his father. Although indebted to some extent by way of arrears of overdue interest that had been steadily accruing during the father's lifetime on loans procured for farming the land, the *bhaktha* however had managed to somehow succeed in agriculture. By the grace of God -- which he sought by worshipping at the temple through daily offerings of fragrant magnolia flowers – and through dint of sheer hard, honest and diligent work, if not through any great skill or efficiency, he did manage to somehow turn a profit from tilling his farmlands which did yield him handsome harvests. With wealth accumulating thus in his household coffer, he was able to fulfil his desire to give away part of his harvest of grains in generous charity.

As per age-old custom and sacred tradition, on the eleventh day of the lunar fortnight every month, he would invite many men of piety and elders in his village to visit his home to observe the holy fast of "*Ekadashi vrata*" and offered them all every comfort of hospitality he could possibly provide. Then the following morning, early on the sacred "*dwaadashi*" day, he would hold a feast for all of them as per the injunctions of the *sastra* called "*paaranai*" – the ritual breaking of *Ekadashi* fast. The lavish hospitality he extended, to all the pious persons assembled as his guests, ensured they were well fed, given token gifts of Rs. 15/- each (*dakshina*) and that they returned thereafter to their homes, satisfied both spiritually and physically upon concluding their *"vrata"*.

As time went by, due to unknown reasons, unfortunately it so happened that in the *bhakta's* village, good-hearted and pious persons were very hard to come by and to be invited as honoured guests at the *Dwadashi* feasts held by him. He found it increasingly difficult to fulfil his desire to host *"Ekadashi vrata"* and *"dwaadashi paaranai"* for at least the hundred guests he desired to so entertain every fortnight. Those persons who did, however, turn up at his home for the feast were known instead to be unsavoury persons, freeloading atheists many of whom were of lowly character or disposition. Some pious-minded guests also came and joined the *"vrata"* only because of the temptation of a good meal and the prospect of the Rs.15/- "Dakshina". They too joined the feast even though they knew fully well that they would be mingling with many undesirable, unholy fellow-guests that were utterly unfit to be part of an *"Ekadashi vrata"*. As a result, such good, pious men too fell from grace.

As days passed by under such unfortunate conditions, the *bhaktha* began to witness a gradual but steep and sudden decline in the harvest yields of his farmlands. Not being able to reason why his lands were turning out such very low yields, he consulted an able astrologer and sought his counsel. The foreteller told Dhanarajan that the farm-yields were declining because the grains harvested were being put to use for very unworthy and impious purposes. What the astrologer meant was that although the charitable act of providing ritually sanctified food on the sacred day of *"dwaadashi"* was no doubt a virtuous or *dharmic* one, nonetheless, if such food was being feasted upon by unworthy rascals and impious blackguards then that would render even *dharmic* deeds as wholly *a-dharmic*.

The *bhaktha* immediately realized the great folly of his ways. He ceased at once the habit of inviting guests indiscriminately without due regard to their good character and piety. He thereafter went to greater trouble than before to seek out where genuinely pious and religious-minded persons lived and ensured they were duly invited to be hosted by him for the sacred fortnightly feast of *"dvaadashi"* (*tadhi-*

aaraadanai). If after hosting such feasts, any money that had been earmarked for the purpose however remained still unspent, the *bhaktha* ensured that it was all donated to the temple for holding "*utsavams*" or other such public religious festivals.

Miraculously it seemed soon thereafter, he began to see his farmlands once again beginning to yield rich harvests! He lived happily thereafter.

***

The fourth *bhaktha* was named Chakrahasthan. He was a suave deceiver, a gambler of sorts and fraudster. However, to the outside world he appeared to be a very upright person. Even those whom he surreptitiously defrauded refused to believe his mendacious nature. So clever indeed was he, Chakrahasthan, in shrouding his devious character behind a mask of respectability.

It was through guile and subterfuge that this *bhaktha* however was able to amass money. With resources so raised, Chakrahasthan often projected himself in society to be a good man … a *dharma-kartha* … by sponsoring and patronizing community events. He took great pride in arranging for conducting many heterodoxic or exogamous mass-weddings for couples from every stratum of society. He also funded the "*upanayana*" ceremonies for young boys with least regard for their familial or social background. He employed dozens of Vedic tutors and then by promising them attractive remuneration, beguiled them into teaching full-fledged Vedic lessons to all and sundry students, with scant regard for antecedents, aptitude or qualifications.

In going about in such cavalier manner with such irresponsible efforts of his, it became clear that Chakrahasthan neither was himself well acquainted with *sastras* nor did he care to seek the counsel of wise elders. The mass exogamous weddings he conducted each cost lots of money. Wherefrom was he getting the money to hold such weddings? It came to be known soon that he was actually pilfering money from temple treasury itself for the purpose!

Chakrahasthan's dear son came of age for marriage. The son was besotted with a tribal girl living in the forests and to the utter chagrin of the father, the son insisted he would wed none other than her. The girl, well, she seemed like she was born out of unholy wedlock of some evil spirit or demon (*peyy, pishasu*) or perhaps of some wild bear, tiger and ape! But in the eyes of the son, the girl from the forests appeared as a celestial nymph of extraordinary beauty! The father was utterly displeased with the son's choice but there was little he could do to dissuade the adamant son.

Much to the father's great disappointment, the marriage was held and the daughter-in-law came to live with the Chakrahasthan family under the same roof. The girl was of a very churlish temperament and from day one, began to pick petty fights with the in-laws on every little pretext…. Her doting husband however always backed her in her fights against father and mother-in-law. So then, hardly anything more needed to be said about the state of domestic harmony in the house of Chakrahasthan! But then, would you have any idea about who the daughter-in-law might have been? *If you wish to know, please read on then…*

Chakrahasthan one day after sponsoring the conducting of a lavish public mass-wedding returned home for lunch. As he sat down for the meal, his daughter-in-law laid down a banana-leaf before him and began serving upon it an elaborate spread of dishes. Do you know what the delicacies were? They were a melange of eatables he disliked most, all tossed together for his delectation! He was enraged and disgusted by what was served! He thundered at his daughter-in-law, *"What rotten melange is this that you serve me?!"*. To which she retorted cooly, *"All rotten melanges will of course rotten be! What else do you expect?"*

From that day onwards, much to his consternation, his daughter-in-law continued dishing out to Chandrahasthan nothing but daily servings of mishmash of the most unsavoury food imaginable… until he could no longer endure it all! But after many such days passed, slowly but suddenly one day, wisdom dawned upon him! At last, he realized the folly of his own ways which indeed were nothing but an unsavoury medley of adharmic deeds themselves! Only he had been convincing himself that they were all such good and charitable deeds. He deeply regretted his misdemeanours.

Chakrahasthan turned over a new leaf completely and became a new man… The mass *upanayanams* and the mass community weddings held indiscriminately were stopped. He now began to sponsor and conduct them as charity but they were now were all strictly organized in accordance with the norms laid down in the sacred *sastras*. And it was in such conduct of charitable deed that he now at last did find a much greater sense of fulfilment in doing good work for community.

Were you able to now guess the identity of that feisty girl? She was none other than Maaya, a daughter that Yashodha was blessed with once upon a time long ago, thanks to the Grace that Lord Krishna had conferred upon her!

***

The name of the fifth *bhaktha* was Bhaktharatnam. He was a muscular, well-built man who prided himself on developing his physique. He took a course on Yoga and went about it with great keenness and vigour. His belief in the yogic exercises he engaged in were rather quixotic. When asked what he was really up to while performing his yogic bodily contortions he would reply, *"This is karma yoga that I am now doing"!* On other days he would claim he was performing *"gnyaana yoga";* and yet on other days, he would insist his yogic exercises were actually what *"bhakti-yoga"* is indeed all about!

If anyone were to press him to explain what he meant by *karma-yoga*, he would glibly reply, *"Practising long and hard the posture of standing on your head on the floor with both feet held firmly high above it is karma yoga".*

If the question was, *"What is "gnyaana yoga?"* pat would be his answer: *"Gnyaana yoga is the daily practice of sitting silently at a spot at home and concentrating mentally on taking an inventory of all household effects and belongings of yours, one by one. Doing this at least for twenty or twenty-five times daily is what this type of yoga is all about".*

When he was asked what he was doing when seen every day in the hour past midnight seated on the culvert of a street drainage-channel, muttering or prattling all by himself, his laconic reply was, *"Oh that! That is what I do daily as "bhakthi yoga"!"*

If anyone puzzled by his strange behaviour were to ask him, *"Aren't you one bit concerned or aware that all your yogic activity, done according to your own whims and fancies, finds no sanction at all in sastras?!",* the *bhakta* would take umbrage and retaliate, *"I don't need any one's sanction or approval to do whatever I know Bhagavan himself has inspired me do and that too in any which way I like! What is wrong with that?!"*

It was in this way that this wilful, fatuous *bhakta* insisted that he would continue his yogic activities believing them to be *"karma, gnyaana, bhakthi yoga"* as defined by himself in his own haughty and self-opinionated way without the slightest of heed being shown to the wisdom of *sastra-ic* or any scriptural tenets. His bizarre behaviour was triggered by a mind probably perverted by a belief in self-importance – the misbelief that it was, after all, only in answer to his own fervent prayer to Bhagavan that the Almighty had blessed him with great physical strength and will with which he was absolutely free to pursue any path he chose in life to be right. This *bhaktha* was totally ignorant of the fact that no true knowledge can be gained, nor any spiritual endeavour succeed, without a yogic aspirant first securing the guidance and blessings of an Acharya.

Self-conceit and inflated sense of self-importance will be of no-good avail for spiritual aspiration. The *bhaktha* could not shed ego. After securing an Acharya's blessings, a yogic student must set out also to genuinely serve fellowmen. In this too the *bhaktha* failed. All that he kept doing however was only submitting constant prayers to Bhagavan with offerings of flowers, while all the time beseeching for nothing else but bodily or material blessings for his very own benefit. They were not by any stretch of imagination true prayers for grant of *"karma yoga"*, *"gnyaana* or *bhakti yoga"* in the real sense of the terms.

Thus, being polluted by egocentric desires for his own physical wellbeing and none else's, the prayers of this *bhaktha* to Bhagavan always ended up being deeply tainted with sinful selfishness.

***

The sixth *bhaktha's* name was Prappanadaasan and he too, like the fifth one, worshipped the temple-deity with daily offerings of flowers.

One day early in the morning, Prapannadaasan and Bhaktharathna both set out to the market to buy flowers for their usual daily offerings to the temple. By the time they both reached the florist's stall, all the flowers unfortunately had already been sold away with just one large, fresh magnolia left unsold. Both wanted to buy it from the florist who, caught in a real bind, asked them, *"Both of you ask to buy it, but there's only one left. What am I to do, tell me, Sirs!"*. Bhaktarathnam retorted, *"Why don't you put the flower up for auction?"*

The auction was duly held but Prapannadaasan being a man of very modest means could not outbid the other *bhakta* in the auction. At that moment a stranger appeared at the flower-stall and in what he felt to be a good-hearted, friendly gesture towards Prapannadaasan, he began to bid for the flower too.

The bidding became fiercely competitive then and the price began climbing to ridiculous levels of a few thousands of rupees! Then abruptly, the stranger stopped bidding and walked away leaving Prappanadaasan high and dry. After thus losing the auction bid, he was deeply crestfallen and tears welled up in his eyes. He said to himself in deep sadness, *"Today, alas, it is not going to be possible for me to worship Bhagavan with flower-offerings to the temple! What shall I do!"*

Bhaktharatnam returned home to fetch the bid money needed to close out the successful auction transaction. And Prappannadaasan too returned home emptyhanded and forlorn. He was met by his wife who rushed to tell him:

"When you were away, an elderly stranger knocked on the door and was asking for you. When I asked him what his purpose was, he told me that you had asked him to hand over to me a basketful of flowers. He handed me then this basket of fresh flowers and left".

The wife handed over to Prapannadaasan a bagful of fresh flowers in which not only were there two lovely marigolds but an assortment of other magnificent flowers too! He grabbed hold of the flower-basket, ran to the temple and offered it at the sanctum as wonted daily religious routine of worship. He was both relieved and very happy at the turn of events... Mercifully, he had somehow been able to fulfil his daily rite of flower-offerings ... *"pushpa kainaryam"* to Bhagavan on a day when it first seemed as though there would be no flower at all to offer...

On returning home, the curious Prapannadaasan queried his wife: *"Did you take a good look at the man who gave you the flowers? Were you able to recognize him? Did you ask for his name?"*

The wife told him: "The man insisted that I should not divulge to you any kind of description or impression I might have formed of him. And as for his name, he told me that he was generally known as one who gets all his work done by harnessing both the sentient and the insentient of the world... He said, he sometimes go by the name of "*chidhachidh-karmakaari*" ..."

On listening to his wife's narration, Prappannadaasan was greatly mystified. He could not fathom who the stranger could be who had mysteriously come calling home... nor why. Still out of curiosity, he decided he must go and make inquiries with a few wise and venerable elders he knew in the neighbourhood; and hoped they might perhaps be able to shed some light on the mystery.

***

After paying off the auction-bid price for his flower, Bhaktharathna proudly took delivery and set off to the temple to make his daily flower-offering as worship. However, by the time he reached the temple gates, to his utter consternation he found that it was already too late in the day and that the priests had long gone to their homes after bolting the doors.

In a fit of frustration, he then spat on the flower held in his hand, cursing to himself, *"Fie upon this wretched, useless flower that has cost me three thousand rupees today!"*. He then threw the flower into the gutter abutting the temple-kitchen and stormed off home in a huff...

Such unseemly and intemperate behaviour on his part was not untypical of him at all since it basically stemmed from his deep and utter ignorance about what constitutes true spiritual *gnyaana*.

One day, Bhaktharathna while engaged as usual in his so-called and almost comical yogic exercises, was balancing himself with his head upon the floor and his legs raised and stretched high in the air. While he remained suspended in that topsy-turvy position for a long while, suddenly a cat appeared out of nowhere and happened to pounce upon him! In an instant he found himself toppling over violently and reduced to a flailing heap of bruised bones, twisted shoulders and a severely sprained neck! The shock of the trauma resulted in his suffering from feverish, fearful tremors! From that day onwards,

Bhaktharathna forthwith gave up performing whatever it was that he had all long believed to be his very own idea of *"karma yoga"*!

As ill luck would again have it, on yet another occasion, when late after midnight, while he was busy piously performing what according to his own idea was *"bhakti-yoga"* i.e., being seated on a wayside culvert under which street-drains ran, suddenly a nocturnal serpent sprang from the darkness and attacked him, winding itself up around his torso in a tight, vicious grip. He screamed in terror for help! Some bystanders came rushing to him, pulled the snake away and killed it, thus saving his life just in time. From that day onwards, a thoroughly chastened Bhaktharathna ceased performing his so-called *"bhakthi-yoga"* exercises too!

It was thereafter that a few wise, venerable men of the village who had Bhaktharatna's wellbeing at heart, counselled him:

"What a foolish fellow you've been! Out of your own ignorance you commit such monumental folly and misdeed but then you also defend yourself by claiming that what you did has been impelled by Bhagavan's own wish or will! How stupid and wrong can you be! Hasn't it occurred to you that by his own admission one of the main purposes of Bhagavan descent into the mortal world in many different avatars was to destroy forces of evil and their misdeeds? Given such clear, stated divine purpose, how can you, dear fellow, ever dare to make the foolish claim that all your own misdeed and folly, born out of your own crass ignorance, are but Bhagavan's own handiwork manifested through you?"

"Never lay the blame on Bhagavan for your own sins of omission and commissions and for your own lapses and transgressions. Never forget that it is to help us all to develop our capacity to discriminate between good and evil, truth and untruth and between the wise and unwise that in Bhagavan's very own design for creation he did carve out a special place in our lives for the invaluable role to be played by our wise and venerable elders, learned in the ancient and sacred sastras. If you pay scant or no heed at all to their wise words of counsel or instruction, then it is you yourself who must be blamed for your own peril and perdition.

"So, if you are to embark upon spiritual pursuit, do so by seeking and following the precepts of a qualified Acharya who will instruct you on the proper way to tread the path of "karma, gnyaana or bhakthi yoga". If you

follow their precepts faithfully then your efforts will surely bear fruit. Never will they be futile".

Bhaktharatna after having heard what the elders had to say to him, fell at their feet in utter remorse He prostrated and humbly beseeched them to give him proper *"upadesam"* (sage counsel) in the matter so that he could begin anew and afresh his journey on the path of spiritual pursuit.

One among the wise elders pleased by his resolve, told him with utmost kindness: *"My dear boy, giving "upadesam" in matters such as this is no trivial matter! It is in fact an extremely esoteric subject that needs very long periods of time to impart properly. Nonetheless, for your benefit and sake, I will try to explain it you as succinctly as possible".*

Below is the gist of the *"upadesam"* that the kind and wise elder delivered to Bhaktharatnam.

***

Gnaayna-yogam consists in being able to meditate constantly upon the nature of the *Atma*, the soul, as being an ontological monadic and imperishable reality, and whose very nature is that of pure consciousness and omniscience. Such meditative effort will be enabled only through the observance of strict discipline such as *"Nithya sandhyavandanam"* daily without fail. The question may arise as to how long such meditative *"gnyaana yoga"* is to be performed. The answer is that the meditation must continue as long as it takes for one's inner eye of self-realization to finally open up and be able to behold the ineffable glory of the *Atma…*

Bhakthi-yogam means *"upaasana"*, i.e., ceaseless visualization of the presence of divinity within one's being. Such visualization can be in many ways --- e.g., one can visualise the divine presence as the personified form of Bhagavan enthroned inside the innards of one's own heart (*hrudaya-mandala*); or as being manifested in blindingly sheer brilliance radiating out as sunrays from the great ball of the solar-centre of the universe; or else visualized in one or more of the several different other forms of divine manifestation or emanation described in the revelations of Vedantic scripture such as that of the wielder of the *"shanka-chakra-gadhaa-paani"* (the wielder of the divine weapons), or as *"Lakshmi-samethan"* (the deity inseparable from the divine consort Lakshmi) or the Almighty whose divine attributes of compassion (*daya*), valour, beauty, power, glory and many other such are all absolute, unparalleled and unsurpassed.

Once again, this *"upasaana"* can be mastered only with due observance of the daily and faithful regimen of *"nithya anushtaana"* (such as "sandhyavandanam" etc.). The *"upaasaka"* must also be possessed of a mind that remains equipoised with control over the senses. Such *"upaasana"* has to be performed without cease right from the day of commencement until the very end of one's life; and it must be practised with unwavering faith and unfading loving devotion to the visualized form of Bhagavan.

Such was the *"upadesam"* in very pithy form that the wise elder imparted to Bhaktharathna who thereafter resolved to begin his spiritual journey in the yogic pathway of *karma*, *gnyaana* and *bhakthi* exactly as guided.

***

The sixth *bhaktha*, Prappannadaasan, who had earlier already performed *saranaagathi* (absolute surrender to the divine will) had all his heartfelt prayers answered by Bhagavan and he was thus able to perform *"Uttara krutyam"* throughout his lifetime i.e., the formal covenants of *"saranaagathi"* which all *prapanna*-s abide by in life.

The covenants which Prappannadaasan faithfully abided may be described as follows:

1. **Anukoolasya sankalpa**: he solemnly resolved to adhere always to the path of righteous conduct as laid down in the *sastras*;
2. **Pratikoolasya varjanam**: he solemnly swore to abjure all unrighteous conduct in life;
3. **Mahavishwaasam**: The trust he placed in Bhagavan as the one and only sole saviour of his soul was absolute and unshakeable;
4. **Goptrutva varanam**: He made a fervent and explicit appeal to Bhagavan acknowledging him as the supreme sovereign of the entire universe who would grant him eternal liberation (*moksha*) from mortal coils.

5. **Kaarpannyam:** The realization of his mortal vulnerability and unworthiness, and of the fundamental abjection of his soul (Atma) was total and genuine.

Besides the above five covenants, this sixth *bhaktha* also renounced completely every trace of personal ownership over his *Atma* which he had hitherto entertained and clung onto within his mind. With the firm conviction that having renounced his soul (*atma bharannyaasam*) and restoring it to where it belonged in the hands of Bhagavan, he now enjoyed the absolute protection of the Almighty. With that firm conviction taking hold of his self, Prapannadaasan went forth in life in good cheer, performing good deeds such as for example, setting out on holy pilgrimages to places like Sri Rangam, Tirumala and Kanchipuram and others while, at the same time, going about performing all individual duties mandated or made obligatory for him by the *sastras*.

***

To end the story, we can say that all these six *bhakthas* who at heart were all rightly resolved in their devotion to Bhagavan, got redeemed by His grace as they were each shown and guided towards and along the right path to spiritual progress and evolution.

Likewise, every one of you too can approach Sriman Narayanan in similar manner, pray for everlasting good and secure his Grace.

***

-13-
Tamizh "*Upannyaasam*" On "*Saranaagathi Tattvam*"

Synopsis: Srimadh Mukkur Azhagiyasingar delivered a public discourse ("upannyaasam") probably sometime in the early 1970s on the lofty subject of **"Saranagathi"** *– the doctrine of* **"Absolute Surrender of the Soul",** *which is the central tenet of Visishtadvaita theology. The lecture was video-graphed and it is probably the only video-recording ever of the Acharya discoursing that is available today in the public domain. The uploaded video can be accessed today on YouTube at this URL:*
https://www.youtube.com/watch?v=qAkx4u-4wMw
The English translation of the entire discourse is presented below.

Our *Bhagavaan* Sri Kannan after taking avatar in the hamlet of Nandagokulam, after spending several happy, eventful years of boyhood frolic there, and in after-years having also mentored and providing Sri Arjuna with the lofty wisdom of the **Srimad Bhagavath-Gita,** finally, at the end therein, also gave for the enduring benefit of all mankind the esoterica of the *"saranaagathi tattvam"* – the **doctrine of self-surrender unto Bhagavaan**. That secret is embedded in the *Gita-shloka*:

Sarva dharmaam parit-thyajja maamekam sharanam vraja I
Aham tvaa sarva paapephyo moksha ishyaami maa shuchah: II

Now, the essence of the *shloka* is only this: *"Do not get anxious! If you are incapable of pursuing the difficult path of "Karma yoga" or "Bhakthi yoga", do not worry! Simply surrender unto me, submit to me as your sole protector! Relieve yourself of all burdens of the spirit simply by relinquishing them unto me!"*

Sri Krishna asks Man: *"What do you seek ultimately in life? You seek* **moksha** .... *Salvation... is it not? Do you know what hurdles there are in the way of your attaining salvation? They are not only the aggregate of all transgressions and lapses ("paapam") committed in millions of your past lives but they include also the outcomes of many virtuous deeds ("punnyam") you performed too!"*

Now, one can understand if *paapam* stands as a hurdle to salvation, but how is it right to say that *punnyam* is also an obstacle to it?!

The answer is that while *paapam* leads one to the state of hellish existence (*"narakam"*), *punnyam* leads one to the state of heavenly pleasures (*"svarga-lokam"*). Thus, both effectively are only obstructions to one attaining *"moksham"*.

Therefore, Sri Krishnan by using the phrase *"sarva paapebhya:"* implies clearly that *"paapam"* or sin is to be understood as including virtue or *punnyam* too.

A sinner, an atheist who detests *Bhagavaan* standing outside a temple-door as well as a pious man beside him praying with folded hands to Bhagavaan there .... both thus happen to be *"paapis"* only since both the **sin** in the sinner and the **virtue** in the pious end up acting as hurdles to attaining *moksha*. One takes the sinner to *naraka* and the other takes the virtuous to *svarga*.... Therefore, to avoid either of such situations, *says Lord Krishna to Arjuna*, I shall show you a path that will lead you unto me forever when you can reside in eternal bliss!

***

As we know **Bhagavaan Naaraayana** had taken ten different other avatars (*"dashaavataara"*). However, in none of those as he did in the Sri Krishna avatar, did *Bhagavaan* make explicit and clear all the fine aspects of the doctrine of *"saranaagathi"*, the nature of *"paramaatma"* (supreme soul), the nature of *"jivaatma"* (individual soul), the nature of *moksha* etc.

Take even the avatar of Sri Rama who proclaimed the great *"saranagathi shlokam"*: **"Sakrudeva prapannaya tavasmeeti cha yachate; Abhayam sarvabhutebhyo dadamyetad vratam mama"**. In the proclamation he does, of course, solemnly guarantee divine protection to whoever it may be who surrenders to him in the spirit of true *saranaagathi*, but then Sri Rama does not go to the full length of explicating how one ought to perform true *saranaagathi*.

Thus, as seen in the *Raamaayana*, Sri Rama granted his divine protection to all those who surrendered unto him viz.: *Bharatha*, the *Rishis* of the forests (of *Dandakaaranya*), *Sugreeva*, *Vibheeshana*, as well as the demonesses (*raakshasees* of Ashokavana in Lanka) at the behest of Sri Sita, his beloved wife, who interceded on their behalf. But in all these instances, none of are able to appreciate the *modus operandi* of the doctrine itself of "*saranaagathi*". Nonetheless, it must be admitted that it is only in these two avatars of Sri Rama and Sri Krishna, however, that the "*tattvam*" or tenet of "*saranaagathi*" got revealed to the world at large.

***

Let us now proceed to see how Sri Kannan propounds the doctrine of "*saranaagati*":

1. If you want to be unburdened of all existential angst, learn firstly to "**Know Thyself**" ... i.e., try to realize "*Who am I? Where do I come from? What is my true nature?*" We often hear people in the world speak about "*Jeevan*" or "*jeevaatma*". Who is this "*Jeevan*"? This *Jeevan* refers clearly to me as an individual. The question is whether this "*Me or 'I*" refers to my **body** or to some other **entity latent within the body** that is understood to be "*jeeva*"? Now, whenever one refers to one's body (*sareeram*) one always says "This is **my** body!" or "This body is **mine**!" Both statements clearly presuppose and imply that he who says he possesses the body... he is separate from that same body whose possession he claims. Take a simpler instance. When I say "*This is my house* (**gruham**)" it is patent that "*I*" or "*Me*" as identity -- or "*Mine*" as possession – is separate from the house that is possessed. **He who possesses is different from what he knows he possesses.** And that "he" is indeed the "**jeeva**" that is spoken about here.

2. Now the question arises: **Who is this "*I*", the "*Jeevan*"?** *What is his nature?* Is the "*Jeevan*" an infinite reality (*nithyan*) or a merely a temporary phenomenon (*a-nithyan*)? Is the *Jeevan* indestructible or perishable?

3. Some schools of philosophy hold that the *"I"* or *"Jeevaatma"* is perishable. Some other schools – like the *"chaaruvaaka*-s" — also deny the very existential reality of the *"jeevaatma"* and regard it as nothing but a myth or fiction! This school postulates the nature of the *"jeeva"* to be as follows:

   3.1. A *jeeva* comes into being as a force when the basic elements of nature – *earth, fire, water, ether and wind* – all combine together. Take the example of what happens when betel-leaves, diluted lime, betel-nuts etc. are rolled into a pellet and chewed by a man. What happens is that by itself when chewed, a strange red-colored spittle forms inside the man's mouth and lips while his tongue and palate all turn scarlet in color! Similarly, when the natural elements combine together, the *jeevaatma* too gets formed all by itself in such fashion. Consider another example: We know that a locomotive engine runs on the energy produced by *steam, coal* and *fire*. A great force gets generated when water is boiled to steam in a coal-fired engine and that force is then used to mechanically propel the locomotive. Similarly, the *jeevaatma* too is nothing but a *natural force* that gets generated when the natural elements combine together. The **Chaaruvaakas** further postulate that whenever the elements eventually dissipate and dissolve, the *"jeevaatma"* too at the same time dissolves and perishes.

   3.2. Not dissimilarly, the Advaita philosophy postulates that the existence of *"jeevaatma"*, its inherent sense of *"I"*, *"Me"* and *"Mine"* or its sense of possessiveness are all nothing but ghostly apparitions having no reality at all in themselves since **Brahman** (*One supreme consciousness*) alone is the only existent universal reality …. All else is but mere mental projection. No such thing as *"jeevaatma"* thus really exists. Whenever the apparitions or mental projections dissipate and dissolve into nothingness, the *'jeevaatma"* too simply dissipates, dissolves and perishes into nothingness, leaving behind only the eternally singular indestructible reality of *Brahman*.

4. It is therefore very important firstly to have thoroughly clarified all doubts and all confusions removed arising from such specious postulates of such speculative philosophies …. Sri Krishna (Gita 2.24) lays this down clearly in the following verse: *acchedyo'yam adaahyo'yam, akledyah ashosya eva cha, nityah sarva gataah: sthaanur, achalo'yam sanaatanaah:"* …. As the scriptural quote says, the nature of the *"jeevaatma"* is that it *cannot be cleaved into two*; it *cannot be incinerated*; it *cannot be in any way expanded or contracted or transformed* in any manner; it *cannot be either moistened or dried*; the *jeevaatma* is *eternal, permanent or enduring reality*….. It undergoes no mutations such as ordinarily seen in bodily forms that grow from youth (*"baalyam"*, *"kumaaram"* etc.) to decay later into decrepitude….

5. So, *Arjuna*, said Sri Krishna, *you who have now sunk into despair and refuse to fight the War (Kurukshetra), must first know well what the true nature of the "jeevaatma" is… Are you going to be slaying bodies or slaying "jeevans"? If you understood the answer properly you would not be descending into this sort of moral pusillanimity at all and be derelict in doing your duty on the battlefield!*

6. It was thus that Sri Krishna went further on to explain to Arjuna the inherent nature of the soul called *"Atma-svarupam"*:

***

7. *"How big is this "jeevaatma"?* In other words, *"what are its physical characteristics, if it possesses any at all"?* The answer to this question is found in profound Vedaantic inquiry and in the form of a famous Upanishad *"vaakya"* (aphorism): ……. *"vaalagra shataa bhaagasya satadhaa kalpitasya cha, bhaago jeevaah: vignyeyah sa cha aanantyayaa kalpate…"*. The size of the *"jeevaatma"* is to be imagined metaphorically in the following way: Take the very end from the tip of a strand of hair on a cow's tail and snip off the tiniest possible part of it. Take the snipped part and snip it into another 100 parts. Picking out form the 100 parts, select one and snip it again into another 100 parts…. Continue the process until finally a situation is arrived at when it is no longer possible to snip the strand of hair any further! The size of whatever part of the hair that can thereafter be imagined to remain in hand at the end of

the process may be said to be also the size of the *"jeevaatma"*! The metaphoric sense in which this Upanishadic process is to be understood is that it is virtually impossible to imagine any entity (*vastu*) that can be smaller than the *"jeevaatma"* …. It is atomic, it is a monad.

8. Such a monadic *"jeevaatma"* indeed inheres and enlivens every bodily form that exists in the universe and the scriptures reveal it to be so …. *"jeevastu prati sareeram bhinnah…"*

9. Such a *"jeevaatma"* also possesses the unique faculty of **Cognition**. It possesses the capacity of discriminative knowledge. It has the innate ability to experience both pain and pleasure. Although it is only atomic in size, the power of its atomic potential is, however, immensely forceful. Which is why it also has the power of free-will and of free choice to act even against the will of *Bhagavaan*. It has the willful power to even rebel against and violate the injunctions of the sacred word of *the* Almighty *viz.* **the Vedas**. There is the example of a scriptural ethic in this regard which warns a man not to entertain evil intentions, not even in a mere fleeting thought, about having illicit or adulterous relationship with another man's spouse. Conversely, it also enjoins man to keep thinking of adultery but only anxiously --- as over the prospect of it being committed on his own spouse by any other man! What the gravamen here is that the *"jeevaatma"*, even though possessing the acuity of discriminative knowledge (*arivu*), possesses equally too the tendency to transgress the limits of free-will.

   9.1. There are of course some speculative philosophical schools that postulate that the *"jeevaatma"* grows, expands or contracts in size in proportion and in sympathy to the extent to which the body (*sareera*) too grows, expands or contracts in time…. such as in childhood, youth, manhood and old age etc…. All such speculations are rejected in the Vedantic school which conclusively establishes the truth that the *"jeevaatma"* is monadic in size, nature and characteristic…. *"esho nu'raatma…"*

10. The next question is: If a *"jeevaatma"* is said to inhere every bodily form in the world, how many *"jeevaatmas"* can be said to exist? The answer is that the number of *"jeevaatmas"* in the universe is as countless as the number of bodily or physical forms we witness in the world in all its glorious ecological diversity of species in flora, fauna and humanity. Every bodily form inhered by a *"jeevaatma"* within it has come to be possessed of such a bodily form as a result of its past *kaarmic* deed and destiny. All such bodily forms are collectively known as *"baddha*-s*"* --- entities that have taken forms in accordance with the character of their unique and respective Karmic legacy. So, it would be a mistake to think that *"jeevaatma"* is a term that refers only to humanity. On the other hand, souls inhere all forms of life in the universe, even non-human ones like those of trees in the woods or insects, worms and millions of micro-organisms in even street-gutters…. After inhering physicality even as tree or insect, a *jeevaatma* through *"kaarmic"* pre-destiny might find itself in the company of other great human souls and even getting enlightened by listening to their words of wisdom or witnessing their sacred deeds … *"smushaane jaayate vrkshah yaathi sthaavarathaam narah…."*

11. *Jeevaatmas* are not eponymous with the bodily-forms they have come to assume. In other words, they are not to be associated with the same identity as that which their bodily-form possess. For example, some philosophical schools --- such as the *Maadhwa's* of the **Dvaita** School --- postulate that even amongst *"jeevaatmas"* it is possible to classify them into categories such as *"manushya-jeevaatma"*, human souls, and non-human souls *"mriga-jeevaatmas"*, or *"pakshi-jeevaatmas"* etc. But in our *"siddhaantham"* we reject such postulates. For us, *"jeevaatma"* is a discrete eternal entity that cannot be categorized in any manner on any basis. It is truly unique. (The jivatma inhabiting the body of a learned Brahmin, an elephant, a dog and eater of a dog-flesh is all the same – there is no difference at all, says Sri Krishna in the Gita: *"vidya vinaya sampanne braahmane gavi hastini, shuni chaiva shvapake cha panditaah samadarshinah…"*) While the *jeevaatma* retains always its pure and natural consciousness (*gnyana and ananda*) of being *"sesha bhuthan"* – i.e., as eternal subservient entity having no other

function other than to serve *Bhagavaan's* purpose and will -- it nonetheless goes on to assume multifarious mortal forms of existence in accordance with its past *"karmic"* deeds and in an endless cyclic series of lifetimes. Thus, it must be understood finally that *"jeevaatmas"* are infinite in number.

***

12. The next question that Sri Krishna addresses is this: In the light of everything explained above, should one therefore believe that a *"jeevaatma"* is condemned to perpetual mortal existence wherein one bodily state of existence follows another in a never-ending cycle of self-perpetuating mundanity? Is there no hope of redemption or transformation in the life of souls? Is there no opportunity for a *"jeevaatma"* to transcend itself to a higher, spiritually superior state of being?

    12.1. Speaking of *"transformation in life"*, let me indulge a brief aside .... Here I am reminded of the unregenerate, lack-luster plight of our youth in South India who lack the same energy, enterprise and pluck that I see in their counterparts in North India. Our boys have been mentally conditioned to look no farther beyond than securing a menial job for livelihood whereas young entrepreneurs up North go about setting up flourishing businesses that earn for them several million times more than what holding down a measly Rs.150/- per month job in ordinary employment earns! So, I too often do ask myself the same question while pondering about the backwardness and fate of our own boys: *"When will they learn to transform their outlook in life, transform themselves from mere job-seekers to become job-creators? Is there no redemption for our lads?!"*

13. Likewise, does the *jeevaatma* have to remain mired too in mundane, unregenerate existence? *Does it have to go on suffering infinite lives caught in the same sorry plight?*

14. The answer is a categorical *"No!"* The *"jeevaatma"* is not condemned forever to such an abject plight at all. On the other hand, it possesses all qualifications and all eligibility to rise, transcend and attain the most exalted state of spiritual grace. The

opportunity to do so is always readily on offer and it is there for the seizing through what is known as the doctrine of "**artha-panchakam**" ---- (i) **realization of the nature of "*paramaatma*"** (ii) **realization of the nature of "*jeevaatma*"** (iii) **realizing the true means by which the *jeevaatma* can attain the realm of "*paramaatma*"** and (iv) **the fruits (*moksha phalan*) or ultimate benefits to be enjoyed in the realm of "*paramaatma*"**. All four elements above presuppose the j*eevaatma* fully realizing that the only thing which in fact had stood between itself and the ultimate fruition promised by the "**artha-panchakam**" is the obstructive **fifth element** in the equation viz. all the "*virodhis*" or spiritual hurdles and impediments of every kind brought about by past *paapam* and *punnyam*, sin and virtue engendered by *Karma*. Once such a deep realization is born, then the individual soul will surely not delay any more commencing its long journey of endeavor to attain the realm of *Bhaagavaan*: ...... *praapyascha brahmano roopam praaptuscha pratyak aatmanah, praapyupaayaam phalam chaiva praapthi virodihi tathaiva cha, vadanti vedaah setihaasa puraanakah...*"

***

15. The first requisite realization is to know the nature of *Bhagavaan*, the *paramaatma*. Is he some furious, terrible or retributive God looking down on us from high in the skies? *Not at all!* If he is otherwise, what is his nature? The quality of the "*paramaatma*" (*guna visesha*) is one of unbounded compassion and tenderness indeed. *Bhagavaan* waits endlessly and most anxiously for a *jeevaatma* to return finally to him even after having left the Lord, its father, as a willful delinquent to go away and wander aimlessly in its cosmic peregrinations. It is akin to a prodigal son, who after having insulted and fought with his father, has chosen to live many years away and totally alienated from him. One day the son however happens to listen to the words of a wise man about the heinous folly of abusing one's father. Suddenly then he is filled with remorse for the injustice he had done unto his father. The prodigal son then hastens back to his father to be reunited with him. In that situation *how overjoyed would the father feel?!* Would

the forlorn father --- having been for so long so very anxious about the whereabouts and wellbeing of his lost son --- would he not rush at once to gather up his son in his arms and smother him with affection and solicitude? Would he not offer him all his wealth?!

15.1. In much the same way *Bhagavaan* too welcomes back the lost *"jeevaatma"* that finally has succeeded in retracing its path in its spiritual journeys and returns to where it always belonged viz. the realm of the *"paramaatma"*. Such a returning soul in plaintive terms has indeed realized finally what a colossal waste of time has been lost in purposeless activity across the expanse of cosmic time, in lifetimes after mortal lifetimes, without having had spared even a moment of worshipful thought towards its father, *Bhagavaan,* or remembering him by uttering even a single sacred *"naama"* of his! On the other hand, even when there had been opportunities in life to grow closer to *Bhagavaan,* the *jeevaatma* had chosen to simply ignore or spurn them...... *"aho me mahatee yaataa nishphalaa janma santatih, anaaraadita govinda charanaamboruha dvayam..."* For instance, whenever the Lord's procession had happened to pass by his abode, the *jeevaatma* had chosen to shut the doorways and remain nonchalantly inside the confines of his home. Not even a small fruit, flower-petal or a basil-leaf *(tulasi)* had been offered to the Deity in a gesture of even symbolic worship, gratitude or devotion.... Such had been the degree of sheer alienation from *Bhagavaan*! And when such a prodigal son does happen to return finally to be reunited with *Bhagavaan* who is indeed *mother, father and all kith and kin* too to all *jeevaatmas,* he of course is welcomed by the Almighty with outstretched arms and a heart exulting in joy!

15.2. After welcoming the *jeevaatma* thus, the Lord then assures the returned soul that there shall be henceforth no more separation from his supreme realm. *"You shall now rest here in my Abode in consummate joy! There shall be not even a moment amiss in the bliss that you will experience here!*

Unlimited will now be, in crores and crores, *of joyous moments you now will enjoy here with all the denizens of this supreme abode of mine --- all these "nithyasuris" and "muktaatamas' who have assembled here to claim you as one of their own!" …..*

15.2.1. Here, let me pause a moment and confess to you all that the phrase **"*crores and crores*"** does remind me momentarily of the crores and crores of funds that I know I am yet to raise for the great project that I have undertaken to raise the magnificent *"gopuram"* tower at the **Sri Rangam temple!**

16. *Anyway, to come back to our subject again*! Once the individual *jeevaatma* realizes the true nature of *"paramaata svarupam"* as being akin to a loving and lovable father who is ever anxious about the wellbeing of a long-lost son, and is ever in eager wait to shower his love, benediction and blessings upon the son once he returns -- that is the exactly the moment when the *jeevaatma* begets absolute trust in *Bhagavaan*!

17. A famous *"paasuram"* (the second stanza) in the Tamizh hymn of the *"tiruppaavai"* helps us understand even better the *"paramaatma svarupa"* --- **"*pārkaḍaluḷ paiyya tuyinna paramaṇ aḍi pāḍi….*"** The usual commentary on this line would read as follows: That a devotee should sing the glorious names of Sriman Naaraayana while mentally dwelling upon his image as the Almighty One who lies supine on his serpent-bed (*"aadi-seshan"*) afloat the great *cosmic milky ocean* (*"paarkadal"* or *"ksheeraabdi*). I interpret the stanza however a little differently. I read it as referring not to Sriman Naaraayana resting on the waters of the cosmic Milky Ocean in the high heavens but as the other *"milky ocean"* (*paarkadal*) at *Nandagokulam* where Sri Krishna as a mere boy had lived with his herds of cows. If the poetess had *Naaraayana* in mind she would have phrased her line in Tamizh as "paarkadalul *sesha tuyinna paraman adi paadi….*" which would have been apt too for the Lord resting upon a serpent-bed called *"seshan"*. Here, the poetess phrases the line however as *"paarkadalul paiyya tuyinna*

paraman adi paadi...." without employing the word "*seshan*". It is clear therefore that the poetess had in mind only Sri Krishna in his avatar on earth at *Nandagokulam* where he, a divine cowherd, was often seen resting supine afloat a "*milky ocean*" ("*paar kadal*") filled obviously with the copious milk of several hundreds of cows Krishna himself shepherded!

18. As Sri Krishna rested thus in *Nandagokulam*, he was absorbed in "*yoga nidra*" – a state of deep meditation. Now, we may ask what the object of Sri Krishna's meditation was. It was these kinds of thoughts that were running through his mind: "*Now that I have descended in this avatar into this mortal world, what should be my mission? Whom all should I save and protect? Whom all should I punish? To whom all should I grant the grace of redemption? How shall I grant to these adoring "gopastree-s" (shepherdesses) of Gokulam a greater bliss than they now experience in my presence and who shower me with so much of their unfading, extraordinary bhakti?!*"

19. Apart from those thoughts, very interestingly, Sri Krishna also kept contemplating upon his own role as the gracious granter of "*moksha*" ("**saranaagatha rakshakan**") to all those who surrender unto him. He wondered to himself why he should not also put to test himself the credibility or veracity of that very role! And so, he began to think up ways in which he might grant salvation to even non-sentient things ("*jada*" or mere Matter) and even rank evil men too that harbored nothing but hate towards him (*bhagavath-dveshis*)! From the accounts of Sri Krishna's avatar, we know thus how he granted "*moksha*" to an ordinary milk-vending *bhaktha* of his named **Dadhipaandam** in *Nandagokulam*. This *Dadhipaandan*, refused to accept the gift of salvation from Krishna unless his great big and favorite milk-pot too was accorded the same favor!! Krishna decided to grant "*moksha*" to a mere pot too! (In our "*siddhaantham*, it must be remembered that even non-sentient matter is said to possess "*jeeva*" or life and hence can also be the recipient of divine grace).

20. Sri Krishna was known next to also grant moksha to the evil **Sisupaalan**, the Kaurava kin who hurled the most insulting invectives at Krishna and shot a barrage of arrows against

Krishna! At the very end of the barrages hurled at him, Sri Krishna revealed his true form to *Sisupaalan* before slaying him…. "*kshanam adbhutha Krshna roopa darshi*…. This was done by Sri Krishna firstly to grant absolution to *Sisupaalan* from all sins since it was, he who in his previous life as one of two gatekeepers, *Jaya* and *Vijaya* of the heavenly realm of *Sri Vaikuntam*, due to a transgression he had committed previously, had fallen from grace and been condemned to live in the mortal worlds. The gatekeepers had themselves requested *Sriman Naarayana* to be granted death and deliverance in the mortal world by the Lord's own hands in three of his avataric appearances on earth. Such was the compassion shown by *Bhagavaan* to even those that hated him.

21. The extremely compassionate nature of "*paramaatma svarupam*" is exemplified in another account of Sri Krishna's *avataaric* exploits. In *Nandagokulam*, Krishna had been accustomed to delighting and frolicking in the company of the comely cow-maidens (*gopastrees*) who were without exception besotted by his divine presence. One day an old hunchback of a hag expressed her heartfelt desire to Sri Krishna that she too partake of the same delight that the young maidens were experiencing in his presence! The handsome Krishna was momentarily fazed by the request of the old hunchbacked hag! But at her insistence he deigned to indulge her amorous desire since he knew that the old lady had been in a previous life (*janmaa*) none other than *Manthara*, the hunchbacked harridan in the Ramayana (i.e., Queen Kaikeyi's maid who had wrecked the palace and peace of the Ikshvaakus!) ….. Sri Krishna gently touched her with his feet and lo and behold hunchback was miraculously transformed into a beautiful young maiden! She too then joined the company of the young "*gopastrees*" and fulfilled her desire thereby to delight in the flirtatious but playful frolicking in Krishna's company.

22. It is such anecdotes and accounts that enable us to appreciate the quality of compassion for devotees that is characteristic of "*paramaatma svarupam*". The "*saastras*" thus affirm that it is out of his unbounded compassion for all those who perform "*saranaagathi*" unto him, that *Bhagavaan* welcomes them as his

very own flesh and blood, *so to say*, into his abode in *Sri Vaikuntam* where he graces them with the same acme of bliss and beatitude that *Bhagavaan* himself is everlastingly immersed in!

23. Now, we must ask: what means must a *"jeevaatma"* adopt to attain such bliss in the abode of *Sri Vaikuntam*? If the yoga of *bhakthi* is beyond one's capability then the only recourse left is to adopt the path of surrender – *"saranaagathi"*. An errant servant who has earned the displeasure of the master, truly repents for his lapse and then begs forgiveness of the master by abjectly prostrating before him. No matter how stern and stone-hearted the master may be, he will not be able to deny forgiveness to such a repentant servant. In the same way, the *"jeevaatma"* that performs *"saranaagathi"* to *Bhagavaan* cannot be denied divine forgiveness…

24. Now, we may ask what exactly is involved in the performance of *"saranaagathi"*. In essence it is nothing more than a very simple sacramental act. It takes no more than 10 or 15 minutes and involves a disciple beseeching an Achaarya to officiate over it for his benefit. The *Achaarya* then proceeds to initiate the disciple into a few appropriate *"mantras"* in Sanskrit the import of which is nothing more than this: *"I have now come to thee, O Bhagavaan, after spending innumerable lifetimes mired in "paapam"! I have nowhere else to go and seek redemption but at thy feet! Here I am now standing before you as your eternally loyal liege beseeching your pardon and grace!"*

   24.1. This act must be done with absolute trust in *Bhagavaan* and abiding faith in his compassion. This is all that is truly required of a *"jeevaatma"* surrendering itself unto the Almighty! It is indeed a very simple sacramental act! *And yet, ironically, its non-performance is indeed all that stands between "moksha" and us!* Furthermore, it costs one nothing, in fact! There is no great paraphernalia involved here in the performing the sacrament as might be required in other great Vedic rites or *"yagnyas"*. Nor is any big amount of money involved…. No more than a few rupees --- one, two or perhaps ten at the most perhaps, these days --- is all that is expected to be given away that too only as a small token of charity on the occasion, *that's all!*

25. The next question to be addressed is: In what *manner of procedure* the sacramental act of *"saranagati"* is to be performed – that takes no more than 15-20 minutes? What mental attitude is to be adopted to be able to genuinely repent for sins and seeking forgiveness of *Bhagavaan*? The answer is one should mentally embrace the feet of *Bhagavaan*. One should then solemnly swear to abide by the will of *Bhagava'an* at all times and to never transgress his word and command. Thereafter, the soul of man must mentally also declare its absolute trust in the certitude of *Bhagavan's* Grace …. i.e., he will never fail to grant pardon and accord salvation to it.

26. Now at this point here, one might imagine *Bhagavaan* querying the *jeevaatma*: *"You declare your absolute trust in me and in the certitude of me granting you eternal divine protection! But tell me then what has made you place such implicit trust in me? You confess yourself to having committed countless sins in a lifetime! Tell me what then gives you still the certitude that if you approach me in total surrender, I will not yet deny pardon and grace?"*

   26.1. An interesting way of answering Bhagavaan's tough question was shown in fact by **Sri Koorathazhwaar** in one of his works: *"My trust in you, O Bhagavaan, was begat only by the many examples of how you granted pardon and grace to so many in the Ramaayana who had simply surrendered unto you! In the same way, I too have surrendered at your feet in the same kind of trust! You did not deny them all your grace, now why would you deny it to me who too have to come ask you for what they too prayed?*

   26.2. **An answer very clever by half indeed!** But *Bhagavaan* does not give up and retorts: *"Yes, indeed I granted them all my grace but then not without valid pretext, did I?! Bharatha sought my grace after giving up a kingdom for my sake.… I granted protection (abhaya pradaana) to Vibheeshana after he had renounced his fealty and place in the royal palace of Lanka… all for my sake! How can you compare yourself with* *their exemplary acts of surrender to me? On what such similar pretext as theirs do you expect to receive my grace?! Remember that you have a record of committing sin, beginning even as while you were in your mother's womb which even a fetus you thought nothing of frequently kicking and causing her pain, didn't you?! It may have been pleasurable pain to her, but it was still pain, wasn't it? So, what then is the cause of your certitude in my grace? Explain to me!"*

26.3. The scriptures come to our rescue here and provides us as aid a very persuasive way of responding to *Bhagavaan's* challenging question: .... *"tam vaayasamapi parayaa dayayaa"*: The example of **Kaakasuran** is to be invoked here to counter *Bhagavaan's* tricky poser. *Kaakaasuran*, a *raakshasa* of the dense forests described in the *Raamaayana*, disguised himself one day as a crow and emboldened by the fact that Sri Rama lay sleeping on the lap of Sita, his spouse, began to molest her physically causing injury and grievous pain to her. When Rama awoke, he became enraged to find *Kaakasuran in flagrante delicto* --- i.e., engaged in act of attempted adultery! He immediately shot the deadly *"brahmaastra"* after the demonic crow!

26.4. *Kaakasuran* fled but the terrifying arrow (*"raama-baana"*) as it began pursuing him relentlessly in the skies... and beyond the skies too in the heavenly worlds of the gods! The terror-stricken bird sought refuge from all the gods and *devatas, Indra, Surya, Shiva, Brahma* even ... None could or would dare to come to his rescue.... *Kaakasuran* then fled straight to the palace of Ravana himself in Lanka and explained his plight. Ravana dismissed him saying, *"Didn't you know that I myself am besotted with desire for Sita? And yet you had the temerity to molest her! Let me now slay you myself, you adulterous creature!"* *Kaakasuran* took fright, took flight and fled Lanka at once!

26.5. Finally, utterly exhausted and demoralized in both body and spirit, and with no one to turn to for help, and the fiery *"brahmaastra"* still in flight pursuing him relentlessly, the petrified *Kaakasuran* realized that he was now hapless and desperate. He flew then to *"svarga loka"* (the high heaven) where he beseeched Sri Rama's father, the great king Dasaratha, to intercede on his behalf! Dasaratha wisely counselled him saying there was nothing or nobody in the universe that could come to his rescue. The only recourse now was for *Kaakasuran* to go and fall at the feet of Sri Rama himself and be resigned to whatever fate may then befall him! *"But hasten now and fall at Rama's feet and beg his forgiveness! He is* **"saranaagatha vaatsalyan"** *(i.e., one who intensely cares for his devotees as a cow might care for its new-born calf!) Go thus at once and abandon yourself at his feet!"* said Dasaratha to *Kaakasuran*. Heeding Dasaratha's words, *Kaakasuran* finally flew back to the forests where Rama and Sita lived and approaching *Bhagavaan* fell at his feet with these words so beautifully described in the **Srimad Valmiki Raamaayana**: *"sa raamaaya namaskrutva raajnye dasarathaaya cha...."*

26.6. *Kaakasuran* fell at Sri Rama's feet by uttering words of repentance thus but one must not fail to notice that they are prefaced by the invocation of the name of King Dasaratha first! That's because Kaakasuran knew that it would behoove him to first acknowledge to *Bhagavaan* that it was Rama's father indeed who had counselled him finally to take recourse to *"saranaagathi"* ... and thereby had acted the role of a true *Achaarya* guiding a disciple on the path of self-surrender! The need for Achaarya's hand in fulfilling the procedure for "saranaagathi" is what is underscored here. *Kaakasuran's "saranaagathi"* was thereafter accepted by Sri Rama and *Bhagavaan*, in keeping with his *"paramaatma-svarupam"* of immeasurable compassion, granted the villainous *raakshasa* too his divine grace!

27. The final conclusion to be drawn by us from all above accounts is thus only this: If Bhagavaan deigned to grant even the villainous

Kaakasuran redemption, why would he look for any valid pretext to justify granting us *"moksha"* when we too go to him and beseech him in the spirit of true *"saranaagati"* to pardon and absolve us of our sins? It is thus out of the example of *Kaakasuran* in the *Raamaayana* that we as ordinary souls can take some courage. And we will be able at last to gain too the certitude of belief that *Bhagavaan* will not deny us the same *"vaatsalyam"* shown even to the demon *Kaakasuran*....

    27.1. Such certitude of the *jeevaatma*, of course, must be accompanied by a solemn undertaking given that it will never repeat the sins of commission and omission of the past, never commit any further transgressions or trespass and spend the rest of its lifetime doing simple and faithful acts of piety -- even if it is otherwise unable to conduct large-scale sacrifices such as *"yagnyas, homa"* etc. Bhagavaan accepts instead even mere offerings of fruits and flowers, chanting his sacred names, doing *"sandhyaavanam"* and other such obligatory rites enjoined by '*saastra*' etc.

28. Once the sacramental act of *"saranaagati"* is completed in the above fashion, we must imagine *Bhagavaan* next telling himself, *"This jeevaatama has truly realized my nature ("svarupam")! Now, there is no reason or excuse for me to deny him the 'summum bonum' he deserves viz: "moksha"! No other pretext is needed! I shall now have to therefore grant it to him!"*

29. Next, *Bhagavaan* beckons the *"jeevaatma"* and tells him this: *"Alright! I am now ready and willing to grant you salvation this very moment! Are you ready and willing to accept it this very moment too? Tell me!"*

30. Listening thus to the sudden offer of *Bhagavaan*, the *jeevaatma* begins to tremble in fear! The offer means departing from mortal existence at once! *Bhagavaan* with a mischievous gleam in his eyes asks, *"Why are you silent?! Tell me, are you ready this moment to accept "moksha"?*

    30.1. Thoroughly rattled by the thought of having to leave the mortal world, all its possessions, desires and unfulfilled dreams, the *jeevaatma*, hesitates to accept the divine gift of salvation on offer! After a great deal of inner turmoil, the *jeevaatma* finally replies, *"O Bhagavaan! …. "ethad dehaavasaane maam tvadpaadam praapya svayam …." …. I shall gratefully accept your grant of "moksha" … but then not immediately please! Please postpone it to my last day in this mortal world… Thereafter you may please take me with you to your abode so that I shall never have to return here again! But until that day arrives, please let me be!"*

31.1. Please let me hasten to add a *caveat* of my very own here just to set at rest some of you who may have niggling doubt in this matter: *Sometimes very soon after a person performs "saranaagathi" he or she might breathe his or her last! Such immediate departure has nothing to do with the performance of the sacrament itself! It should not therefore tempt anyone to go around cautioning another against approaching any Azhagiyasingar for fear that if the Achaarya were to initiate anyone into "saranaagathi" then death usually is sure to follow very soon as night follows dusk! It must be understood well that for one who has surrendered in the true spirit inhered in the "saranaagati" rite, departure from mortal realms happens as soon as Karma ceases).*

32. *Bhagavaan* then asks the *jeevaatma* a further searching question by way of testing its true intentions: *"Since you say that you wish the grant of "moksha" to you to be postponed to the time of your final release from mortal coils, I ask you for what reason you seek then such reprieve in time? What will you do on earth in the meanwhile? What do you propose to do with the time left to you that is going to be any different from what you've have been doing all along so far in life…? Eating sumptuously, gratifying coarse tastes, getting involved in petty dissimulations and cheating? What else do you really intend doing in the time left on earth?"*

33. The *jeevaatma* listening to *Bhagavaan* remains silent, shamefaced for a moment but then gives a timid reply: *"In the time left for me, O Bhagavaan, I shall discard all unwholesome, petty and quotidian habits and activities of mine that were my wont. I shall instead embrace*

deep lifestyle changes: ..... "*nalluravaal naam isayum kaalam....*" such as going on distant pilgrimages to the "*divya-desam*" temples in the land, sit at the feet of wise and pious men and listen to their religious discourses and homilies, celebrate festivities for Deities in temples, conduct special prayers like "*dolotsavam*" etc.... And generally, involve myself deeply in other such religious deeds..."

34. Bhagavaan replies: *"Are you telling me then that after "saranaagati", and being engaged continuously in such religious activities, you are going to do nothing else in life?! Will you not exert yourself in other activities at least to earn a decent livelihood for the sake of your family at least.... for the sake of your children, for the sake of your own and their comforts and mundane enjoyment in life?*

35. *"O Bhagavaan",* declares the *jeevaatma*, *"I do admit that I am not entirely going to give up activities to earn a living for the sake of my family-needs and for the wellbeing of my home and hearth. But I shall no longer look upon such exertions in life of mine as though they were intended for the sake of my family, kith and kin.... but indeed, I shall dedicate all of them for your sake alone in the spirit of a liege who works contentedly for the sole pleasure and will of the master only.... "maam madeeyam cha nikhilam chetanaachethanaathmakam, svakainkaryopakaranam varada sveekuru svayam..."* and *"....Atma raajyam dhanam chaiva, kalatram vaahanaani cha, Yat tat bhagavatah sarvam, its tat prekshitam sadhaa..."*

36. Bhagavaan then again teasingly asks the *jeevaatma:* "*Since you are a seeker of "moksha" why haven't you knocked on the doors of the great Paramashivan or Brahma and beseech them to grant you the favor?*"

37. And the *jeevaatma* answers: *"I did not go to them to seek favor since those mighty gods have neither the capacity, authority nor competence to grant the grace of "moksha". It is you alone, O Bhagavaan, and none else in the universe who can grant such grace. Hence, I came knocking on your door to beseech you for the ultimate favor!"*

   37.1. We all know that a guest would be turned out at once as unwelcome indeed if he were to be so indiscreet as to tell his present host that although he had been invited to a meal in another's house, he had nonetheless chosen to come and patronize only the present one! That would be an insult to the present host, wouldn't it?! In the same way *jeevaatma* seeking salvation and having come to *Bhagavaan* to beseech him for it, would never even think of going elsewhere to other gods and *devatas*? *Never!*

37.2. Furthermore, it must be understood that to grant moksha to a *jeevaatma* it is necessary first to extinguish all its *"paapam"*. Given that all such *"paapam"* committed by a *jeevaatma* are transgressions against *Bhagavaan*, how can they all be forgiven by any other god or *devata* like *Shiva* or *Brahma*? They are not the aggrieved after all. They would simply wash their hands off such a situation claiming lack of any jurisdiction in the matter, wouldn't they? Therefore, for having committed sins against *Bhagavaan*, the *jeevaatma* will have no other alternative but to approach him alone for pardon, redemption and absolution.

37.3. It must also be understood that a *jeevaatma* surrenders unto *Bhagavaan* through *"saranaagati"* only with the full and terminal realization that it is utterly incapable of attaining salvation through any other means of effort or endeavor such as *"tapas"* …. i.e., ascetic practices of yogic control over the senses, abnegation of objects of pleasure and desire and other such severe methods of austere self-flagellation.

38. Sri Krishna under the obvious pretext of counselling an utterly dispirited Arjuna (on the battlefield of Kurukshetra) delivered thus the great sermon of **Srimad Bhagavath-Gita** through which great work, that was born out of his infinite compassion for all creation, he specially revealed also for mankind's benefit and redemption the sacred and simple but esoteric doctrine of *"saranaagati"*.

39. A question might arise now in our mind if it is only seekers of *"moksha"* who can approach *Bhagavaan* Sri Krishnan. *Not at all!* Sri Krishna besides granting salvation to the seeker also bestows upon him all manner of earthly riches and goodness upon him.

This truth is attested in the account of how **Kuchela**, an utterly destitute Brahmin and old friend of Sri Krishna attained riches equal to a *Kubera*! – *"Dhaana musti muche kuchela munaye datte sma vittesathaam…"* (*vide* "Vairagya Panchakam-1")

40. This destitute Brahmin decided to visit Sri Krishna in his palace in search of aid and succor for his family's dire and pathetic circumstances. Not wanting to go empty-handed without as much as a token-gift for his old friend, *Kuchela* requested his wife to find something of a morsel at least that he thought she might be able to somehow manage to scrounge from their virtually empty kitchen larder. Since she was being asked for something to be given as offering to *Bhagavaan* Sri Krishna as a humble gift, the distraught wife could not confess forthright that there was nothing indeed left in the house-kitchen that could even be scrounged! That was the degree to which Kuchela, his wife and family was poverty-stricken!

    40.1. The poor wife therefore rushed out of the home to beg from her next-door neighbors for some grains or millets that could then be taken by Kuchela as a gift to Sri Krishna. The neighbors refused until at last one of them reluctantly parted with a handful of half-rotting paddy good perhaps only as animal fodder but hardly fit really for human consumption. The wife rushed back home with it, de-husked the paddy and with the handful of rice-grains collected boiled and roasted them into parboiled-rice (*"avvul"*, in Tamil). She then handed it to *Kuchela* inside a tiny, ragged cloth-bag. *Kuchela* tucked the bag under his waist and set off to meet Sri Krishna in his grand royal palace.

41. Sri Krishna welcomed his old friend Kuchela (also known as Sudama) into his palace with great joy! After offering the poor Brahmin with all kinds of lavish hospitality (*upachaaram*), Krishna finally turned to Kuchela and asked, *"My dear friend, what gift have you brought for me?!"* Kuchela was overcome by shame! He hesitated to reveal the measly gift of a few grains of *avvul* tucked in a ragged cloth-bag under his waist. Momentarily, he thought

he would simply deny having brought any gift for Sri Krishna rather than present him with the shabby gift in his possession.... Sri Krishna however quickly espied *Kuchela's* predicament and reached forward to himself snatch the little cloth-bag! Opening the bag, Krishna immediately emptied the contents and began eating the *avvul* to his heart's content and even delighting in its taste! *Kuchela's* joy knew no bounds! A moment later, Sri Krishna's consort Rukmini also partook a morsel of the same food as *"bhaagavatha prasaadam"* and delighted in it!

Krishna Washes the Feet of His Guest Sudama

42. At this point in the story of Kuchela, a humorous scene of mischievous banter takes place between Sri Krishna and his consort Rukmini who was verily the avatar of *Goddess Mahalakshmi*.

    42.1. Rukmini asked Sri Krishna what gifts she must gather to be given to *Kuchela*, the honored guest who had come visiting their palace. Sri Krishna smilingly replied, *"Left to me I would like to give my good old friend everything in this*

177

palace! Why, I would even prefer to gift you to him!" What Sri Krishna meant was that since *Sri. Mahalakshmi* was the *Goddess of Wealth,* if she were to even as much as merely let a single beauteous glance of hers fall upon the *Kuchela* .... i.e., *"lakshmi-kataaksham"* .... all his poverty-stricken conditions would simply vanish in a trice! But then Rukmini, who too like her Lord also possessed a streak of harmless mischief in her, took Sri Krishna's words literally. Thus, she in a playful mood pretentiously gave a tongue-in-cheek reply to her husband: *"My Lord, I do not mind if you give me away to Kuchela but then beware that he belongs to an extremely austere "vaideeka" family that scrupulously adheres to all the domestic regime and codes that apply to all "vaideeka" homesteads.... A lady of a "vaideeka" home must be well-trained and adept in the daily routines of "vaideeka" house-keeping – i.e., she must know how to sweep the front-yard and water it with fresh cow-dung, she must know how to wash the utensils meant for household worship and other rituals, she must know how to cook food and serve it as sacred victuals for offering to God .... And many more such strictures....! You know, my Lord that I on the other hand come from a royal family unschooled in the "vaideeka" way of life... So if you must give me away to Kuchela as gift, please do so only after giving me some time and an opportunity to first visit his house and become apprenticed there in the art of conducting a household strictly according to "vaideeka" ways and lifestyle! Otherwise, what you give to Kuchela as a gift would turn out to be quite useless to him!"*

42.2. Sri Krishna guffawed at Rukmini's' clever retort! And then smilingly whispered to her with a mischievous twinkle in his eyes, *"All that must be given to my friend may be deemed to have been already given!"*

43. Krishna thereafter showed *Kuchela* all due courtesies and bade his old friend stay with him for the night in the palace. Both could spend long hours of the night recalling all the old days of their boyhood and youthful adventures! Krishna embraced his friend as

they lay together recalling those old times… Next morning, after showing *Kuchela* all due courtesies again, Krishna bade his old friend farewell from the palace doors. *Kuchela* set off on the return journey to his home.

44. Retracing the steps back home to his village, *Kuchela* arrived at where he knew his dilapidated house was located. When he arrived there, he however found no home! Instead, a magnificent, imposing mansion stood there, all illumined with gorgeous lighting, sprawling beautiful gardens, opulent furnishings… it was a spectacle of pure riches! Momentarily, he thought to himself that he had probably lost his way and had meandered into some strange new neighborhood! But then looking again hither and thither he was able to ascertain he had made no mistake in directions he had taken to his home and that he was indeed at the very spot where his residence had always been situated! *Kuchela* stood there utterly befuddled and dumbstruck, *"Where I have come?! Where is my old house! What is happening here?!"* he cried.

    44.1. It was at that moment that *Kuchela's* wife who had been watching out for his arrival from the grand balcony of the mansion, noticed that her husband had returned. She had been awaiting the arrival of *Kuchela*, eagerly expecting that he would be returning in truly grand style in a procession of pomp and pageantry, seated perhaps on a golden palanquin in a royal parade of honor arranged for him by Sri Krishna! After all, she had reckoned, Krishna had already bestowed upon her unimaginable riches by transforming her shanty home into a magnificent mansion full of dazzling wealth …. So wouldn't Sri Krishna have also showered similarly his munificence on his old friend *Kuchela* too?! Thinking thus to herself, she was a little disappointed to see her husband return home in the same tattered clothes and in a condition that had, in fact, been made even more unkempt thanks to the all-night palaver Kuchela and Sri Krishna, old companions, had had the previous night in the palace…. She saw thus that there was no change whatsoever in her husband's poor demeanor!

44.2. Before she rushed out to meet *Kuchela*, she paused then a moment to think: *"What could be the reason my husband has returned from Sri Krishna's palace in the same destitute state but then, even before his return home, Sri Krishna has miraculously transformed this house to a magnificent mansion, filled it with all kinds of opulence and even bedecked me with this priceless jewelry and costliest silks?*

44.3. *"I am sure Sri Krishna would have readily bestowed all riches on Kuchela too... but then I am sure too that my husband would have declined it all! He would've told Sri Krishna so long as he had Krishna's friendship, he would need nothing for himself personally. All he might need is all only that which must be provided for the sake of his wife and children back home! And that is why, perhaps, why Sri Krishna sent my husband back home empty-handed but then by his grace transformed my house and gave me all this – a mansion, lavish furnishings, diamond bangles, emerald bracelets, necklaces, coral pendants, ear-rings and tiara on me with clothes of the finest silks! Look at me now! I seem to glow like a royal queen!!*

44.4. **But then shame on me!** *Sri. Krishna recognized my husband's own humble nature of self-denial ("vairaagyam") but did not think of me as being equally self-abnegating too!* **Oh, Shame on me!** *I shall now remove all the finery I am bedecked in! I shall not go out to meet my poor husband looking now like some dressed-up royal queen! I must renounce all these magnificent riches around me! I must revert to my old humble self before I go out to meet my husband!*

44.5. When the wife rushed out of the mansion to the street, she came near *Kuchela* to greet him and welcome him back home. But he could not however recognize her at all! He only knew his wife from her generally famished deportment. He thought it was some strange lady who was merely seeking a Brahmin's blessings by humbly prostrating at his feet with the words. However, on closer look at her, he finally ascertained that it was indeed his wife ... (*veekshya patneemitia gnyaatva...*)! Then they rejoiced in reuniting! She took hold of Kuchela's hands and led him gently into their new magnificent mansion. The couple were a sight to behold indeed as though they were a replica of the divine couple itself – *Bhagavaan* and *Mahalakshmi* in the awe-inspiring surroundings of the new mansion! While *Kuchela* and his wife went around on a tour around the spacious precincts of their mansion, they were admittedly overwhelmed but not too overawed by it since they realized that all that they were witnessing was nothing to gloat over. None of it was their own possession.... It was all nothing but the great handiwork of Sri Krishna's grace and compassion only that had been showered upon them! *Kuchela's* wife then led her husband to the special alcove in the house exclusively reserved for the idols of *Bhagavaan* to be installed and worshipped as part of the ritual of *"bhagavath-tiruvaaraadanam"*.

44.6. *Kuchela* stood in front of *Bhagavaan's* sacred idols, and closing his eyes, lost himself in deep meditation upon these very poignant thoughts: *aho bata mama durbhaagasya saasvat daridrasya sammrdhm....:* "O Lord! I have been an abject destitute stricken by unspeakable poverty **("parama daridran")** for countless past lives besides this present one! A destitute in both mind and spirit, have I been always! And yet now all the "daridram" has vanished in the blink of an eye! What is the cause? What has made this transformation! There is no question that it is all because of **"Sri Krishna kataaksham**!" ("mahabuteh avalokanam ....) the miraculous grace of Sri Krishna alone that has brought about this change in my soulful and physical condition! I pray now to You, O Krishna, for nothing else but to grant me only this: that I shall remain your true "bhaktha" for now and all times to come!"

44.7. When Kuchela then opened his eyes, he witnessed again that his wife was once again bedecked in all the dazzling jewelry and finery as before! Moreover, he found himself too all decked in fine silk vestments, golden chains, diamond rings and ear-rings etc.! He turned to the Lord and spoke, *"Oh Lord! Why are you forcing me now to wear and flaunt these trifles too! Do I have any need for them?!"*

44.8. To which *Bhagavaan* replied that the gifts he bestows upon his devotees out of his own will and pleasure must never be rejected. They must be humbly and wholeheartedly received and accepted as token of divine affection given so generously by the Almighty – *"bhagavath prasaadam"* …!

**"*raamaanuja dayaa paatram gnyaana vairagya bhushanam I
Srimath venkata naathaaryam vande vedaanta desikam II*"**

***

-14-
"*Sri Vaishnava Sampradaaya*": Clarification of a Few Doubts on Doctrine

Synopsis: *The doctrine of "Saranagathi", is the bedrock of Sri Vaishnava Theology. It is a lofty conception of soteriology which is sometimes difficult to understand even by devout members of the laity. Doubts and skepticism arise in the mind and it is not surprising to find many "sishyas" of Srimad Mukkur Azhagiyasingar appealing to him to provide clarifications and comfort. In this epistle, the Acharya addresses some of those doubts on Saranagathi doctrine raised by disciples.*

A few "*doubting Thomas's*" ("**sandeha praanigaL**") of our community have been constantly requesting me to provide them clarifications to certain doubts on a matter of doctrine in our **Sri Vaishnava Sampradaaya** which they say they have been for long trying to seek. I shall now explain the subject at length to impress upon them all the correct position to be taken on such doctrinal matters.

The doubt in their minds can be summarized as follows:

- "In accordance with the injunctions laid down in the relevant "*saastra*", let us say that a soul abides faithfully in the guidance given him by his lineage of Acharyas who have instructed him to do so;

- "Furthermore, let us say the soul places its complete trust in the words of Sri Krishna in the **Bhagavath-Gita**, "*maamekam sharanam vraja*", the solemn promise that the act of a soul's absolute surrender or "*saranaagathi*" unto Him, will surely fetch it salvation and a permanent place in *Sri Vaikuntam*, the Abode of the Supreme Almighty, is assured;

- And where in Sri Vaikuntam, in the company of other souls like itself who have previously been already liberated (*"mukthaatmas"*), this soul too will begin enjoying infinite spiritual bliss while being engaged as eternal servitor to **Srimann Naaraayana**, the Lord Almighty resting upon the body of the divine serpent, **Adi Seshan**, along with Consorts, ***Sri, Bhu*** and ***Neela*** attendant upon their Lord!"

- "The question asked now is when such a soul has thus duly performed "**saranaagathi**", why does it not get transported or ascend to the heavenly realm of *Sri Vaikuntam* ***immediately?*** Instead, why does it continue to linger in time and remain mired still in these mortal realms for quite a long while?

- "Does it mean therefore that the doctrine of "*saranaagathi*" is ineffectual?

- "Or does it mean that the *Achaaryaas* who initiated the soul into the rite of "*saranaagathi*", did so improperly and thus let the soul down?

- "Or does it mean that the very doctrine of "*saranaagathi*" is nothing but myth?

Such indeed are some misgivings of Sri Vaishnavas who have raised similar doubts to me and they seek my clarifications.

Our Achaarya Swami Vedanta Desikan in a "*prabhandham paasuram*" (Tamizh devotional hymns) of his wrote this stanza:

> "*malaadha vinai annaithum maaLa nampoyy*
>
> *vaaneri malarmagalaar anbu poonum*
>
> *tholaadha maamanikku thondu poondu*
>
> *thozdhukandhu thothirangal paadi yaadi*
>
> *kelaadha pazhamaraiyin geetam kettka*
>
> *kidayaadha perinbam peruga naalum*
>
> *meelaadha peradimaikanbu pettrom*
>
> *medhiniyil irikinnrom vidhiyinaale*".

The above hymn can be appreciated through several annotations but I shall explain only a few of them here.

Before this lifetime of ours we have all journeyed through innumerable past lives. In each of them we have committed countless deeds of good and evil (*"punnyam"* and *"paapam"*). But by any account, the evil would certainly outnumber the good. Those countless deeds of sin and virtue are what have been referred to in the above hymn as *"maalaadha vinai"* --- an interminable, inestimable and intolerably oppressive series of bondages caused by deed after deed after deed....

Yet, would we believe it if we are told that we have been freed from such an inextricable series of *"paapam"* and *"punnyam"*? Yes, in truth, we are indeed freed from the clutches of that terrible cycle and do you know why? It is because of the solemn promise made by Sri Krishna, the Acharyan who delivered to us the Bhagavath-Gita: *"sharanam vraja; sarva paapebhyo, moksha-ishyaami"*. If we but surrender our soul at his feet, then it is certain beyond doubt that he will absolve us of all our sins, of commission and omission, and grant us everlasting liberation.

Now, to address the question: *"Why then don't we experience "moksha", the bliss of eternal salvation, in the very same instant that we perform the act of "saranaagathi"?"*

Let me explain.

Moments after we perform the act of "**saranaagathi**", our soul stands in the presence of the Almighty who shines with the effulgence radiating from his divine consort who resides in him (**lakshmikaanthan**). After obtaining solemn oath of allegiance, He then asks the soul, *"Tell me when you would like to receive the grace of "moksha"?* If the soul were to reply then, *"I want eternal deliverance at this very moment"*, the compassionate Bhagavaan would certainly and readily grant him the wish. But then the soul at that moment is faced with a grievous dilemma. It knows well that salvation is bestowed by Bhagavaan only on those souls that have shed mortal coils. Bodily death always precedes spiritual Salvation. So, the soul is filled with dread at even the mere thought of mortal death. And the fear of losing life and all earthly possessions takes hold of it. In that moment, caught between its desire for *"moksha"* and fear of mortal death, the soul hesitates to answer the Almighty....

Bhagavaan then asks the soul again, *"Why don't you answer me? What are you thinking?!"*

To which question, the surrendering soul sheepishly answers, *"Swami, I do wish to be graced by "moksha" but I wish for it only at the very end of this lifetime of mine. When it is time for me to shed this mortal coil at the end of my days here on earth, please do not let me fall back into the abyss of yet another lifetime in this earthly realm. Please come to my aid then and take me away with you to your glorious abode of Sri Vaikuntam to live there in everlasting joy with you as your eternal servitor!"*

What happens next is that the compassionate Bhagavaan then does grant to the surrendered soul a brief but blessed further lease of life on earth wherein it is able to enjoy the fruits of its residual good deeds (*"punnyam"*) even while its past, accumulated and innumerable sins (*"paapam"*) all stand entirely cancelled and absolved.

It is such an act of compassion of Bhagavaan which the soul enjoys that is described by Swami Vedanta Desikan in his above *paasuram* as .... *"medhiniyil irikinnrom vidhiyinaale"*.

In other words, even though we may have performed *"saranaagathi"*, and become thus instantly eligible for eternal salvation, nonetheless, it is because that we out of our volition and desire have beseeched Bhagavaan to extend our existential condition (*"medhiniyil"*) on earth as described above, that we continue to still live during the course of time remaining for us on earth, even though mired, as it were, in this vast vale of mortal joys and sorrows (*"samsaara mandalam"*).

Not a speck of blame thus can be said to rest upon Bhagavaan who was willing and ready to grant the soul the *"moksha"* even in that very moment it performed *"saranaagathi"* and surrendered unto his feet. It is the surrendered soul alone that had, out of its own petty desires, sought to postpone receiving salvation only at the very end of its present lifetime. It is for that reason alone that even after offering Surrender through the rite of *"saranaagathi"*, a man continues however to live through all the vicissitudes of this worldly existence .... And that too is exactly as Swami Desikan (in a Sanskrit *shloka* in the "**Nyaasa Dasakam**") has observed through the expression *"etat dehaavasaane maam tvath-paadam praapaya svayam…"*

***

In the moment we surrender unto Bhagavaan we must know that we have instantly earned his love and grace. Until that very moment of our surrender, Bhagavaan is, of course, gravely unforgiving of our sinful selves. But the moment we fall at his feet and genuinely beseech his pardon with these words:

"Lord! Please absolve me of the countless sins and transgressions I am guilty of committing in innumerable past lives. Please bestow your infinite compassion upon me! I prostrate myself now before you my Lord and my divine mother, your consort! Bless me as I lie now at your feet!"

Once we have uttered those kinds of words sincerely, Bhagavaan's ire subsides instantly. He then comes forward to shower his grace and blessings upon us. And Bhagavaan grants what we have prayed for:

He arrives at our side in the moment of final departure, arouses the soul within us as it sheds this body and helps it free itself through the cerebral aperture on the crown of our head, and then, as pure spirit, helps it to begin ascending high into the celestial spheres.

Thereafter, the soulful journey is undertaken with the aid of divine chaperones --- the angelic *"suryarashmi-s"* -- and all along the way into the high heavens the soul is offered pleasantries and lavish hospitality too by the celestial archangels (*"aadivaheeka-s"*).

Finally, the *"aamaanava-s"*, the divine agents of the Almighty, ceremonially lead the soul onwards into the realms of **Sri Vaikuntam**, the eternal abode of the Almighty Sriman Naaraayana!

It is in that highest of celestial worlds that we begin to then live in an eternity of infinite bliss as described (by **Swami Nammaazhwaar**) in the expression: *"ozhivil kaalamellaam udanaai manni…."* In the presence of Sriman Naaraayana, that ineffable bliss is accompanied by the euphonies and melodies of Vedic chants that were never heard before! Such indeed is the divine ecstasy that we earn in eternal **Sri Vaikuntam** thanks to the act of *sharanaagathi* we performed! That indeed is the *summum bonum* of our existence!

Thus, what in fact should be understood clearly from all the above is only this:

Bhagavaan out of compassion for us does heed the special request we make to him while performing *saranaagathi* i.e., to let us continue to remain in these earthly realms until the terminal moment arrives to shed our mortal coils; and that it is only thereafter that he should convey our soul as described above into the realms of his abode in Sri Vaikuntam. In other words, it must be understood clearly that our present unexpired term of a lifetime on earth is itself one of the benedictions conferred upon us by the Almighty who is pleased with our act of "*saranaagathi*" unto him.

In fact, such an insightful reading of the doctrine has been revealed to us by many of the spiritual masters of our tradition in the past. And none other than our Acharya, Swami Vedanta Desikan himself has opined that the Destiny that herded and guided us finally in the direction of steps leading towards "*saranaagathi*" is verily the same Destiny that grants us, too, the fresh lease of our post-"*saranaagathi*" lifetime on earth.

This is how the various *saastra*-s (scriptural texts) in our tradition have expatiated upon the esoteric doctrine of "*saranaagathi*" which is a unique means of salvation propounded in our Sri Vaishnava *sampradaayam*.

There are some people who express their own personal interpretations of it according to their whims and fancies. They are free to do so. No one can stop them from doing so.

***

I shall now address those amongst us who are stone-hearted.

"Don't we see that even in the ordinary world, protection and safe haven are granted to one who is hapless and seeks safe asylum? So why must it be doubted that Bhagavaan who by his own declaration has resolved to grant asylum likewise to all abject souls would ever refuse to grant the wish of any person who approaches him with these sincere words: *"I surrender to you, Lord! I have no other means to save myself! Please pardon all my sins and grant me the exalted state of grace! I have come to you to seek asylum in the hope that you who have granted asylum to even such evil persons like Kaakasura and Gandaakarna, will not refuse me your grace! You will see me too as one amongst them and grant me your protection...!"* Now, why would Bhagavaan abandon any person who beseeches him thus?

"I forswear all the wicked ways of my past. I now swear also that henceforth I shall abjure all evil until my dying days!" Anyone who has firmly resolved thus will never be deserted by Bhagavaan. The Lord **Achyutha** can never bring himself to abandon any soul that has taken oath thus: *"Until I breathe my last in life, I shall remain ever firm in my loyalty to you and to your will, my Lord!"*

"This possession of mine that I call **"I, Me and Mine"** *I have now surrendered to you, my Lord... I am now nothing but your chattel! The responsibility for its safekeeping and the duty of ensuring its wellbeing is now all your very own!"* Would Bhagavaan betray anyone who has so completely surrendered to Bhagavaan and placed such absolute trust in him? Why cast any doubts about it?

What does it cost a soul to cling to the sacred feet of Bhagavaan with the plaintive cry of *"You are my one and only last resort, there is none other to save me!"*? Even in the ordinary world, such a desperate appeal made by anyone is succored at once, is it not? Under the circumstances, when Bhagavaan has himself declared that he will rush to save all those who surrender absolutely unto him, why would he fail them? **Not to worry, it is certain that he will not fail them. He will surely rescue them. He will surely reach them to safe shores. He will grant them his protection.**

***

What is therefore crucial is to have faith in Divinity (*deiva-bhakthi*). It calls for little time or effort of thought to easily dismiss Divinity. But then even the most intelligent of humans fails to conclusively prove the validity of such dismissal or denial. Thus, what we ought to do is to do the contrary: we must constantly affirm through our words, deeds and thought that Divinity indeed exists and always prevails. That is how men of piety hold forth in life with the slogan *"Dharma alone triumphs!"*

But it is the general lot of mankind to live unmindful of the Divine. If a man were to be stricken with severely painful and incurable stomach-ailment, he would then in such a condition cry out for divine help. The moment he is cured, however, he will forget God and proudly claim that it was the medication he took that did wonders! Similarly, when adversity strikes a man, he is likely to bemoan the spitefulness of God. But when the adversity passes and he enjoys again happy times, he will boast that it all came about by the dint of his own efforts!

Thus, amongst mankind there is none whose faith in the Divine is ever steadfast.

By contrast, Divinity is never as fickle-hearted as Man.

He grants his blessings even upon the man who even only accidentally approaches a temple sanctum with palms folded. The man's gesture even though made with no intention to worship the Deity at all is nonetheless regarded by Bhagavaan as having been offered to him only with genuine feeling! Bhagavaan does not therefore deny the man the blessings due to such offerings! Even if a man were to heap ill-will upon and foul thoughts and words against Bhagavaan – as *Sisupaalan* (in the Mahabharatha) did -- at the end, the grace of God still gets bestowed upon such an ingrate. The reason why is that God thinks to himself, *"Even while heaping invectives upon me, the fact is that this person's mind was fixated upon me alone! Without the mind focused on me, it would not have been possible for him to abuse me so vociferously! I must reward him for that effort alone!"* Thinking thus, the Lord then out of enormous compassion sows the seed of **Bhakthi**, devotion to Divinity, inside the mind of the man. It takes root and then grows and flourishes.

***

One day a very intelligent disciple posed a very pertinent question to his guru.

"Sir, can you describe to me any place in the universe where the presence of Divinity is not immanent?"

The guru pondered over the question for a moment before answering as follows:

"The Divine does not reside in the man who denies Divinity. God is not present in that man who ekes a living through dubious, untruthful means. There is no presence of Divinity in the woman who deserts her lawful spouse and consorts with another man. God never chooses to inhere in persons who are slaves to lust and anger. God is never present in those who spread hatred or pollute morals in society. Divinity never is at home among those who are antipathetic towards the Vedas nor does God live amongst those who go against the spirit of the Saastra-s in destroying places of worship. There is no Divinity in those people who decry and desecrate the legacy of traditional beliefs and faith that their elders have long embraced and then try to replace it with their own willful new-fangled practices".

The guru ended then by saying, "*Our ancient scriptures have revealed to us that God does not exist in people and places as listed above*".

The quick-witted student however retorted, "*Swami, what you say seems to contradict the claim that everything in the universe is imbued with Divine presence! Only if God is omnipresent can many scriptural pronouncements such as for example:* "**vaasudevasya sarvam**", "**nirkinnradhu ellaam nedumaal**" *or* "**vastu parichedha rahitan**" *all be said to be valid and true? Sir, haven't you yourself many a time explained to me the Vedantic aphorism* "**ya aatmani thishtann**" *to mean that God inheres within the souls of all?*"

The guru looked at his disciple and said, "*You have posed indeed a very formidable question for which a convincing explication can be quite difficult to grasp. Difficult for whom? It will be difficult for fools to understand it. But it should not be difficult to grasp for someone I know is as intelligent as you. So, listen to me as I explain the matter to you:*

"*I enumerated for you above the persons in whom the scriptures say that Divinity does not reside. What that means is that God resides even in such persons but then does not reveal himself to them as being existent. Bhagavaan exists in every man ... even in men of other faiths and beliefs... but then Bhagavaan does not reveal himself to be present in them and they too are not able to be aware of his presence. Even within the atheist who denies the existence of Bhagavaan, Divinity does exist but then the atheist is neither aware of its presence or its immanence. This is the sense in which one must understand the statement of the "saastra-s" that say that Bhagavaan does not exist in certain kinds of persons as described above.*"

Hearing the explication of his guru, the disciple was thrilled and exclaimed, *"Sir, today you have dispelled doubt on the matter and enlightened my mind! I am so grateful to you!"*

***

To summarize now all that has been said above: Anyone, irrespective of caste or creed, who submits to Bhagavaan, the Divinity residing within every soul, through the genuine act of "**saranaagathi**", will have all his or her desires fulfilled and will earn divine protection. Bhagavaan is said to be in Vedantic thought to be *"sarvasya suhridh"* …. The unfailing friend of all, the savior of all! Therefore, in placing complete faith in the potential power of the *"saranaagathi"* doctrine, you must strive to reap and enjoy the beatific fruits and grace of salvation (*moksha*) being verily the consummative realization of the very purpose of human life.

***

-15-
The Good that Virtuous Women Do

Synopsis: Srimadh Mukkur Azhagiyasingar had a very high opinion of Womanhood. He regarded the womenfolk of the family as the true legislators of moral values and virtuous behavior within the home. He considered women as eminently capable of providing the best moral compass for menfolk in society. In this very lively and engaging epistle of his, the Acharya pays handsome tribute to the ideal of the virtuous woman of the house.

In a town there lived a man whose atheism was so rabid that he may well have been crowned the King of Atheists. The man would abide by nothing and disdained everything related to Faith.

He detested temples as fraudulent institutions invented by a bunch of cunning people who were only out to make a comfortable living for themselves. Pointing to the idols of the Deity in temples, he would mock them as mere metallic toy. He rejected all *"saastras"* and sacred scriptures as superstitious fairy tales. He dismissed the wise men and elders of the community as a motley crowd of charlatans. Charity and philanthropy he disdained as nothing but seeking vainglory. If he were asked whether he saw no difference between Good and Evil at all in the world, he would reply that there exists nothing as Evil. When asked if he saw no evil in thievery, he replied nonchalantly, *"So what is so evil about stealing?"*

His personal habits, deportment and attitudes also often reflected his atheistic nature. For instance, he was known to bathe only once every three or four days. The food he consumed on any day was stale, perhaps cooked two or three days ago! While sitting down for a meal, he would invite his two pet dogs to eat with him and they would gobble the same food on the same plate at the same time! Even while defecating, he was known to crunch away merrily on snacks like "*cheedai*", "*murukku*" etc.!

Whenever the festive procession of the temple-Deity passed through in a palanquin his street (during the time of religious "*uthsavam*"), he would rudely ignore show his annoyance at the holy pageant by slamming shut the front doorways of his home as it went by.

He was never in the habit of reading any book to expand or improve his mind.

If anyone, by way of polite, preliminary self-introduction, were to inquire of him, "Sir, may I know who you are?", he would turn on them fuming, *"Are you blind? Don't you see who I am standing right before your eyes?!"*

If during a conversation, a friend of his happened to engage him by posing a serious or weighty question to him such as, for example, *"Sir, what do you think resides within this mortal body (sarira) and enlivens it?"*, the man would only reply facetiously, "Yes, within this *sarira* of mine is the meal and drinks I have just had a while ago. It all now resides as un-alimented stuff in my bowels --- the food as fecal matter and the drink as un-expelled urine! Nothing else resides inside here".

If such a line of serious questioning persisted, and the friend asked him thus:

"Sir, you are capable of speech… Now, can you tell me wherefrom within you Speech emanates? Who is it really that is speaking?". The man would blandly answer: "It is from the tongue within me that all speech emanates".

"Sir, without an entity called soul or *jeevaatma* within you, how can mere tongue by itself cause speech?".

"Why not? Look at a big wall-clock. It chimes too… Inside the wall-clock, tell me, is there a *jeevaatma*?"

"Sir, when a man dies, he goes totally silent. Does his tongue then continue to cause speech?".

"Tell me then, can a wall-clock that is permanently damaged, ever chime again?".

"Don't you think, Sir, that it's a little miraculous that sons and daughters are born?".

"What is so miraculous about tamarind and mango trees being born from tiny seeds sown into the soil of the earth?"

The man would go on in similar vein whenever anyone tried to engage him in any such serious and thoughtful discourse and would simply counter meaningful questions with irreverent insouciance.

If someone asked him, "Do you ever consider anyone to be superior to you in any way?", he would retort arrogantly, "The only person superior to me is I, me and myself".

"Don't you ever show any deference on any account to any other person?"

His reply was: "If I did show deference to any person, would not that person become my superior?".

***

This same man had a wife, a fine, God-fearing lady. She found him to be utterly incorrigible in his ways and, hence, had a long time ago, given up, after trying extremely hard in all sorts of manner and effort, to reform him.

However, one day, she hit upon a very bright new idea to reform him.

"If I too started behaving like a rabid atheist, and began mirroring his own arrogant traits too, as well as his insolence and crass behavior, maybe it might make him begin to realize and repent the folly of his ways and he might probably try reforming himself?", she thought to herself.

She thus resolved to henceforth behave towards him in the most obnoxious of ways possible, not so much to annoy or disobey her husband, but to simply mirror his own very unsavory character.

***

One night the man turned up at his home extremely late at night and (thinking his spouse to be fast asleep) immediately set out again to visit the quarters of his concubine. Quickly realizing what his intentions were, the man's wife emerged out the house, and went out at the same time as her husband was exiting it; and while he headed in one direction to reach his concubine's house, she began walking in the opposite direction.

The man was astonished by her action. He stopped her and demanded to know where she was going out at that late hour of the night.

She spun around and asked him in turn, *"Where are you off to now at this time of the night?"*

"I am on my way to meet with her in her house", he replied arrogantly.

And to which she replied laconically, *"And I am on my way to meet him in his house"*.

"What for? What purpose", he asked her sharply.

"The purpose for which you are heading towards wherever you are going, it is for the very same purpose for which I am now headed."

Shocked and stunned by her words, the man meekly turned back and re-entered his home. She too at once followed him.

Inside their home, he confronted her: *"How could you stoop to commit such an evil thing as you were about to do?!"*

She retorted, "Well.... Isn't it you who has always said that there is no such evil in the world? Besides, is not it your own habit every night to frequent that house of your concubine? Tell me is that evil or is it good?"

"I tell you that I visit her home every night but then I don't do anything there that I should be ashamed of", he protested.

"By the same token", she calmly replied, "I too visit the home of my paramour and I don't do anything there that I should be ashamed of either".

"What?! Do you expect me to believe it? That you visit that scoundrel's home at night, and you do not do anything shameful there!", he thundered at his wife.

"And what about you, then?" she countered back at him, "You expect me to believe that you visit the house of ill-fame of that slut there who welcomes into her boudoir ten more other men like you every night, and *that you don't do anything shameful with her?!"*

This kind of furious exchanges between husband and wife flared up frequently over the following few days on all kinds of pretexts.

By the end of the third day, the man quietly and completely gave up his wicked habit of visiting the house of ill-fame.... Forever!

***

One day before he was due to return home at dusk for his supper, the wife took the two dogs to the backyard and let them loose to roam around for a while. Later, just when she knew her husband would he home soon she went out to the backyard again, went looking for them, and fetched the roaming dogs back to the house and leashed them securely.

She went back into the home and laid the table and the plate for her husband who was readying himself to sit for his meal. When he noticed that his pet dogs were not present with him as usual at the dinner table, he was surprised and asked his wife crossly, *"Where are the dogs? Why aren't they here?"*.

"I have leashed them in the backyard" she said to him tersely.

"Untie them, right now!", he told her sternly.

She remonstrated. He rebuked her saying, "If the dogs are not here to join me in at dinner, then I will not touch this food you've served me.... *Those pets are like my children.* I cannot dine without they dining with me too."

She threw an angry look at him, shrugged her shoulders in exasperation, went out into the backyard, untied the dogs, and brought them into the home to him and let them loose to do what they usually did daily – begin slurping and gorging the same food that he ate from his plate himself.

As he began eating with his dogs, halfway through the meal, he suddenly began to sniff, pucker his nose in distaste at a strange, foul, and fetid smell that seemed to arise from nowhere particular. He lifted the plate to see if there was anything under that probably emanated the noxious smell.

The wife who stood by watching, asked him "What's the matter? Why do you lift your plate and look beneath?"

"The food smells horrible… I'm looking beneath the plate to see if anything is stuck there that gives off this foul smell!", he said.

"I laid the plate for your meals only after ensuring it was fully washed and cleaned. So, the plate cannot smell. It is those dogs of yours, sitting there eating with you, that must be causing the stench", she told him.

"Don't you ever blame my darling dogs", he snapped back at her, "they should not be faulted for any reason!" Saying so, the man put his arms around the yapping dogs and began kissing them and they too, in turn, began licking their master with affection.

No sooner had the dogs started licking his face than their overpowering stench enveloped him!

He recoiled in disgust, pushed the dogs away, beat them and yelled, *"Oh you filthy, coprophagous curs! Get away from me!"*

The poor dogs cowered in sheer fright. The wife then restrained her husband from further violence and spoke to him gently:

"Don't beat up the dogs, please. It is in their nature to feed upon excrement…. Haven't you heard of the saying that even if you bathe a dog clean and bring it inside the home, once you unleash the creature, it will slink away wagging its tail to feed once again on what it likes best-- faeces on the streets! That is the very nature of this specie! How can it help its basic instinct?! It is we humans who should know at what proper distance even pet dogs must be kept; instead, we hug them, kiss, and even let them lie down and sleep with us in our bed! It is all improper and can end up in undesirable results. When these two dogs were let out, I found them loitering around in the marketplace today. So, I brought them back home and leashed them in the backyard. It is possible the creatures might have fed themselves upon something filthy back there in the marketplace."

After he had listened to his wife intently, the husband suddenly realized how unnatural and unhygienic had been his misplaced love of dogs. He resolved to shed it forever and stay away from unclean canines for the rest of his life.

***

One day, many months later, the man returned home to find his wife relaxing and seated sprawled on the floor with her legs languidly stretched out. Unmindful of her husband's presence she made no move to modestly fold her legs and sit properly. Her disrespectful attitude enraged the husband. He yelled at her, *"Insolent woman,* don't you know to show modesty becoming of a lady? *Why don't you fold your legs and sit properly in my presence?"*

"Why must I fold up my outstretched legs?" she retorted.

"Am I not your husband, elder to you in age? Do I not deserve due respect?", he asked her sternly.

"Oh, in that case, please tell me, do you ever show due respect to many venerable elders who pass by our house in the streets…? Many times, have I seen you sit lolling about with your legs outstretched towards them. *Did you show them all due respect and courtesy?'*, she shot back at her husband.

"Those men are not really all that venerable", he countered.

"Then you too are not venerable", she replied.

"Woman, I shall thrash you!", he screamed at her.

"Go ahead, but by beating me you, will you become venerable?", she replied coolly.

"You are a rebellious wretch!", he shouted. And she defiantly told him, *"It is you who are a horrible, recalcitrant man!"*

***

As days went by, and after several such similar tempestuous exchanges and incidents between man and woman, it slowly began to dawn on the husband that he ought to start introspecting upon his own unpleasant personal traits and undesirable, offensive behavior and perhaps do something to correct them.

***

One day, the wife secretly slipped a deadly, live scorpion into the folds of the mattress of her husband's bed. She did it with a certain purpose and design in mind. The idea had occurred to her as an effective feasible way of delivering her husband a fitting lesson since he was stoutly resisting her entreaties to begin duly performing the daily sacred rite of "*sandhyaavandanam*" mandated by the "*saastra*-s" for all men. Despite her constant badgering, he adamantly kept resisting, telling her, "*Get lost, you woman! I will not do it! I don't believe in all this mantra mumbo-jumbo, which is all waste of time!*"

That night, the foolish man retired to bed and as soon as he had slipped between its covers, the scorpion lurking there at once stung his back.

He screamed out in pain, "*Aiyo! Aiyoo! Oh!*" and jumped out of bed, crashing to the floor, and writhed in distress.

The wife rushed to him and asked, "*Oh dear! What happened?! What's the matter?*"

"*It's a scorpion! It has stung me! I just cannot bear the pain! I am going to die now! OH!*"

The wife then rushed out at once into the street to fetch the medicine-man who lived as neighbor only three houses away.

The medicine-man, who was a doctor in herbal cures and adept in magical chants and ritual incantations, came and examined the scorpion bite.

Beseeching the doctor, the man said to him, "*OH, swami-ji, please save my life, I beg you!*".

The swami-ji pacified the man's fears and said reassuringly, "*Do not worry, I shall expel the poison in a matter of minutes…*"

So, saying the medicine-man, by uttering some mantras, succeeded in transferring the poisonous strain that was pulsating through the body of a man and transfused it into the body of the man's friend who had just arrived on the scene, to commiserate with his friend's dire plight. With the poison excised out of his body, the man immediately felt relief and recovered but then saw that his friend, poor fellow, who had come to merely to help, was now writhing and screaming in severe pain! The poison now transfused into his body through the magic spell of incantations the swami-ji had cast upon him now pulsated and raged! The swami then soon uttered a few more mantras and once again magically transferred, as it were, the poisonous strain from the friend's body onto a nearby tree that stood outside the house. The friend recovered and his life too was saved!

The following day, when her husband had fully recovered from the painful experience of the previous night, inquired:

"At least now, do you realize that sacred mantras do possess a certain magical, curative potency?"

He replied, "Yes, I do realize that truth fully now!" He then continued, "Please do not go now and say anything more to that medicine-man, the neighbor, about me or my disbelieving nature... lest he transfers the poison latent in that tree, back into my own body again!"

"Instead, please why don't you now go and fetch me a book on how to quickly learn, memorize and begin performing the "*sandhyaavandanam*" mantras and ritual. I shall begin doing the rite from this very day onwards....!"

The wife was gladdened and at once did what he wished. She gave him the book on *sandhyaavandanam* which he duly memorized and began practicing the rites.

"Will that swami-ji deign to teach me all about how to cure poison through mantras? I'd like to learn that useful skill....", he asked his wife curiously.

She reaffirmed it to him in these words:

"Although born a Brahmin, you were guilty of many unpardonable wrongdoings-- of omission and commission. If you forever abandon all those wicked ways of yours, you can be sure that Swami-ji will impart to you all the sacred mantras of healing ailments and diseases that he knows".

"If I must now turn an entirely new leaf in life, please tell me about everything that I should now be doing...", the man asked his wife.

She then began detailing to him the **Do-s and Don't-s** to abide by if he wanted to truly reform and redeem himself.

***

First, you must totally give up using and abusing substances such as snuff, tobacco, cannabis, toddy, arrack etc.

Next, you must forever cease declaring your unbelief in God. You must desist from ever mocking venerable and wise elders.

You must give up gambling. Never must you utter lies to deceive and mislead anyone.

You must stop ridiculing and denigrating religious sacrificial rites, customs, and observances.

You must never consume stale, putrid food leftover from previous days.

You must cleanse yourself thoroughly with daily baths taken with the chant of appropriate mantras. You must regularly perform the obligatory rites to ancestors such as *"tarpanam"* and the annual *"divassam"* etc without fail."

As the man was listening to all this, suddenly, he raised his hand and cried,

"Hold it, hold it right there!", and so saying, he ran to a corner of the room, opened his trunk-case and pulled out a diary. He flipped through the diary and remarked loudly, *"Oh dear!* My father passed away on *Ekadashi* day of *Aadi* month of the lunar calendar (the eleventh day of the fortnight in June-July)! *Tomorrow happens to be the anniversary!* Should I not be performing the *"divassam"* ritual tomorrow for my father's spirit?", he asked his wife.

"No question about it!", she answered, "you must conduct the rite tomorrow since otherwise, as the scripture declares, "**mrudaaham samadhikramya chandaalah: koti janmasu…**" -- you will be reborn into a family clan of a thousand heinous sinners. It will behoove you therefore today to forthwith tonsure you head, sport the traditional *"kudimi"* (tuft of hair) and perform all the due expiatory rituals to atone for all past sins and transgressions. Only then you can be sure that tomorrow for the *divassam* rite, your invitation to good-souled Brahmins to come home and duly partake the funerary ritual-feast will be accepted by them."

Thereafter immediately, as his wife had suggested to him, the man performed all the requisite expiatory rituals, and on the following day --- duly dressed in the traditional attire of *"kaccham"*, with his body also duly smeared with the 12 holy symbols of Vaishnava custom, and with generous sacrificial donations given away to the brahmins – he conducted the annual sacrificial rites to the spirit of his departed father. He then arranged for a photographer to come home and had him take a portrait of himself with his proud, comely wife! At the end of the day and after concluding the ceremonies around 5 PM, he finally asked his wife, *"What else must I do now?"*

She then told him, "You must fast on al *Ekadashi* days (the 11th day of the waxing and waning fortnights); completely stop behaving in an oafish manner like beasts of the streets, like cows and goats; and you must henceforth respect all other womenfolk as if they were your mother and/or sisters."

"Alright, now tell me", he then asked his wife, "how should I now henceforth look upon you, my spouse?"

She replied, "You can consider me as if I were your liege. Or else, as your factotum. As your wife. You can also look upon me as a God-given gift to be enjoyed in all wholesome ways. And as I have already told you earlier, you can look upon me also under certain situations as if I were your mother or sister too."

"Alright, that is fine", he told her, "Now tell me more".

So, she continued, "Books that have a corrupting influence on one's mind should he avoided; watching drama or theatre-plays that are corruptive should also be shunned. Never should you accept to dine in the houses of hosts who you know are of dubious character and morals nor in homes where no daily worship is offered to the Almighty".

"My dear, darling wife, I have a wish…", he suddenly told her,"Let us also perform *'puja'* in our home too and offer worship to our own household deity… Please remind me to do so tomorrow…", he said cheerfully.

"Sure, I will", she replied, and added, "There are so many other such virtuous deeds that you must now henceforth begin doing… I shall tell you about them as and when the right occasion arises".

Thus, ended their exchange and the couple retired very delighted with each other…. Little by little, the man began to transform himself for the better and to become a better human being.

***

\It was around this time that the man had the occasion for the very first time in his life to ever attend a religious public lecture (*upannyaasam*) delivered by a respected, learned theologian. The theme of the talk was **"Atma Tattva"** – *the Reality of the Soul.* The speaker began with a preamble to his discourse saying:

"Let me tell you at the very outset that in this talk of mine, I will be expounding on **Atma Tattva** as expatiated in the school of Sri Vaishnava Philosophy known as **"sri raaamaanuja siddhaantam"** and none amongst you in the audience should have any misgivings about it".

He commenced his oration with a scriptural quotation:

"Nayam devo na marthyo vaa na tiryak sthaavaropi va I

Gnyaananda-mayastvaatma seshohi paramaathmanah: II"

(*Vide: Vedanta Desikan* – *"upakaara sangraham"*)

(**Meaning**: The soul is neither God nor man, neither beast nor tree. Its essential nature is knowledge and bliss, and it is entirely dependent on the Supreme Being and exists solely for His purposes (*SEsha*).)

"The *jeevaatma* is none of these things in form or nature – it is not deva, it is not human, nor that of any creature such as an elephant, horse, lion, bird, serpent, a tree, plant or creeper…

"The *jeevaatma* is pure Knowledge, pure Bliss that enlivens all bodily forms described above. He exists in each as discrete, separate soul and existing in each such individual condition, he serves the supreme '*paramaatma*' as liege. He is monadic and there is no other entity that is smaller than he. He is endowed with intelligence. He is imperishable; he was not created and like God Almighty, he too exists eternally. Acting in accordance with the will of God, the *jeevaatma* can seek and attain a sublime state of divine grace and live in everlasting bliss in the highest of heavens. Have you all understood what I have said so far?

"Now, there might be some people who might argue that a *jeevaatma* is no different an entity than pure energy that gets generated when coal is burnt to produce intense fire, which then is used to boil water, which in turn produces steam, which then is used to turn the wheels of a locomotive engine. Similarly, it may be said that the soul-energy too is really nothing more than, but a certain force generated by various elements of nature that have combined to energize the physical body and drive it – much like a locomotive engine – to move, act and conduct all tasks of life in this world. It is only such energy, or that force, which one might wish to call as *jeevaatma*.

Those that argue as above are putting forth nothing but untruth and utter fallacy.

Ask yourself, if that energy or force which is said to drive the locomotive engine possesses anything called Intelligence or Volition? Let us assume that there is a locomotive engine that is driver-less. Then can you imagine a such self-driven locomotive travelling full steam ahead on rails being able to all by itself avoid a head-on collision with another similarly speeding locomotive engine travelling in the opposite direction on the path of the same railway-lines against it? Would such a driver-less locomotive engine on its own be able to avoid collision by reversing its own course quickly?

That is simply absurd and impossible, isn't it? What is the reason? It is because the locomotive can neither set the course nor navigate its travel direction all by itself nor is it capable, on its own, of regulating its speed. But unlike such a locomotive, the *jeevaatma* inside the body, is possessed of intelligence which enables him to sense the danger ahead and to accordingly respond to it by acting appropriately to save himself. The *jeevaatma* is thus to the *'sarira'*, the body, what the engine-driver is to the locomotive. The energy or force that is generated by a whole host of natural elements combining within the body is quite different in nature from the *jeevaatma* who alone drives the body. The body with all its force and energy acts only and solely at the behest of the *jeevaatma* and exactly as he directs it to do too. Therefore, one should never fall into the trap of believing the false theory which suggests that the intelligent *jeevaatma* and the unintelligent body are really the same. One can very easily infer why the body possesses no intelligence merely by observing it in the state of sleep. In that state of sleep, would the body by itself become aware of a burglar breaking into the house? Can the body then by itself apprehend the burglar or drive him out? Nothing of that sort can ever happen!

There are thus only two ever existent realities – *Paramaatma* and *Jeevaatma* – that are endowed with sentience and intelligence, and none other than these two entities in the world can accomplish anything on its own.

Therefore, in view of all that has been said above, we humans being all *jeevaatmas* and being endowed with keen and discriminative intelligence, should wisely abjure all folly and untruths in life, seek to attain our full spiritual potential and aspire to enjoy everlasting bliss in the realm of God Almighty".

Having spoken thus, the learned theologian further elaborated upon the theme of the talk with other quotations, excerpts and allusions drawn from the scriptures such as the *Vedas, Divya Prabhandhams* of the *Azhwars,* the *Itihaasas* and *Puraanas* before concluding his public oration for the evening.

***

The man who had listened to the whole of the public religious discourse in rapt attention returned home that evening.

At once, he beckoned his wife, and, quite astonishingly, he recapitulated to her exactly all that he had listened to and absorbed from the riveting *Upannyaasam* that he had just heard!

After he had finished, he grew somber and began self-pitifully lamenting to his wife:

"What a waste my life has been so far! I have foolishly squandered away my life living the life of an atheist in unholy and futile pursuits! Alas, how am I going to ever redeem myself?!"

His wife immediately consoled him with these soothing words:

"Do not worry, do not wallow in regret and self-pity ... for it has been said by our wise elders:

"yadh vaa tatth vaa yaadrusho vaa
yathaa vaa katham sositoham naarhasitvam I
uttame cheth vayasi saadhuvruttah:
tade-vaasya palati netharaani II

Let the past begone. Henceforth, if you associate yourself intimately with men of religion and god-fearing devotees, you can engage yourself in many virtuous deeds which will cancel out all the sins of your past. Thereafter, further honorable deeds of yours, going forward, will please Bhagavan who will keep you always protected by his grace. So, do not worry!"

The next day, the man performed all the prescribed rituals and observances. He presented himself thereafter to the Swami-ji, his next-door neighbor. Prostrating before him, he beseeched the healer to take him under his tutelage as a disciple and student.

For several years thereafter, the Swami-ji taught him all the skills and secret knowledge of mantra, tantra, magical potions and incantations to cure ailments and diseases caused by poison and other deadly toxins.

Becoming an expert healer himself in time, the man served society for long years as an apothecary, medicine-man, and healer whom everyone respected and hailed. He helped convert many atheists too into true believers like himself. He became an ardent votary of Bhagavan, earned the Almighty's grace in life and lived happily ever after with his wife.

***

The moral of this whole story is this: If women set their mind to the task, then they have the capacity and power to change even this age of evil **Kali yuga** into virtual **Treta Yuga.** They can raise and groom good offspring. They can be a virtuous influence on siblings and other family members, even parents. They can also reform and help redeem their wayward husbands.

Through thrift and prudence, they can raise the prosperity of their respective families. They can prepare excellent meals at home for the delectation of the whole family. They can show great warmth of hospitality to guests and relatives who visit their homes and earn thereby great goodwill and pride for their own families.

It is precisely for all the above reasons that our venerable elders have always exhorted even womenfolk to learn Sanskrit language. Our traditional scriptures and historical literature reveal that there were many women who were adept in a wide range of Vedantic subjects. In fact, religious instruction and sermons delivered by women can be far more persuasive and appealing to the mind than that delivered by menfolk. The reason is because there is sweetness and striking qualities of lucidity and conviction in what womenfolk teach us.

Therefore, let me address the womenfolk here: If all of you also come forward to learn and equip yourself with deep Vedantic knowledge, then you can all surely accomplish a lot of good for the whole community and society. You can exert great moral influence on the menfolk and your spouses, guard them from going astray in life and even help in reforming them if they fall prey to wicked ways.

In fact, in our scriptures, there are so many accounts of how it was women who indeed reformed the characters of men and transformed them into great men. It is to such virtuous women of sterling character that even very great and eminent men of the past in our country were fortunate to have been born. When we hail such great men in society for their lofty accomplishments, it is to their mothers and wives' support and influence that we should really ascribe so much of their greatness. You must all therefore commemorate such women of high character and caliber and try to emulate their example.

***

To conclude, let me give you an example to prove that the exhortation of a woman is indeed more efficacious, and indeed has a more lasting impact on the mind, than those delivered by a man.

Bhagavan (*purushan*) in his avatar as Krishna gave his sermon as the Bhagavath Gita. In the same manner, **Bhudevi**, the Consort of Bhagavan, in her avatar as **Sri Andal** delivered her sermon through the *Tiruppaavai*.

The lofty message of the Bhagavath Gita is not all that easily comprehensible to men. To the question *'What is Absolute Truth?'*, Krishna's answer in the Gita is simply this *"It is I, and it is none but I!"* ... but then never do we all understand what exactly Krishna meant to reveal about such Absolute Truth, do we? It is only with much effort and difficulty that we can determine what the truth is.

Turn now to the sermon in the verses of the *Tiruppaavai*. In a single line like many found in the hymn, such as "**naaraayanane namakke parai tharuvaan!**", we find so many truths expressed therein so clearly, and they reveal and truly illuminate for us the ultimate truth about the Almighty.

It is thus that I say to all womenfolk:

You, the beloved daughters of Goddess Mahalakshmi, are fully equipped to be competent teachers indeed for menfolk who are but the beloved sons of Bhagavan.... And this fact of you being superior to men in this regard is known commonly to everyone as **"nahi nindhaa nyaaya** (a rule of dialectic reasoning, according to which the praising of one person more than another, need not necessarily mean that the latter is any less praiseworthy than the former).

***

-16-
A Tiff Over Tiffin! ("*Saapaatu Sandai*")

Synopsis: *Mukkur Swamy had an impish, at times irreverent sense of humor which would often surface in a flash to lace his discourses and delight his readers and audience. This epistle is an example of how easily he could convey lofty matters of "siddhaantha" and "Vedanta" in a very light-hearted manner. From what begins as the recounting of a rather petty incident at a meal table involving two irate persons, Mukkur Swamy goes on to derive and convey important lessons on the theme of* **"aahaara shuddhi"** *– Food and Health.*

One day at a wedding banquet, an unseemly spat broke out between two men who were seated beside each other at the table. One of them had already finished his meal and wanted to leave the table to go to the washroom to rinse his hands; the other one was tardily and merrily savoring his meal unmindful of the other restless guest who then snapped at him impatiently:

*"Why don't you get a move on, you glutton? ("**saappaatu-raama**")!"*

The other fellow took umbrage immediately and retorted acerbically, "**Me a glutton!** And what about you then?! This morning at tiffin time didn't I see you tuck in fifteen **iddlies** (fluffy rice pancakes) for breakfast right here?!"

The exchange was enough to spark off next a very heated tiff between the two fellows.

A third man who was witness to the ugly quarrel tried to step in and cool things down but then the two irascible gentlemen turned on him and said, *"What the hell do you know here mister... mind your own business!"* and to which he retorted right back testily, *"Eh! Both you silly fellows! Unlike the two of you let me tell you I do know a thing or two about good manners at eating at a banquet!?"*

A very elderly, wise gentleman who was nearby and watching the nasty imbroglio between the three guests getting completely out of hand decided that he must intervene to put a stop to the squabble before it descended into something worse than mere verbal tiff.

"Oh, oh, hold it gentlemen!" he called out to the warring three....

"Gentlemen, please, why this unwarranted scuffle over eating?! Don't you all know that eating heartily and sumptuously is a virtue in life and that it leads to one's higher well-being?! Why do you quarrel over this matter? In fact, he who eats well and wisely is said to be spiritually advanced!"

Hearing the old man's words, all three fellows stopped quarreling and turned to him with astonished looks.... And so did other wedding hosts, guests and families who had gathered now around the spot to see what the commotion was all about.

The wise old man, with a mischievous smile and gleam in his eye, spoke, *"Why do you look at me with such astonishment?"*

The three fellows then sneered at him saying, *"What a ridiculous thing you say, Sir! Maybe you are only mocking at us?! How can what you say be true?!"*

The old man replied, *"No! What gain do I get by mocking you, Sirs?! What I say is fact and nothing but fact indeed!"*

When the old man said this, everyone who had gathered there around them were intrigued by his words. All the wedding hosts and guests then urged the old man to explain what he had meant to say and sat down at once in a large circle around him and entreated him to address them. Seeing a fairly large audience that had suddenly collected around him eagerly waiting for him to expatiate on what he had uttered to the three squabbling fellows; the wise old man was pleased to deliver an impromptu sermon to them all.

My dear friends, the primal cause of universal well-being is indeed nothing but Food. It is only a plenitude of good Food that can promote the progress of both individuals and of society.

However, such wellbeing and progress is possible only when first we are able to know what Food is good and what Food is bad for us. Only when we consume food which has been ordained by the sacred scriptures (saastra-s) will our innately good nature – i.e., "**sattva guna**" – manifest itself, get nourished and glow forth. Such "saatvic" nature nourished by good food will impel good divine thoughts and tendencies in us and which in turn will encourage us to tread the path of devotion to Bhagavaan. It will then be possible for us to be rid immediately of other evil tendencies and urges lurking within us. This is what is sought to be conveyed to us by the words of the **saastra** below"

"Aahaara shuddhow sattvashuddhi: sattvashuddhow dhruvaa smritihi: smriti lambhe sarva granthinaam vipramokshah:"

Thus, if a man consumes unwholesome and improper food, he only ends up being afflicted by "rajoguna" and "tamoguna" -- i.e., the propensities of unruly passion and degeneration -- and thereafter invariably falls into folly and misdeed and finally plunges into the abyss of a hell of his own creation.

First and foremost, amongst all kinds of food that is fit or unfit for consumption – and which will or will not land us in a hellish state of existence – which I am going to tell you about at length is Milk. If any of my explanations arouses doubt in your mind, please stop me for clarifications... I shall clear your doubts to the best of my ability.

1. The milk of animals that have hoofs without a natural cleft in them should not be consumed e.g., the milk of donkeys, horses etc.
2. Milk from an animal such as a cow which has more than two calves to suckle should not be consumed.
3. The milk of camels is unfit for consumption.
4. Milk that has been mixed with salt or yoghurt or butter-milk should not be consumed.

Someone in the audience interjected: *"How would milk ever get mixed with salt?!"*

The old man smiled and explained calmly, *"Suppose you were to mistakenly add salt to milk thinking it was a glass of buttermilk, and then you had realized your mistake? And suppose you then hastened to simply remove the salt crystals from the glass and then drank the milk? I am saying that should not be done".*

Another person in the audience raised another query: *"You say that milk mixed with butter-milk should not be consumed. How is that possible? Please explain clearly".*

The wise old man patiently responded: *"After boiling the milk what does one do with it to turn the same into buttermilk? One drops into the milk a small dollop of buttermilk to ferment it. That in effect is what is milk mixed with buttermilk. That milk which has not yet fermented fully to turn into curd or yoghurt should not be consumed. In fact, our elders who know the saastra intimately go further to say that such milk mixed with buttermilk should not be even seen by us until it fully ferments overnight as yoghurt. If you want to know more about such saastra, please meet me separately in person when you have the time and I will reveal it to you".*

Another one in the audience raised a further query rather incredulously: *"you said that the milk of donkeys, camels and horses should not be consumed. Who would ever imagine drinking the milk of such animals?! I don't know how you can imagine such a thing!"*

The old man replied: *"Why, haven't you ever heard of people administering donkey's milk to patients suffering from certain diseases and ailments? Similarly, the milk of camel and horses too are sometimes fed to patients suffering from rare diseases or conditions --- (sometimes in cases to boost the physical strength of extremely emaciated persons, for example). Also some people consume such milk purely as medication. All the same, even in such circumstances, there is no escaping the sin (**paapam**) arising out of consuming such milk and the requisite atonement or "**praayaschittham**" has to be performed for it. This matter has been well recorded in the ancient scriptural manuals of praayaschittam such as "**Hemaadri**", for example, and if one reads therein about the dire consequences of such sins going un-expiated, it is quite terrifying indeed'.*

***

The wise old man continued his impromptu discourse to the gathering:

5. The milk of a pregnant cow should not be consumed. This fact has been attested by some medical doctors too who say that such milk can cause diseases.
6. The milk of animals such as cows separated from their calves should not be consumed.
7. The milk from cows that have suckled calves other than its own calf should not be consumed.
8. If ever a man were to deceive a cow in any way, you can be sure, he will somehow someday be paid back with the same coin i.e., he will become the victim of deception under some circumstance or the other later in life and will come to no good at all. Which is why it is said that the milk of a cow that has been extracted by showing it merely a straw-stuffed effigy of its calf should not be consumed since such milk is the product of heinous deception of the mother cow.
9. Milk that has turned rancid should not be consumed. One needs no *saastra* to reveal to us that milk that turns rancid only because it carries some unknown pollutant or bacteria. To consume such milk is to consume such pollutant and suffer resulting disease.

One from the audience interjected at this point: *"Sir, but who would ever knowingly consume rancid milk which is distasteful?!"*

The old man replied: *"If milk has gone slightly rancid, it is not uncommon for chefs in the kitchen to add it to sweet porridge (**paayasam**) and other such sweetened beverages. If the milk becomes too rancid, then they may quietly add it to dishes like sweetened milk-stew (**therrattipaal**). Whatever may be the reasons for milk turning rancid, rancid milk is not good for consumption".*

10. Furthermore, the milk of cows that have been either painted or tattooed with the names and symbols or insignias of gods, spirits etc. should not be consumed.
11. Some owners cruelly brand their cows with hot-irons or tridents…. Their milk should not be consumed.

A member of the audience posed a query: *"If a cow were to be tattooed with figurines of goddess Lakshmi or the sacred Lotus flower… or has been branded with the sacred symbols of Vishnu such as the Sankham (divine* conch) and Chakram (divine discus) .... Can the milk of such cows be consumed"?

The wise man said: *"If milk from such a cow has been obtained by a person, then such a person can be regarded as having been bestowed with rewards and benediction for the virtuous deeds of his in past lives. Yes, of course, such a person can wholeheartedly accept such milk for consumption and its consumption will surely advance their spiritual progress".*

12. The **"Saandilya smriti"** clearly proscribes the consumption of milk from a cow in the following cases: (a) the animal's hind legs have not been tied together while milking it; (b) not even ten days have elapsed since the animal gave birth to its calf; (c) the animal has been milked at untimely hours, day or night; (d) cows whose fodder or feed has included unwholesome, unfit substances such as garlic etc.

13. The milk of wild goats, milk purchased from Brahmin households for a price, and milk stored in copper vessels should not be consumed.

***

I have taken pains at length to explicate all the above with regard to Milk alone because it happens to be a staple diet and I have singled it out as an example amongst all other Foods only to underscore the fact that Food can be good and bad, wholesome and unwholesome. And it is only our ancient scriptures --- the **"dharma saastra-s"** – that show us what is good and bad for us in the case of so many other varieties of food.

Our Achaarya **Swami Vedanta Desikan** has delved deep into such dharma-saastra-s, culled from and distilled their vast contents in one excellent work on dietary regimen titled **"aahaara niyamam**". In that work of his, there is one passage from which everything now that I have explained to you all about Milk, has been excerpted. Here I quote that passage (Paasuram 17 of Ahaara Niyamam) by way of concluding my talk:

"orukuLambi yirukanRi yotta kappaal uppudanpaal
mOrudanpaal maadhar thampaal karuvudaiya vaRRinpaal
kanRi laappaal maRukanRaaR kaRandhidumpaal thirindhi

dumpaal thirumagaLaar kaNavanalaath dheyvath thinpEr sinnamudai yavaRRinpaal semma Rippaal parivathilan^ thaNarvilaippaal sembi niRpaal theethaampaa livaiyanaitthum parugaap paalE.

MEANING: *Forbidden milk: Milk from one hoofed animals like horse or donkey, cow that has twin calf, or camel milk Salt added milk Milk from women Milk from pregnant cow Milk extracted with the help of calf that does not belong to the cow Milk from Cows that belong to temples Goat milk, milk bought from Brahmins Milk kept in copper vessels, rancid milk.*

Whatever I have explained above at length has been spoken pithily in the above single passage of Swami Desikan.

If only we could memorize the above "**paasuram**", we will always remain mindful of what kind of milk we consume. It will enable us to avoid the many types of milk that is bad and unfit for consumption. By simply avoiding the bad we can easily obtain a lot of good.

***

Thus ended the brief and impromptu talk delivered by the wise old man at the wedding banquet. Those hosts and guests who had listened to him in rapt attention applauded him finally in the end, "Sire, we are so grateful to you for the wealth of information you have given us! At the behest of His Holiness Srimad Azhagiyasingar this wedding is going to be conducted in the traditional way i.e. over the course of five days. We would very much appreciate it if on every single day you regale all of us as you have done today with many more such valuable guidance found in the scriptures".

The old wise man was given warm and affectionate hospitality and after which the assembly dispersed.

***

-17-
On Forbearance and Patience

Synopsis: *"There is one effective weapon in the world which if possessed enables Man to prevail over all enemies. That weapon is not made out of any metal, such as copper, silver, iron, steel or wood. Rather the weapon is fashioned using the human mind. And the weapon is called "kshamaa":* **Forbearance,** *also otherwise known as* **Patience** *("porumai"). If a man possesses this quality of forbearance/patience, then there is no antagonist in life who must be feared".*

क्षमा शस्त्रं करे यस्य दुर्जन: किं करिष्यति ।
अतृणे पतितो वह्नि: स्वयमेवोपशाम्यति ॥

"kshamaa shasthram karey yasya durjana: kim karishyathi I
athruNE patito vanhi: svayamevopashaamyathi II"

नरस्याभरणं रूपं रूपस्याभरणं गुण: ।
गुणस्याभरणं ज्ञानं ज्ञानस्याभरणं क्षमा ॥

"nasyaabharaNam roopam roopamyaabharaNam guNa: I
guNasyaabharaNam gnyaanam gnyaanasyaabharaNam kshamaa II"

क्षमा बलमशक्तानां शक्तानां भूषणं क्षमा ।
क्षमा वशीकृती लोके क्षमया किं न सिध्यति ॥

"Kshamaa balamashakhthaanaam shakthaanaam bhooshanam kshamaa I
Kshmaa vasheekruthee lOkE kshamayaa kim na siDhyathi II"

***

No man is born who does not make enemies and who then become the cause of much unhappiness in life. Therefore, serious thought must be given to how even when surrounded by enemies one can remain untroubled and happy. Is it possible to overcome all enmity through sheer physical strength? That may not be possible since our enemies may be much stronger than we and may easily subdue us. If we think that with the aid of weapons, say, like knives or swords etc., we may be able to prevail over our strong enemies, again, we might only end up discovering to our utter chagrin that by virtue of might which is superior to ours, our enemies actually are able to turn our own weapons against us. It is thus that men of the world often find it difficult to live peacefully with so many enemies around them.

However, there is one effective weapon in the world which if possessed enables one to prevail over all enemies. That weapon is not made of out of any metal, such as copper, silver, iron, steel or wood. Rather the weapon is fashioned using the human mind. And the weapon is called *"kshamaa"*: **Forbearance,** also otherwise known as **Patience** (*"porumai"*).

If a man possesses this quality of forbearance/patience, then there is no antagonist in life who must be feared. Adversaries and enemies may spite a man, harass him, mock or humiliate him, or even assault him, but if the man remains unperturbed and meets and resists all their attacks with this weapon called ***calm, patient Forbearance*** that he wields by hand, they will all ultimately realize the futility of their attempts to cow him down and, eventually, they will withdraw muttering to themselves, *"This fellow is a harmless, virtuous man... there's nothing to be gained by harassing him. Let's leave him alone"*.

Now, you may ask me: "Just a moment ago, you told us that this special weapon is to be *fashioned out of one's mind* and invoked mentally... And yet now you are saying this weapon is to be *wielded by hand*... How is one to understand what you say?" Let me then explain it all to you.

Forbearance of course is a quality possessed in the mind, but is it not necessary that it should be manifested too? An inward mental quality ought to be exhibited through external behavior, and that is why I say that *"kshamaa"* as a *mental weapon* has got be *wielded by hand*.

You may ask now how is one to express an inward, ethereal quality of the mind through outward physical gesture. I say that expression can be made by us through *the joining of the palms* with folded hands (i.e. the humble *'namaskaara'* or *"anjali mudra"*). That single gesture of ours denotes not only the absence of haughtiness in us but also that, instead, we possess the quality of enduring Patience (*'porumai'*) against which our adversaries soon find they really have no defense at all and hence find it best to retreat saying to themselves, *"poor man… he can harm no one… let us leave him alone"*.

An analogy will help understand this fact. Assume there is a piece of barren land in the wilderness where a wild fire breaks out. If the land is so completely barren that not even grass or weeds are found growing upon it, what happens? With nothing to feed upon and burn further, the wildfire by itself dies out and disappears, does it not? In the same way, when our enemies find nothing of arrogance or other such aggressive qualities in us, and instead they confront only the tranquil quality of *"kshamaa"* in us, realizing then that there is no fuel to inflame their enmity, they discover there is really no choice other than to quietly withdraw and fade away.

A profound thinker who has studied very deeply this human quality of Forbearance has explained it indeed very beautifully… (i.e. through the 3 *shloka*-s above).

There is no doubt that there is such a thing called natural beauty or what is known as *"physical attractiveness"* … in both man or woman… and it gets greatly enhanced by ornamentation. But can mere ornamentation by itself add to the beauty to either a man or a woman who is completely bereft of natural beauty or grace? Ornamentation in that case only makes the man look a bit simian. And as for the woman who, although endowed with no natural beauty, yet lavishly adorns herself with jewels, she only ends up looking like an overdressed old hag or a harridan of a monkey – and almost exactly as the old saying describes her: ….

'வ்ருத்தவாநரமுகீ விராஜதே'

"vruddhavaanaramukhee viraajathE".

Thus, wherever we find beauty not being naturally present in either man or woman, no amount of ornamentation is able to enhance or embellish his or her looks; and attempting to substitute natural beauty with ornamentation results only in enhanced ugliness. But when attractiveness and beauty are both naturally present in a man or a woman, there ornamentation certainly enhances their looks. So, one might therefore conclude that true ornamentation for either man or woman is nothing but *natural attractiveness* itself.

But even if one regards natural beauty of a woman or the attractiveness of a man as being an ornament by itself, it must be realized that there is yet another one which further embellishes such an ornament. You may wonder how on earth one ornament can be ornamented by yet another? It most certainly can. If a beautiful necklace is worn round a neck, wouldn't adding a nice sparkling little pendant to it make it look even more beautiful? Likewise, doesn't an ear-dangler or nose-ring dazzle more if its centerpiece is another brilliant studded gemstone? In a great assembly of scholars, is not often said of one who presides over it that it is his very presence that indeed adds greater luster to the gathering? In the same sort of way, it may be said that if *natural beauty* is an ornament for a human being, then such ornament is ornamented by yet another one which goes by the name of *"guNa"* --- human qualities or virtuous attributes.

Just think for a moment deeply about what happens when someone approaches a person because he is momentarily attracted by the other's striking handsomeness or beauty. But then he soon finds out that the person is full of haughtiness, airs, pretensions and snobbery… What happens then? All the physical attractiveness perceived earlier suddenly makes no impression at all! Similarly, let us imagine a father is looking for a suitable groom for his daughter. He gets carried away by the handsome mien of a young man. But then upon further inquiry into antecedents, the father discovers the young man has a reputation for ill-temper as quick as that of a choleric dog. Wouldn't the father then immediately shrink away from the handsome man? Would he not think to himself then, "*Thank God, good riddance, this chap is not for my daughter!*" So, it becomes very clear that it is only when *"guNa"* i.e., good and noble human qualities, reside together with physical beauty in man or woman that personality becomes truly attractive.

Now, there is also an ornament that adorns even *"guNa"* to make it even more lustrous. Do you know what it is? If you don't know, let me tell you about it.

We said that first there is natural beauty; then there is *"guNa"* that is ornament to such beauty. Now, there is yet one other ornament that adorns both. It is called *"gnyaana"* or knowledge ... i.e., knowledge about *"bhagavath vishayam"* or knowledge about *Bhagavaan*, the Almighty. A person who possesses no knowledge about *Bhagavaan* lives a life of utter waste and purposelessness. Therefore, we say, that he who possesses such knowledge indeed possesses the greatest of all ornaments in life.

We must know now too that even such knowledge called *"bhagavath vishayam"* stands ornamented by the quality called *"kshamaa"*. A man may possess knowledge of God but if he is bereft of the attribute called Forbearance then even such knowledge serves no purpose at all to him. If he has no *"kshamaa"* in his heart, he will find no disciples or followers to whom he can impart his great knowledge of God. A man known for his knowledge but known too for his lack of forbearance and patience thus will not be able to command the respect of fellowmen. Without *"kshamaa"* there can be no *"bhakthi yoga"* that can be put into effective practice; and when there is no such effective effort, no yogic benefits can be reaped either.

Where there is no forbearance in the heart, there Anger and Passions – **"*kaama-krodha*",** the two greatest enemies of Man, begin to breed easily and force him to go astray. The best weapon to use against these two mortal enemies of Man is *"kshamaa"* indeed. With forbearance one conquers *"kaama-krodha"* and attains *"brahma-gnyaanam"*, the knowledge of the soul. It is with such knowledge of the soul that one then begins to gain knowledge of the yoga called *Bhakthi* which in turn leads to knowledge of *Mukthi*, or eternal Liberation --- the liberation that is granted by the grace of the Almighty.

Considering all the above, therefore, it may be said that *"kshamaa"*, Forbearance indeed is the most priceless ornament for a human soul.

This is what as profound truth has been revealed to us so beautifully by the wise man who spoke through the *shlokas* (quoted at the beginning).

If one were to read and re-read the second *"shloka"* to understand its message, a doubt may arise in the mind.

It is all well to say that *"guNa"* is ornamentation for physical attractiveness, *"bhagavath-vishaya gnyaana"* is ornament for *"gunA"*, and in turn for such *"gnyaana"* the true ornament is *"kshamaa"* ... and all that. But then we might ask ourselves what happens to the case of men and women who, in the very first place, possess no physical features of any distinction worth ornamenting at all? It is utter folly to think that simply with good looks and an attractive physique one can easily gain everything else one desires in life. Let us examine the matter a little more closely.

A man may be very handsome but then he happens to be a dumb. Will any father desire a groom who is a dumb for his daughter? A young man looks most attractive but is known to be rebellious wastrel... Will such a man be a desirable groom for one's daughter? Or, a young man is dashingly handsome but then knowing him to be one who keeps constant company with friends who are habitual drunkards and carousing with them... would any father seek him as a groom for a dear daughter?

And vice versa, it is the same case with beautiful young nubile maidens too. Their physical attractiveness alone will not be desired unless it is accompanied by the other virtues too that are mentioned.

You may now ask me: *"A person is not physically attractive at all, but is found to have all the other virtuous "guNa" you mention. Is that acceptable?"* My answer is yes, it is indeed acceptable.

It is *"guNa"* that is of prime importance. If it is accompanied by attractive physical attractiveness (*"roopam"*), of course, that would be ideal; but if one of them has got to be absent, then rather, better it should be *"roopam"* than *"guNa"*. *"Guna"* can be compared to a rough gold-ingot while *"roopam"* can be likened to sweet-smelling perfume. A perfumed ingot (if ever there was one) might of course be most desired but then without the sweet scent of perfume, is the value or preciousness of the ingot going to be any the less? The value of "*kshamaa*" as a "*guNa*", likewise, is thus incomparable and it just cannot be overstressed.

In the third *shloka* quoted, the wise man who inquired into the quality of "*kshamaa*" gives us a unique insight into it which all of must really appreciate.

க்ஷமா பலம் அஸக்தானாம் ....

"*kshamaa balam asakthaanaam*" ... For one who lacks strength and who yet wishes to thrive in life, he or she can find source of great strength in "*kshamaa*".

ஸக்தானாம் பூஷணம் க்ஷமா .....

"*sakthaanaam bhooshanam kshamaa*" ... For one who is able to achieve what he desires in life through pluck and resourcefulness, if he were to possess "*kshamaa*" too, it then greatly enhances his stature. People look upon such a person and say admiringly, "*How enterprising this person is and yet how forbearing, calm and patient he is while going about his work!*"

க்ஷமா வசீக்ருதி: லோகே ....

"*kshamaa vaseekruthee: lOkE*" .... It is through the power of one's calm forbearance and patience alone, besides other virtues, that one is able to easily win the affections of one's fellowmen. There was this son-in-law who was continually heaping scorn upon his father-in-law for all manner of reasons. But the father-in-law patiently ignored his son-in-law's deprecations. Instead of reacting in kind the man went about speaking in glowing terms to others in the family about how praiseworthy was his son-in-law. After a while, the son-in-law's antipathy towards the father-in-law began to diminish by itself and he came to his senses on his own! This works the other way too, as we sometimes see, when a son-in-law showing great forbearance in dealing with a rather cantankerous father-in-law is gradually able to bring about a change of heart in the latter, who then later showers affection upon a son-in-law whose praises he cannot sing enough.

There is also this example of an employer who thinks nothing of abusing and taking to task severely his servant for every little lapse in doing his duties. But the servant is a man of great forbearance and so instead of returning abuse for abuse, he gently tells his boss, *"Sir, whenever you abuse me like this you do remind me of my own father who, when I was young, used to similarly take me to task very harshly for any little transgress of mine"*. The following day, the employer had a change of heart... and for all we know he might well even perhaps have rewarded the poor servant out of soft sympathy for him!

We know that mothers out of the great love they have for their daughters never make too much ado about the faults and foibles of their daughters. Such mothers when they show the same forbearance and patience towards their daughters-in-law when they are found guilty of any fault, by showing such kindness and *"kshamaa"*, instantly earn the latter's affections manifold.

There is another little story about this poor but philanthropic-minded person who used to go around town to homes, ever so frequently beseeching donations from wealthy persons and their families to enable him to organize religious charity-banquets (*'thadhi-aaraadanam'*) for scholar-*vidwaans* as well as for the poor and destitute.

One such wealthy person to whom the person had gone home to make his humble appeal, turned on him with great annoyance and yelled at him, *"Don't you have any other useful work to do other than going around like a busybody pestering everybody? Why don't you do some real hard work to earn a living ... maybe serve as a porter lifting sacks of grain in a farm or warehouse?"*

To this rude outburst the man did not react as one might have expected. He was a man of great forbearance and calmly, without showing any trace of anger, he replied to the wealthy man:

"Sire, what else am I to do to help my own cause? The Almighty seems to have ordained that I should go about in life only as I do now. When I go around town beseeching donations, many times have I had to bear the brunt of unkind words similar to yours thrown at me... in fact, I have had to hear and bear much worse abuse hurled. But having heard such rude words so often I have now actually become inured to them. Sire, but this is exactly how for the last ten years I have gone about organizing "thadhi-aaraadanam" events, thanks to the donations of generous people of this town. I have been

able to conduct on occasions even great feasts such as the ceremonial *"7-day aaraadanam"* where hundreds of people are served. Each day after the last of the honored guests at the festive feast, fully gratified, leaves, I then feed myself with whatever food is there as leftover. You might say, Sire that it is all those leftovers upon which I have fed myself all these years which has turned my nature into the thick-skinned one I now possess and which knows no shame, no compunction and no squeamishness in continuing to do what I do in life. But then good Sire, I do understand very well why you are so annoyed and vexed with me and with my appeal too. Sire, it does not matter if you do not oblige me this time... There is always next time when I can count upon your generosity. But meanwhile, Sire, may I at least appeal to you to direct me now to any other wealthy donor in this town you might know well, and who might perhaps favor me with charity at this present time?"

When the wealthy man had heard the above outpouring, he felt duly chastened and regretted immediately the churlishness he had earlier shown the man who had come looking simply for some help. To make amends he told him, *"Look here, man, please don't get offended by my hasty words!"* And then he duly proceeded to make a handsome donation for the *"thadhi-aaraadanam"* that even exceeded the latter's expectations.

Next, let us look at the expression in the *shloka* that says:

"kshamayaa kim na siddhyathi?"

Through the practice of Forbearance, even the impossible becomes possible to achieve... In other words, *"kshamaa"* has the power to break down all barriers of communication and can bring about unity of very wholesome feelings amongst Mankind.

There was this man who was a wife-beater. He abused and harassed her in every reprehensible sort of ways possible. He kept her half-starved; let her remain in tattered, shabby clothes; gave her nothing to wear as decent jewelry... not even a simple ear-stud... and the only *"jewels"* she received were the daily, cruel body-blows he dealt her! All the physical and psychological abuse she received at his hands, the wife bore it all with extraordinary forbearance and continued serving her husband with uncomplaining, unstinted, untiring faithfulness. But he would neither acknowledge nor appreciate her for her loyalty to him. And even in the moments of intimate conjugality which he enjoyed with her, he remained sadistic towards her. On the other hand, she remained submissive, telling herself that she ought to be content and grateful that despite all the abuse he heaped on her, at least he had not thrown her out of home and left her helpless on the streets.

To such an unhappy couple, in time was born a bonny baby-boy who soon became the father's darling and apple of the eye. He was so besotted with the baby that he would spend hours with the child fondling and playing with it. One day while enjoying the pleasure of playing with his little son, he suddenly observed that while the baby always kept giggling at him and giving him broad, beaming but seemingly derisive grins, he did not do so while looking at his mother. This made the man think that the baby in some inexplicable way was mocking him with its grins as if to wordlessly convey to him this:

"You fool! You are besotted with me so much that you shower me with cuddles, kisses and fondles! It's because you think of me as being so precious to you. But then why are you not able to understand and realize that she, your wife, who it is who has begotten me ought to be much more precious than I and therefore that much more worthy of your love and affection?"

From that moment onwards, every time the baby grinned at him, the more it began to dawn on him that his wife was indeed the true cause of his happiness in life, being the mother of his beloved child. Gradually, the handiwork of God began to have its effect on the man's soul and soon thereafter the relationship between the couple changed for the good, forever. Forbearance began to work its magic and what once had seemed a relationship impossible to repair and restore to normal, happy conjugality, was achieved easily by the Grace of God!

Similar such instances abound in the world. There are, likewise, many instances known to me between *Acharyas* and their disciples where hopelessly dysfunctional relations were miraculously restored to a state of wholesome goodness thanks to this peerless quality called "*kshamaa*".

There is one other very important matter I must hasten to share with all of you and let me do it now.

Men and women, and their families too, whom we come across in this world, we often find them to be undergoing great trials, tribulations and sorrows in life. They might have suffered setbacks of all manner and faced much humiliation. They might have suffered painful, grievous bereavement – through loss of near and dear ones like, say, a child, a grandchild, a spouse even. Or else, they might have suffered a great loss of property and wealth. They could have been struck down otherwise by severe disease and illness too. They might have been orphaned even from a very young age…

There are so many such innumerable sufferings that people are known to have the misfortune to experience in the course of life. Even in the midst of all such grievous mishaps in life, it must be remembered by all of us that we should never let the quality of Forbearance, *"kshamaa"*, desert us. If we do so, then it would be easy in such moments of adversity for us to fall into wretchedly cursing our fate and bitterly blaming God for all the suffering we undergo. We must never under any circumstances allow such a reaction from ourselves even if it seems to be almost natural or reflexive. The God who is ever solicitous of our wellbeing should never be accursed like that by us out of sheer despair or under any other circumstance. Instead, we must only tell ourselves that *"All the misery and grief I am experiencing now is just dessert for my sins of either committed in this lifetime or my previous ones"*. It never behooves Man to cast aspersion upon the Divine under any circumstance for any reason whatsoever.

One should never entertain even a single disparaging thought towards the ever compassionate Almighty nor ever utter even a single critical word while speaking to others about Him. I have come across persons spewing words of scorn upon *Bhagavaan* on occasions such as when a parent bewails a son of his who has just failed in an examination! *"Oh, how cruel is Bhagavaan to let my son fail like this?!"* they moan. That is wrong. Even though it is natural human tendency to blame the Almighty for one's plight, one should resist it. Instead, one must say, *"My son's failure is perhaps a way for me to atone for some past sin or transgression of mine…The fault lies not with God but in me."*

When Bhagavaan sees that we truly and solely blame ourselves and all our own transgressions for the fate we have come to suffer, and that we do not shift it all upon Him, then God's attitude towards us is clearly described in these words spoken by himself:

तं प्रसादं करिष्यामि देवैरपि सुदुर्लभम् ।

"tam prasaadam karishyaami devairapi sudurlabham" I

i.e., *My blessings that I rarely bestow upon even the 'devas', the gods, I shall surely shower upon such a person!*

In this context we must remember with how much remarkable forbearance Sita (of the Ramayana), even while enduring the excruciating misery of solitude and imprisonment in the Ashokavana in Lanka, said this silently to herself about the cause of her own pitiable self:

ममैव दुष्कृतं किंचिन्महदस्ति न संशयः ।

"The cause for my miseries is none else but my own past transgressions"

We are fated by divine order to undergo the punishments that we deserve for our lapses, our sins of omissions and commission. But by being so punished, as so many of our wise *Acharyas* have said before, our spirits get cleansed of impurities and all the taint of sin. It is for this reason that even in the face of mortal adversity we must never think or speak disparagingly of *Bhagavaan*. And when we enjoy the fortunes of life, we should, at the same time, sincerely feel that it is all due to the Grace of the Almighty.

At all times through a man's life, if he clings firmly to this quality of forbearance, *"kshamaa"*, if he were to deserve to be consigned to hell even because of his many sins, wittingly and unwittingly done, it is enough if he were to humbly join his palms together with folded arms… Bhagavaan will simply condone all sins, protect him from hell, and pave the way for him to attain the higher, happier worlds of the heavens. He who knows how to humbly join his palms together to symbolize the great quality of *"kshamaa"* within his heart, soon comes to realize that the simple act, by itself, is enough to elevate him to states of heavenly bliss and divine grace.

***

-18-
"*Daana Mahimai*": Charity's Value

Synopsis: *The idea of Charity in Vedanta Ethics is a very unique one and quite distinct from the popular sense in which it is known throughout the world in other religions. Sri Mukkur Azhagiyasingar in this "arul mozhi" expatiates on what is true "daana" or Charity in the Vedantic sense.*

Of all the gifts of life that we are blessed with by Bhagavan, only a certain few may be given away by us in charity or donations (*daanam*). Wealth, Foodgrain, Land, Cattle, Raiment, Rice, Water, Buttermilk, Fruits *etc.* are a few examples of such donations.

Charity is said to be of 3 types: Saatvika, Rajasa and Tamasa.

Examples of *Saatvika Daanam* can be said to be the following: It is being charitably disposed towards even those from whom one has never once received any favour of any kind; out of pure humanitarian feelings, extending charity to a person who is deserves it in his hour of need; donating anything out of a sense of genuine care and commitment; and giving with a humble sense of godliness.

Examples of *Raajasa Daanam* can be said to be the following cases: "If I donate something now to this fellow, maybe at a later time I will possibly be able to get something equally valuable if not more precious from him in return?"; "If I donate now to this cause, I know it will later surely yield the benefit I desire"; "What I give away in charity now is anyway of little use or value to me… I lose nothing from parting with it as a donation?"

Examples of *Taamasa Daanam* can be said to be the following cases: Charity given to men of low, dissolute character and to atheists; charity given for unworthy causes tainted by moral turpitude; charity given on wholly inappropriate occasions; Gifting of objects that are not worthy to be given as charity; Charity given arrogantly or in a spirit of condescension; Charity given with the intention to belittle or humiliate the receiver... and so on.

***

The pious elder of a family once made up his mind, determined to give away in charity the household sacred *"Saalagraama"* (ammonite fossil stones symbolic of Lord Vishnu) to none other than a certain relative or near kin. He would not brook any suggestion otherwise. So, very adamantly, the *Saalagraama* stone meant for worship as verily Vishnu's form residing in the house as *"archa murthy"* or sacred idol, for well over the lifetime of two previous generations of the family was given away by the family-elder as *daanam* unto another home without proper or prior due diligence...

Only Lord Vishnu who had been residing within such a *"saalagraama"* in the house truly knew the piteous circumstances he had had to endure all those years... He had been kept in a perennial state of malnourishment if not total starvation while being kept in the custody of the donor's household-shrine! As can be well imagined, the Almighty was actually very happy at the prospect of a change of residence! *Who knows?!...*

Alas, the change of residence for the Bhagavan Vishnu as a *"saalagraama archa-murthy"* turned out, however, to be case of moving from the frying pan into the fire! The person who had received the *"saalagraama daanam"* turned out to be an even worse host than the donor! This man was addicted to sniffing tobacco snuff-powder every now and then throughout the day. While receiving the *"saalagraama"* stone as *"daanam"*, the man knowing nothing about its sanctity, nonchalantly wrapped-up Bhagavan inside the folds of his handkerchief – the very same piece of a rag that he was using to pick his own dirty nose to clean it of traces or particles of snuff-powder! It doesn't need much effort of imagination to understand, on our part, what a real, unfortunate predicament our Bhagavan Vishnu had landed himself into! After all, how could our poor Bhagavan ever have known anything called *"substance-addiction"*?! Needless to say, the snuff-sniffing man too hardly knew what grave sin he had committed.

So, the long and short of the story is this: This sort of charity is "*daanam*" indeed but since it is given with mindless fecklessness it turns out to be exactly what is "*taamasa daanam*".

***

Quite similarly, there are also within some families you may all know, a father who hell-bent on doing "*go-daanam*" – the gifting of cows or cattle -- to none else than his son. The receiver of "*go-daanam*", however, would happen to be a pucca business-minded person... say, a dairy wholesale milk-vendor. For him milking cows was nothing but means for milking ever more profits! So, undoubtedly, such "*daanam*" too is nothing but "*taamasa daanam*".

Further, there are also some people who pride themselves in doing "*bhoomi-daanam*" – i.e., gifting landholdings to some near kith or kin. Here, the undeserving receiver happens to be a race-horse punter! The promptly pawns away the land received as gift, raises loans and simply loses all the money away on betting at the races upon *horse number 7*! Such kind of "*daanam*" is yet another instance of "*taamasa daanam*".

The gift of one's daughter hand in holy matrimony is known as "*kannika daanam*". If out of pecuniary considerations alone, a greedy father was to get his young girl gifted away in such "*kannika daanam*" to a groom who in age is way far above hers, then that too is "*taamasa daanam*". Or else, if such marriage is arranged with a groom who is known to be afflicted with some chronic disease, then such "*kanyaka daanam*" too qualifies as "*taamasa daanam*". Why, it goes without saying too that the same applies to a father marrying his young daughter off to a groom knowing fully well that the fellow does not possess robust health nor is he of good character.

It becomes possible thus for one to get to know many more such illustrations of misguided and utterly inappropriate acts of charity by heeding the guidance and counsel of wise elders. Before proceeding to donate in charity one therefore must exercise a bit of caution and responsibility, consult wise elders and then follow their advice.

Generally speaking, it is quite safe to give wholeheartedly in charity as far as possible only to those who are steeped in poverty, or who are weighed down by the heavy burden of having to provide for their large families; and to also give alms to those who are of good character and God-fearing.

***

Out of all acts of charity, the one known as *"anna daanam"* i.e., the giving of food as alms to the hungry and malnourished, is considered to be the best and most virtuous.

Any man suffering from the pangs of constant hunger, as we all know, is incapable of survival. If food is gifted to him, he survives and recovers. With such recovery, he regains strength. When strength is gained, it becomes possible again for him to strive hard in life to earn a livelihood… i.e., to do what is called *"tapas"*. Long and hard striving in life leads then gradually to great mental resolve in pursuing noble goals in life. This resolve is known as *"shraddha"*.

Great *"shraddha"* results in the maturing and blossoming of *"buddhi"* i.e., the power of intellect and discriminative wisdom. Such *"buddhi"* soon awakens spiritual yearning for Bhagavan and an ardent desire to pursue and realize him. With such spiritual awakening arrives a great sense of mental fulfilment. When the mind experiences such fulfilment, it begets great serenity … *manas shaanthi*. Such *"shaanthi"* then ensures that all other mental afflictions and infirmities are destroyed. That state of mind renders the man fit and ready to walk along the path of *"karma yoga"*. The path then leads next to the dawn of what is called *"smriti"* i.e., the gateway of *"gnyaana yoga"* walking through which a man's true self gets revealed – *Atma-gnyaanam*. It is then that he is also rendered fit to experience *"vignyaanam"*, a higher order of awareness which empowers and enables him to journey forth on the path of *"bhakti yoga"*. That journey then finally reaches its destination: the knowledge of *Brahman, the very acme of bliss surpassing all other!*

The above process has been revealed to us by the Vedas. It establishes the truth that he who out of charity gives *"anna daanam"* to any man suffering from hunger-pangs, actually paves the way for the unfortunate soul to realize its own full spiritual potential and destiny! It is for this reason that charity in the form of *"anna daanam"* is held in such high esteem in our scriptures and our culture and it has been explained here in very dramatic sequential process only to drive home precisely that point. The inner significance and deeper verities of this subject can be learned further by delving deeper into the relevant Vedic scriptures.

***

A few important points that must be observed:

Once a donor has earmarked a gift to be given in charity to a certain person, thereafter it should never under any circumstance be given to any other person. However, if the former happens to decline the donation, then there is no bar to the gift being given to the latter.

Sharing knowledge with others or imparting it to those who seek such knowledge is called *"vidya daanam"* and it is one of the noblest forms of charity. However, he who gives *"vidya daanam"* should have no expectation of gaining from it any great fame, profit or praise. Those who are recipients of such generous *"vidya daanam"* however should be aware that if the knowledge so acquired is to turn out to be valuable or useful to them in any way, then they must not fail to duly compensate the one who freely gave such *"daanam"*. The recompense could be through some token of gratitude expressed in any material form that is both befitting and affordable. Other recipients with no adequate means to afford such material compensation for the donor of *"vidya daanam"*, may then simply at least wish the donor well with this sincere and heartfelt prayer: *"May this person who gave me so much knowledge be always blessed with all goodness in life!"*. There is no need in such a case for other means of expressing gratitude to the giver of *"vidya daanam"*.

"Should I, if the occasion demanded it, be willing to give in charity to persons I know are inimical or ill-disposed towards me?" Some people might answer such a question with a resounding *"No!"*. However, the Veda demurs and insists that if such persons happen to be of good character, then they should not be denied gifts of charity…. *"daane bhavanthi dishantha: mitraa: …"* (Please note that the order of words of this famous Veda *"vaakya"* (aphorism) quoted has been slightly changed by me only for the sake of emphasis).

The gift of *"anna daanam"* to hungry people or destitute may be given to one and all irrespective of creed or caste, especially if they happen to be unfortunate victims of fire-accidents and have lost their homes and all possessions. All kinds of charitable aid and support– with the exception of *"kannika daanam"* – may be extended to people in such dire situations. All such acts of charity are to be regarded as lending a helping a hand to unfortunate fellowmen in times of crisis.

In time, even *"taamasa daanam"* does yield some *"punnya phalan"* (fruits of virtue) for the charitable donor. But such *"phalan"* is bound to be far less than that which *"raajasa daanam"* bears fruit. Surpassing all other *"phalan"* yielded by all other kinds of *"daanam"* is however only that which is the fruition of *"saatvika daanam"*.

***

A man with a family to provide for in life should never bequeath all of his wealth to charitable causes without first ensuring that he will leave behind for his offspring adequate endowments with which to live with a modicum of comfort in their own lives. If he, on the other hand, deprives his children of their inheritance by leaving everything in his will to charity, then he is guilty of sin.

Let us take next the instance of a man who has no offspring other than a young nubile daughter. He chooses not to give the girl away as bride in the sacred act of *"kannika daanam"* and instead decides to keep the unmarried maiden at home out of a misplaced sense of possessiveness. He thinks to himself, *"After all, what is wrong if I keep her at home since she happens to by my only daughter? Where is the need for me to gift her away in marriage to anyone else? Whatever wealth I possess is anyway going to, after all eventually, be her very own, is it not?"* The *"sastra"* condemns such a man as a *"maha paapi"*, a sinner of the worst order. It is the bounden duty of every father to give away his daughter in marriage as *"kannika daanam"* to a suitable groom coming from a family with a different *"gotra"* or genetic lineage. (Those of you who happen to be fathers of sole daughters should not take offence if you feel I am overstressing this truth. It is the good that this question has arisen and I have dealt with it exactly as I know it ought to be…).

Many other aspects of *"daanam"*, and several other fine nuances of how charity is to be given, one should be able to find and learn from the pages of quite a few *"Nrsimha Priya"* magazine-issues where many other learned scholars have expatiated upon the subject too.

***

It is possible that one may feel urged to do charity after having heard about similar good deeds done by someone else; or else, after having seen someone else do good; or perhaps after being persuaded to support, endorse a certain charitable work; or else oneself undertaking on one's own initiative such charitable work. The fruits or *"phalan"* of all charity acts as described in the foregoing are actually yield granted by none other than Bhagavan himself in the proportion that each such deed of charity deserves. This truth must be well and thoroughly appreciated. One should never, instead, engage in *"daanam"* thinking *"It is I who am the principal donor in this act of charity"*. Nor should one think, *"This act of charity of mine will surely return to me the desired benefit, some well-deserved "phalan""*. On the contrary, the thought-process should be as follows:

"Nothing I possess is really mine. Bhagavan is the true owner. It is he who has endowed me with all these possessions and wealth. It is he who decides how much of whatever I possess must be given away in charity to whom or to what causes... I am merely Bhagavan's agent. It is only in that capacity as agent, and that too at his command, that I have been enabled and mandated to give away whatever is at my disposal to worthy causes -- donations to elderly citizens, construction of temples and temple-ponds, feeding the poor and providing relief to them from poverty and suffering etc."

When one engages in charity with such a humble attitude of mere agency rather than overlordship, then Bhagavan is pleased to bless him or her with the fruits or *"phalan"* of charity that even exceeds what is ordinarily deserved. Such divine blessings enable one to mature in wisdom (*buddhi*), advance spiritually and ultimately attain everlasting experience of bliss.

***

To illustrate further all that has been said above, our wise elders are often wont to narrate a short-story which I must recount here. The title of the story is "The Broomstick".

There lived a very wealthy man in a town who people of the town, behind his back, called him *"the broomstick"! Do you know why?*

What does a broom do? It sweeps up all grain strewn and scattered everywhere upon the ground and collects them all into a heap. Although the broom gathers up all that grain, the fact remains that the grain so scooped up is hardly of any use to it – the broomstick cannot feed or feast upon grains collected, can it? …

Likewise, this man too was known to accumulate wealth but hardly ever intended to enjoy it any sort of way. Every day it was a habit of his to open the vault where he kept his stash of riches, gaze at it and be overcome with emotion and become tearful. *Can you imagine why?*

He used to shed tears over the prospect that after his death, since he had no heir to survive him, all his rich estate would probably only land up in the hands of some unknown stranger! The man thus would wistfully think to himself, *"All these riches I have worked so hard in life to acquire and accumulate, alas, is going to be enjoyed by some unknown fellows!"* and then heave a huge sigh of sadness and shed copious, maudlin tears!

This man's miserliness knew no bounds. He was a born miser! Do you know how he went about buying vegetables from the market to take home to his wife in the kitchen?

In the marketplace at the street-corner was kept a large garbage-skip into which the vendors at the end of the day, used to dump all the merchandise of their left-over stock of vegetables that had gone rotten or unsaleable. This wealthy man under cover of darkness, would later unobtrusively steal up to the street-corner and forage inside the garbage-skip for such rotten, discarded vegetables. He would then fill everything he could so collect inside a bag and secretly take it home!

At home, he would take all the rotten vegetables out, peel out parts of them that gone wholly rotten, salvage the rest he thought was good enough to be edible, and handed it over to his wife, ordering her to use it for cooking meals the following day!

Now, the poor lady of the house was never able to detect the rotten state of the vegetables her husband brought home to her for her for the simple reason she had no clue where it came from. She also had no awareness at all of what the difference was between quality and rotten vegetables since she had never before had any occasion to set sight on fresh vegetables. *Why so?* Because she rarely ever stepped out of the four walls of her house to know anything about marketplaces or vegetables!

The reason why the man's good wife never stepped out of home was because the poor lady was clothed always in ragged sarees... Her wardrobe consisted of only torn and ragged sarees barely sufficient to drape around herself to even conceal her modesty. How could she then ever venture out in those shabby clothes?

It is truly shameful pity how even today in some of our homes in our communities, our otherwise so very intelligent womenfolk -- like the wife of the wretched miser—are often ill-treated. They are forced to undergo unspeakable humiliation and suffering at hands of uncaring husbands such as this miserly man of this story.

Usually, in such pathetic cases, even if the lady of the house might have no other choice but to wear only such ragged workaday clothes while going about her daily household chores, she would nonetheless have carefully kept aside in safekeeping at least one saree in fairly good condition, anticipating that she would be able to wear it for special family or social occasions such as an important wedding event. Now, although such grand weddings, as is wonted custom, get celebrated over the course of 5 continuous days, this poor lady wearing the one and only fine saree she had in her possession would not dare stay for the wedding festivities beyond a single day... *Why?!* For fear that after being seen in one saree on the first day of the wedding, it would be very embarrassing for her to be seen by wedding-guests wearing again the very same one every other day following! So, to avoid such embarrassment, the poor lady would gracefully excuse herself from the wedding festivities soon after the first day ended and return home, and denied herself the pleasure of joining in the gaiety of the rest of the family...

The poor wife of the miserly man of our story, alas, did not possess even one such saree in good condition. If ever she gathered up courage to ask him for even just a small piece of jewellery, he would mock at her, *"Why do you need jewellery? To what purpose? Only to please* me, is it not? Let me tell you then that even if you are bereft of any jewellery, you still do look pleasing enough to my eyes! So where then is any need for you to wear any jewellery?"

He would find such rude and crude ways to dismiss her and would never indulge her little womanly fancy for a piece of jewellery. It was such a miserable existence that this poor lady, always trembling with fear of being humiliated, had to endure domestic life with her miserly, surly husband. It was so much like cohabiting with an evil demon – a "*brahmaraakshasa*" -- under the same roof!

***

The poor woman, what could she do? She almost half-starved her way through life while the coerced frugality of her existence, on the other hand, on the other hand, only helped enrich her husband's coffers evermore. And by simply watching his accumulating wealth swell day after day, the miserly pervert of a man shed even more copious tears bemoaning to himself, *"Oh, these riches are all fine, but alas, I cannot bear to think that at the end of my lifetime, it will all only land up in someone else's hands! Oh, how pitiable am I!"* The man still did not care to lift even a finger at any time to give even one bit of his growing riches for any charitable purpose, to help anyone less fortunate than him.

Despite knowing him to be an absolute miser and misanthrope, sometimes on occasion, a few people did knock on his door seeking alms. He at once used to turn them all away without parting with a single dime out of his pocket!

That this man was an incorrigible miser came to be only too well known in his community. Nonetheless it did not dissuade some persons from still keep calling on him now and then at his home beseeching him for charity. The reason why was that, quite interestingly, they found they did not eventually have to return empty-handed at all! Which is why many persons continued to make a beeline to his house in expectation of the fortuitous gain they hoped would result from their visit.

How were such expectations met? That is yet another interesting part of this short-story….

***

On the very same street, a few blocks away from where he resided, there lived another very wealthy man in a large mansion. This other gentleman was known to be not only extremely wealthy but also very large-hearted and who never turned away anyone who came looking for alms or support from him. In fact, it was said of him that as a benefactor he was no less charitable than even the legendary Karna of the epic *Mahabharatha*! So well-known and appreciated by the community was the philanthropic good-naturedness of this other wealthy man on the street.

The miserly man of wealth was consumed with great envy and ill-will he felt towards the other wealthy neighbour. He could never tolerate his presence. He deeply resented the rival both for his greater wealth as well as for the enormous goodwill he enjoyed within the community as an extremely charitable person. Thus, he was always secretly plotting within his heart some way to discredit or defame the other man and to have him driven out of town for good, on some pretext or the other...

It was out of such vicious envy and ill-will that whenever persons turned up at his doorstep with appeal for alms, the miser would at once refuse to give anything by way of charity but instead he would take them by hand, point them out in the direction of the mansion of the other wealthy man and then say to them:

"Hey, you fellows, do you see yonder that big mansion? There lives a very wealthy man. Go to him now and make your appeal for alms to him... He might ask you then if you also visited me and inquire about how much it was that I gave you as my donation. Tell that man that I gave you each the handsome sum of Rs. 250/-. Don't baulk now even if you have to speak untruth... It will fetch you good returns in the end, for that man will only then want to give you even more money thinking he must outdo me in charity! Go now, and make your way to that man's house and seek alms for yourselves there. Begone from here for I shall not give you a farthing!"

On hearing what the miserly man told them, the persons who came asking for alms, would shudder at the distastefulness of his suggestion to go and speak untruth to the other wealthy man and to try manipulating him into giving them alms. Gently remonstrating, they would instead turn then to the miser and make another sort of polite appeal to his sense of generosity:

"Sir, without at all receiving Rs.250/- from you, how can go and tell the other gentleman that we did receive it? It would be blatant deception on our part, wouldn't it? On the other hand, if we did receive from you, let's say, at least something -- why anything at all -- that perhaps could be equivalent to the measure of 250 ... say for instance, at least a fistful of paddy which might after all well contain 250 seeds of grain.... What we would then tell the other wealthy gentleman was that we received 250 pieces from you and that then would not be an utter lie. So, now Sir, we beg you.... Please at least give us each a handful of paddy-seeds, if not Rs. 250/-, that we can take with us!"

Hearing this, the wretched miser would retort: *"What?! Give you paddy?! No way! You may as well ask me to give up my life!"*

"Then Sir, if not paddy, couldn't you please be good enough to at least spare us 250 pieces of tamarind-stalks? We will gratefully accept it from you?"

On hearing this, the wealthy miser exploded: *"What?! How do you expect me to give you tamarind-stalks from my own kitchen when I already have set them aside for my use? They are going to be used for cooking sauce for my ritual-meal this new moon day (amavaasai)?! If I were to give it all away to you fellows, what will I do? Never! So, begone now at once! You will get nothing from me! Do as I tell you and go to that other wealthy man over there and beg for his beneficence in the way I have told you to!"*

It was in such an unseemly and haughty manner that the miser used to similarly turn away any person that came home to him humbly asking for alms and rudely directed him to the other wealthy man's house on the street, for whom he harboured nothing but evil feelings.

***

One day, a very wise scholar, a *"vidwan"* turned up at the miser's house seeking alms. He too was similarly treated so shabbily – the wealthy miser pointed out to him the home of the other wealthy man and asked him to go try his luck there.

The *vidwan* gently demurred at the unseemly suggestion. He took the liberty of even counselling the miser against carrying out such misdemeanour. The man however shot back at the *vidwan*:

"Hey *vidwan*, if you were now to somehow trick me into giving Rs.10/- as alms, later at some time future in my hour of dire need, are you going to rush to my succour? Not a chance! You won't be seen anywhere near me! In that moment of need, it is my money, not you, Sir, that will save me."

To which the wise man replied, "Don't you know that even in the direst of moment in life, when Death is imminent, it is only one's own stock of sin and virtue (*paapam, punnyam*) that a man can take along with him to the other world. It is not his money-chest that will go with him".

"*Mind your tongue, vidwan*! Not one of you who comes here begging for money or alms is ever going to be around me when the time arrives for my death! Why then should I waste any money on charity for people like you?! *Be gone now from here at once!*".

Watching the *vidwan* walk away sadly, the miser's wife took pity upon him. Turning to her husband, she said, "This wise man is a very respectable elder. Please give him at least something for his need. It would be virtuous deed on your part". He told his wife, "These wonderful words of yours themselves have now earned you much virtue! You deserve a reward! Come closer to me and let me give you your reward!". When the wife came close to him, he caught seized her and resoundingly slapped her cheeks saying, *"Never say such insolent words to me again!"*. Shocked by his violence, she fled into her kitchen, weeping all the way...

It was thus that this miserly wretch of man continued living... Whoever came to him seeking alms was rudely turned out at once, directed to go to the other wealthy man in the neighbourhood, from whom they were able to secure the alms they needed and were able thus to return to their homes contented.

***

Time passed by... this miserly man reached the age of 75.

One day he fell very ill. His body was wracked by seizures and he was rendered unconscious. Fearing that the end was near for him, the family decided to move him to the forecourt of the house (*rezhi thinnai*), laid his limp body out on the stony bench, to await the inevitable end.

At that moment, another *vidwan* appeared on the scene. The man looked at the limp, almost lifeless body and felt pity for the wealthy man. Turning then to the wife, the *vidwan* asked her to fetch a one-rupee coin and placed it inside the palm of her husband. She did as she was told.

The *vidwan* then whispered into the ears of the miser, *"Please, Sir, will you give me the one-rupee coin in your hand as a final and token act of charity?"*

On hearing this, the nearly unconscious man suddenly sprang to life, and cried out*"Aah!"*, then closed his palms and clasped the Re.1/- tightly and close to his chest, unwilling to part with it! Instead, the man lifted the other hand, and with the forefinger, pointed it out to the *vidwan* in the direction of the home across the street belonging to the other wealthy man!

The wife who was watching all this happening, sighed to herself in deep sadness, *"Even in the terminal moments of your life, you stoop to do only this?!"*

The man finally breathed his last. The agents of Yama, the Lord of Death, dragged him to face sentencing in Yama's celestial court. In the realm of Yama, the man after having shed mortal coils, had to assume another corporeal form. He now awaited sentencing. The miser trembled in terror.

Yama summoned his courtier, Chitragupta, and asked him for a complete account of all the miserly man's sins and virtues in the mortal world. Thereafter, Yama felt he must consult with his advisory panel of wise *"maharishis"* before passing sentence on the man. He spoke thus to the rishis:

"This man has to be credited with having pointed out to everyone that came to him for alms the house of the other neighbour who was even more wealthy. They all went there and did receive the charity they were seeking. So, although this man here did not himself give anyone any charity, he nonetheless did enable them all to secure it by directing them towards another surer source of charity. So, even in his miserliness, there was present a certain

small element of charitableness. There must be a way to reward him for that? What would that be?"

The consultant *maharishis* told Yama, *"All his life, this man never gave in charity but then to his credit it must be said that whoever came to him begging for alms was shown the means to procure such charity. They were asked to go to the other wealthy neighbour. That was done by use of a finger to point in the direction of the home of the other benefactor. Therefore, in spite of his miserly nature, there was a streak of latent good intention which he possessed. As a reward for such good intention, we recommend that while this man is being subjected here in hell to all other harsh and painful punishments he surely deserves, his finger alone should be spared. While the rest of this man's body undergoes all manner of pain and torture, his finger should on other hand be kept wrapped in the soft, cool and fragrant petals of fresh flowers sprinkled and sprayed with even cooler perfume and balm".*

Heeding the recommendation of his advisors, Yama passed sentence on the man accordingly. While his body was wracked with lashes and lacerations in punishment, he screamed in pain. But then when his finger alone was exempted from such punishment and was instead kept wrapped in cool petals of fragrant flowers exactly as Yama's *maharishis* had ordered, he was able to immensely enjoy the pleasurable sensation.

After a while, it came to be known to Yama's agents that they had inadvertently erred in bringing to Yama's abode the miserly man out of the mortal world a little prematurely. When they reported the matter to their Master Yama, he decided that the man still had a few more years left to live on earth and experience mortal existence. So, Yama ordered that the man to be returned forthwith to earth to serve out the rest of his allotted lifetime.

***

Meanwhile on earth, in the home of the miserly man who had been pronounced dead, elaborate preparations were afoot for his funeral. Pall-bearers were summoned to carry the corpse for cremation. Priests too had been called to perform due obsequies. But when they suddenly found that the miser had come alive after having risen from the dead, as it were, they all became terrified. They ran helter-skelter and fled from the scene… The pall-bearers did not even want to collect their wages… nor did the priests even look back once… *They vanished!*

The wealthy miser rose and now came to his senses. He sat up and recollected everything he had just experienced in the land of Yama, the Lord of Death. He narrated it all in full detail to his wife.

The wife after listening to his horrific tale of her husband's visit in spirit to Yamaloka calmed him down and told him gently, "Do we really need all this wealth of yours! Why keep it hoarded?! Why not you please give it all away now for good charitable causes?" To which, the man who had just returned from Yamaloka replied firmly, *"What?! Give my wealth away? Never! I shall not give it up until I breathe my very last in life. Before the moment I pass away, my eyes shall remain transfixed on all my wealth, even if that was for the last time ever!"*

***

After the entire community in his town had heard all about the miraculous return of the miserly wealthy man from his near-death experiences, and after the 10-day funerary period had elapsed, a group of Vedic priests one day knocked on the doors of the man, wishing to seek his financial support for a great sacrifice, a Vedic Yagnya that they were planning to conduct in prayer for the general welfare and wellbeing of society at large.

They beseeched him, "O Prabhu, our beneficent lord, we believe that at least now after everything that we have heard you experienced in your recent encounter with death, you probably at last realize the truth that there is nothing of material wealth that any human can ever hope to take along with him into the other world! Sir, realizing that truth, perhaps now you will deign to help us in our cause? We humbly beg you to grant us aid to conduct our planned Vedic *yagnya*… We would be so grateful if you could even preside over it as our honoured chief guest". The man asked then the Vedic priests, "How much is conducting the *yagnya* going to cost?"

"Sir, we estimate about Rs.50,000", they replied.

When he heard this, the miser was overjoyed! He thought to himself, *"With this great opportunity, surely, now I'll bring about the end of that very wealthy fellow living across the street! The fellow will now surely have to* part with Rs. 50,000 from his wealth in one go! That will be the end of him!".

He beckoned the Vedic priests out into the front yard of his house, and as was his wont, he pointed out to them first with his finger at the mansion of the other wealthy man, the neighbour across the street. He then told them, "Go there to that fellow over there! He will surely give you the amount you are seeking as alms!".

Saying so again and again, the man next began to use not only his finger to point in the same direction but also *his head, legs, back, midriff and every other anatomical part of his body!* He then began to repeat his actions, rolling over and over again, and swivelling around on his feet again and again in contortions… pointing out all the time the Vedic priests to the house where the wealthy philanthropist lived across the street!

After dismissing the Vedic priests, the miser retired into his home extremely pleased with the turn of events. He thought to himself, "If only I get a few more opportunities like this one today where I know the other fellow across the street will be stripped clean off more instalments of Rs. 50,000/- each all in one fell swoop, I am sure he will be doomed very soon! I can then rest content and happy ever thereafter!".

Entertaining such evil designs in his heart, the miserly wretch continued living out his days….

***

The miser's last days finally arrived. He died and was promptly dragged again by Yama's agents into their master's presence.

Once again, Yama summoned Chitragupta to give a complete account of all his good and bad deeds on earth. Yama was amazed at what he learned. So, again he had to call to confer with his *maharishis* to help decide on the sentencing. When the rishis too heard about what the wealthy miser had been up to during his time spent on earth, they too were put in a quandary.

Earlier, Yama had ordered both punishment as well as a little reward for the man. The reward was in the form of cool, soft and fragrant flowers wrapped around *the man's finger*! This time around, Yama wondered how to extend the same sentence to the entire body of the man who had used not only his finger but every limb of his and his whole midriff too to perform the same act of earlier virtue i.e., pointing out to those come seeking alms at his doorstep in the direction of his wealthier and generous-hearted neighbour?! *Going by earlier precedent, did Yama have to pass sentence that the man in hell should be all rolled up and ensconced in soft, cool, fragrant rose-petals?!!* Both Yama and his *maharishis* were flummoxed!

Yama and wise rishis huddled conferring and finally decided that this man cannot be held in hell but should be returned to earth to live out yet one more lifetime as a human. But this time around, he should be predestined to lead not the life of a nasty, wretched miserly hoarder of wealth, but as a noble *"dharmishtan"* – a large-hearted wealthy person well-disposed towards showing charity and generosity to one and all for the greater good of society…

The man was thus returned to earth as per Yama's decree. And that was how he then went on to live life and fulfil his destiny….

And that is where the story ends!

***

I do not wish to underscore the many moral lessons contained in this short-story. Each of you must contemplate upon it yourself and come to your own conclusions. But there is one clear lesson that must be learned:

A man like that wealthy miser so bereft of good intention, so lacking in morality and charitableness, had his sentencing in hell by Yama extenuated. Why? Because it was reward for he having at least enabled charity through another man even though he himself had been so very uncharitable and selfish all his life. Amidst all the sufferings in hell he was otherwise condemned to undergo in hell, Yama ordered that his finger would be exempt from any punishment and instead that he be rewarded with rosy, soft and perfumed petals!

That being the case of how leniently and compassionately our *sastras* deal with human sin and virtue, crime and punishment and in delivering justice, there should be no doubt in our minds at all about what awaits us as great and wonderful rewards from Bhagavan if we go about doing charity for the larger good of one and all of our fellowmen – such as building a temple, constructing a temple pond or donating generously for noble public causes etc. Hence, without any misgivings of any sort in your hearts, go all out into the world to do as much "*saatvika daanam*" as possible, each according to one's own capacity and means.

-19-
"*Daaney Dvishantho Mithraa Bhavanthi*": Charity

> ***Synopsis:*** *This epistle expands even further upon the theme of Charity in Vedanta. "Gifts of charity must be made in favor of those who are truly needy and in utter poverty for much the same reason why medicines are to be administered only to the grievously ill --- the medicine relieves their suffering and cures them. What is the purpose of giving medicines to perfectly healthy persons?! Far from curing them, it might actually create in them only disease or affliction, will it not? Likewise, when one bestows charity on persons who are already well-to-do, able-bodied and resourceful, the surfeit of beneficence at their disposal might only end up tempting them to either misuse or even abuse it to their own detriment."*

Few in this world realize the blessed quality of charity. But from whatever I have learnt about it from the words of our wise forebears, I shall now write about and share with you in the hope that you shall then be sufficiently urged to engage in generous charity in life, each in accordance with your own means and capacity.

Try imagining a lake or a pond whose water-level is rising to dangerous levels due to incessant inflows. What do you think the person responsible for its safe upkeep ought to do about it? You would all say he should immediately see to it that a channel is cut to allow excess water from rising levels of the lake drain out slowly, and thus prevent breaches in the lake's embankment resulting in far greater loss of its precious waters. Similarly, we can say, that as the levels of the wealth we go on earning begin to rise steadily as we progress in life, we must let it percolate out little by little through the channel of generous charity. Otherwise, there is every possibility that we might end up losing a greater part of it through sudden, unfortunate vagaries, mishaps or accidents in life such as theft, taxes or expropriation. Therefore, we must understand that both spending and giving in charity, in generous measure, do go a long way in life to not only help retain but also protect our larger stock of wealth.

A wise man once said this: *When we neither spend our Wealth in living well ourselves nor do we give it in charity for the wellbeing of others, the Wealth very soon gets reduced to naught --*

दानं भोगो नाशस्तिस्रो गतयो भवन्ति वित्तस्य ।
यो न ददाति न भुङ्क्ते तस्य तृतीया गतिर्भवति ॥

"daanam bhogho naasha-tisro gathayo bhavanthi vitthasya,

Yo na dadaathi na bhunkthe tasya tritheeyaa gathirbhavathi."

People often ask, *"How is charity to be given? What is the proper way?"*

The answer is short and sweet: "Whenever done, any act of Charity firstly must be made with a pure heart? What does that mean? It means when I give in charity, I must feel that the act itself is verily the fulfilment of my life".

I am often asked this too: *"To whom must be charity done and in what proper ways?"*

Listen then to the answers I shall give you now:

First and foremost, one should proceed with an act of charity if it is known for certain that what is about to be given away in charity to a person will in turn get used by the latter, either directly or indirectly, but solely and surely for true, godly purpose only (*bhagavath aaraadanam*).

Next, persons who have studied and imbibed well the Vedic and Vedantic body of knowledge as well as those who do no more in life than sport a tuft on their crowns (*kudumi*), and are satisfied with performing no more than the '*sandhyaavandanam*' rite, are both deserving of charity but then the former should get the first priority and the latter the last.

Charity should also be timely and made appropriately... It has been said in the **Bhagavath Gita**: *"paatrey anupakaariNey"*

If one gives to another in charity with the tainted thought *"If I gift this man now at this time, I can expect him to owe me something valuable in return at a later time"*, then such charity carries really no merit at all.

Secondly, one must know that to be able to give in charity from out of one's wealth, one must know first the means of its proper enjoyment. Merely possessing wealth means nothing if one knows not the means to experience delight out of it. No delight ever accrued to a man of wealth who simply wore it on his sleeves and strutted about. Real delight is derived from one's wealth only when it is enjoyed collectively with one's kith, kin and friends. But greater is the delight derived when it is put to use for godly purposes – for *"bhagavath tiruvaaraadanam'*, for preparing varieties of delicious and wholesome food-offerings to *"bhagavaan"* and thereafter enjoying them (as *prasaadam)* in the holy company of other devotees… that is certainly one form of delectation to be derived from one's wealth.

Another way of putting to use one's wealth in a wholesome way and derive delight from it is to regard oneself, one's own family members and one's own community at large as though they were all temples or places of worship. Thus, when one's wealth is spent in providing them all with all material wherewithal and good things in life, it can be likened to spending generously on erecting festive festoons to the temple, and lavishing rich clothing, finery, jewelry and other ornaments and embellishments for the Deity and the sanctum.

However, on the contrary, spending one's wealth for nothing more than self-gratification in so many profligate ways that are sinful, ungracious and are prohibited too by *'saastras'* as being the cause for *"bhagavaan's"* displeasure is indeed the surest path to perdition and can in no way secure any kind of delight or wellbeing to the owner of such wealth. The perils of squandering away one's wealth in such fashion is severely condemned by the *"paasuram-s"* of the holy *"prabhandhams"* well known to us such as this one for example:

"வம்புலாங்கூந்தல் மனைவியைத் துறந்து"

"vambulaankoonthal manaiviyyai toorandhu…"

To contribute through charity towards the celebration of temple *'utsavam'* (public religious festivity) and to be able to enjoy the fervor and fanfare is indeed one of the ways to delight in the use of one's wealth. So is being able to offer beautiful and lavish floral tributes to temples and enjoying the sight of the Deity adorned with them. Similarly, donating a bit of one's wealth towards organizing the temple-kitchens to provide sumptuous and wholesome food-offerings to *"bhagavaan"* and then having it all distributed to vast assembly of devotees and pilgrims (*bhaagavatha goshti*) can also be a source of immense mental pleasure and fulfilment for the donor.

Just as one spends one's wealth in the periodic renovation and refurbishment of one's dwelling, and then he is able, along with his family, to feel tremendous pride and pleasure from simply watching the new surroundings, so can a man of wealth who uses a part of it to gift it to the temples of our deities like Rama, Krishna, Ranganatha or Lakshminrisimha and others then able to savor the great delight of witnessing their precincts renovated and beautified with his donation and beginning to shine and sparkle again with new life and energy (*"jeernOdhaaranam"*).

There is yet another source from which springs very great satisfaction and enjoyment for the man of wealth: when he decides to gift a part of his wealth to arrange for young boys from underprivileged families to undergo the ritual investiture of *"upanayanam"* or to conduct the weddings of daughters (*"vivaaham"*, *"kalyaanam"*) hailing from such very poor families.

It is through the vehicle of such charity as described above that one may ensure that what is given away through generosity or philanthropy ensures in turn that what remains as wealth thereafter continues to be a fund worthy of respect and honor. It is akin to water inside a well. If the copious store of water inside the well is not periodically drawn out from it for use in a variety of ways in domestic, household life, the well is sure very soon to turn turbid and the water will begin to smell putrid. Likewise, we can say that periodic drawing out of excess wealth that accumulates with us and given away partly in charity helps to render the residual wealth free from the taint of sinful selfishness and the stigma of miserliness.

A great message on the subject of Charity was once conveyed by Sri Krishna to Yudhishtira in the following words (in the *Mahabharatha*):

दरिद्रान् भर कौन्तेय मा प्रयच्छेश्वरे धनम् ।
व्याधितस्यौषधं पथ्यं नीरुजस्य किमौषधैः ॥

> "daridra Bhara kowntheya maa prayaccheshvarey dhanam,
> vyaadhitasyowshadham patthyam neerujasya kimowshadhaihi."

"O Dharmaputra! Take it upon yourself as duty to give generously in charity to 'saadhus', 'yogis' and "bhaktas" who suffer silently in dire poverty... And there is no need at all for you to gift anything of any value to those who are already well to do."

What Sri Krishna meant in the above *shloka* was this:

"The gifts of charity must be made in favor of those who are truly needy and in utter poverty for the much the same reason why medicines are administered to the grievously ill --- the medicine relieves their suffering and cures them. What is the purpose of giving medicines to perfectly healthy persons?! Far from curing them, it might actually create in them only disease or affliction, will it not? Likewise, when one bestows charity on persons that are already well-to-do, the surfeit of beneficence at their disposal might only end up tempting them to either misuse or even abuse it to their own detriment."

Even today all of us hear about and cherish in our hearts the glory of King Mahabali's act of extraordinary charity in giving away everything he held as his empire to *Vaamana bhagavaan* who came to him disguised as a poor "*brahmin brahmachaari*" begging alms and made a demand for just 3 yards of land. The king's royal counsellor, Sukraachaariar, when asked his opinion, voiced his suspicion and warned Mahabali not to give away the gift the boy was demanding and told him that it would mean the loss of his entire kingdom, crown and all his wealth. But Mahabali as a benefactor, even knowing fully the impending consequence of his charitable deed, went on still to confer the gift of "*daana*" on the boy and lost everything... Such is the glory of Mahabali and his exemplary generosity!

Have we all also not heard about the famous legend of Karnan (in the Mahabharatha) whose act of charity was magnificent and simply takes our breath away? And that when asked to be given it, he did not hesitate even a moment to rip out from his chest the coat of protective armor which had been conferred upon him at birth as a divine boon and gave it away in charity!

Then isn't there also the legend that we all know of about how King Sibi Chakravarthy, in order to save the life of a mere winged creature, a poor pigeon, did not hesitate to slice out with his own hand a piece of flesh from his body to give the bird a lease of life?

A wise man once illustrated through a very telling analogy indeed how the many acts of genuine *daana* or charity by a person all raise him to very great heights of status and nobility. He compared the oceans and the rain-bearing clouds in the skies in this context. The waters of the vast seas are always held down by it and never given away for any great use by the rest of the natural world. Whereas the rain-bearing clouds shower down every bit of the moisture that they are laden with in such abundant measure upon all creatures and life on earth. And so, we find that it is the clouds which for their self-less charity, get rewarded with a place of great prominence in the lofty heights in the vast skies of the heavens… and why too, the selfish oceans that do never part with their waters, get relegated to such a lowly, earth-bound status in nature.

Another wise man had this observation to make about Charity:

A man's wealth is much like the stream that springs forth from the high mountains. That stream empties itself incessantly by letting its waters gush down the slopes of its meandering course. Does anyone need to spell it out to anybody at all as to what great dangers might arise if the mountain stream did not drain itself of its waters that way constantly? And instead, if it stored or dammed itself up somewhere high up there in stagnant condition on the mountain slopes?

It is much the same with Wealth… even as it springs up and accumulates, so must it also be continually drained through charity. If it is allowed instead to amass and stagnate, such wealth only ends up attracting unwanted attention of covetous people including taxmen and other authorities. It then becomes difficult to account for such disproportionate accumulation of wealth and the mode of its disposal. (These days we hear often about some people, caught unable to properly account for their wealth, being hauled away from their cozy homes to live out their days in other very "specially protected and secure kind of homes", don't we?)

On the other hand, when a part of wealth is wholeheartedly given away in charity -- to the needy, the orphaned and to the destitute men of learning (such as learned Vedantins) of this world -- such large-heartedness yields unseen but very certain blessings to one.

Thus, when all is said is done, a prudent man of the world will ensure that a third of all his income and wealth is put away as his savings, a third is spent well in enjoying the pleasures of all good things in life together with family, relatives, friends and community; and finally, a third will be earmarked for charity to be given for worthy causes described above as '*daanam*'. At the same, without first accumulating a basic corpus, he should never begin to freely spend his earnings and wealth.

One of the blessed qualities of Charity or "*daanam*" is that it has the power to turn even foes into friends. Those who harbor any sort of enmity or rivalry against a man known well otherwise for his philanthropy usually end up making light of the rancor and making much more instead of his generosity. Charity (of the kind with no strings attached) indeed conquers all and that is why it is said (in the Veda): "*daaney dvishanto mithraa bhavanthi*"

The Upanishad also goes on to say this of Charity: "*daaney sarvam pratishTitham*" i.e. All good things in life that a charitable man may desire get realized by him, sooner or later, by virtue of those very own charitable deeds of his. Many indeed are the gifts of "*daanam*" which are revealed to us by our ancient "*dharma saastras*":

foodgrain (*daanyam*), apparel (*vastram*), meals (*annam*), utensils (*paathram*), milk (*ksheeram*), yoghurt (*thadhi*, or *thayeer*), a son for adoption (*puthra daanam*), a bride in marriage (*kanya daanam*), jaggery (*vella daanam*), salt (*uppu daanam*), cows (*go daanam*), land (*bhu daanam*), cereals (*tila daanam*), gold (*swarnam*), butter (*aajya daanam*), silver, property, trees or grove (*vruksha daanam*), temple elephants (*gaja daanam*), horses (*ashva daanam*), camels (*ushtra* daanam) etc.

Amongst the many "*daanams*" one can give as a gift of spiritual knowledge (intellectual property), the most priceless is that of "*Sri*

Bhaashyam" (the commentary of Sri Ramanujacharya on the Brahma Sutra of Bodhaayana), "*bhagavath-vishayam*" (the commentary of Sri Kurugoor Piraan Pillaan on Nammazwar's "*tirvoimozhi*"), *Srimad Ramaayanam,* and books on the sacred *Stotra* works of great Vedic and Vedantic Acharyas. The exposition by very learned men of the deep meanings and significance of such great works can also be deemed to be very valuable intellectual gifts given away by them. Some peoples' learning is all out of sheer vanity and they keep hoarding valuable books in their private libraries and gloat about it without sharing their treasure with others. In time, those libraries used by none become moth-eaten and waste away. Rather than let such intellectual treasures decay, books of knowledge should be given away as gifts to young students and sincere seekers of knowledge.

***

I must now dwell a bit upon an important aspect of charitableness:

Imagine a father of his only child, a beloved daughter, saying, "*She is the only child I have! How can I give her away in marriage (kanya daanam)? Should my home not be blessed with the presence of at least one loving child of mine?*" Irrespective of such paternal sentiments, one must yield to our '*saastra*' which stipulates that a father soon after his daughter attains age of puberty must seek out a worthy *brahmachaari* groom for her; one who belongs to another "*gotra*" (genetic group); is able bodied, well-educated; and the father should then dutifully confer all ceremonial honors on such a groom --- with gifts, flowers, perfumed offerings and to the sound of *mantra*-chants for the occasion --- and forthwith give away his daughter's hand in marriage to such a worthy man. Such a gift of nubile daughters ("*kanya daanam*") must be performed whether a father has only one or fifty daughters! If a father fails to perform the sacred duty of "*kanya daanam*" in a timely manner, and instead continues to keep her in his own paternal custody indefinitely at home, he is deemed by the *dharma-saastras* to be guilty of such heinous sins as "*bruNa hathya* (feticide), "*maathru hathya*" (matricide), "*pithru hathya*" (patricide), "*brahmahathi*" (slaying Brahmin), homicide, thieving, felony, crime, and social treason.

A daughter born to a father ought to be parented with love and care as a child. But the day she attains the age of puberty, it is the duty of the father to gift her away in marriage to a worthy groom; no delay in the matter for any reason should be brooked. That duty when performed in a timely manner is said to please all the gods (*devataas*), sages (*rshi*-s) and men of *Vaideeka* ancestry (i.e., I mean the venerable persons of our past who were wedded to the Vedic way of life). It is so common these days to blame the secular laws for the late marriage of our daughters -- and thus marriages get postponed to even ages far advanced as 30 and 35 years. Lack of financial resources is yet another excuse for postponing the marriage of our daughters. There is also the pretext of the evils of the dowry system. And then these days, we also come across nubile girls in our community who baulk at the prospect of getting married to grooms who are of orthodox mien and demeanor (such as wearing the traditional *kudumi*)! Anyway, so long as the daughters (*kanni*-s) in our community are married in time, that in itself should be a cause for happiness, and welcomed and encouraged as a form of '*daana*', an act of good charity. At least, let us hope that the groom believes in and knows how to offer "daily worship" to his household deity ('*saalagraama poojai*' or "*tiruvaaraadanam*").

Then there is the gift of "*anna daanam*" to be spoken about. It is the gift of feeding masses of common people. How is this to be done by a man of wealth? This "*daana*" must be made only for the benefit and heartfelt satisfaction of those poor people who truly know and have experienced the pain and pangs of hunger and have no other reliable or sustainable means of providing themselves with at least one square meal a day. Food given as gift to such people provides instant relief and sustenance to them, energizes them, makes them active and in turn enables them to offer thanksgiving and prayers to "*bhagavaan*" ... Hence, the merit of such "*daana*" accrues and arises immediately and in abundant measure too to the "*anna daatha*", the donor.

The gift of cows – "*go daanam*" – can be made to worthy men devoted to Vedic learning (*vedaviths*). But such gifts should be given only to those who can be expected to protect and husband the animal and enjoy the copious milk it yields. The donor must ensure that the recipient of "*go daana*" is not negligent in protecting the cows. Also, once the gift of the cow is made, the donor should never, later on, try to regain or claim it back for any reason whatsoever. Several scriptures condemn it as heinous sin. Again, no man should make a gift of a cow to *vedaviths* knowing it to be frail of health, sick, decrepit, disabled, infecund or unproductive of milk. Such gifts only earn for the donor all manner of ill fate in life.

Giving away one's son by way of gift to foster parents for purpose of legal adoption is *"puthra daanam"* and it is approved by our *saastras*. But such *'daana'* is best made when the adoption is accepted (*sveekaara*) by one's own kith (*gnyaathee*-s). Next in order of preference, the gift of adoption may be given to relatives belonging to the same *"gotra"* lineage. The least preferred mode of *"puthra daanam"* is to arrange for adoption of a son on mere pecuniary considerations.

Another praiseworthy mode of gifting particularly to temples and religious monasteries (*mattam*) is what is known as *"gaja daanam"*, elephants. But the gift of these magnificent animals was once made only by maharajas and noblemen who had both the resources and willingness to make such munificent endowment.

Then there is also the custom of gifting to great temples massive accessories for use in the temple festivities (*utsavam*). Such accessories are great big umbrellas known as *"kudai"*. They are ceremonially carried to provide shade and cover to the idols of the deities when they are taken out in procession – with all attendant pomp, pageantry and parade – and are admired and witnessed by delighted, awe-struck crowds of teeming devotees thronging the streets along the way. There have been a few great donors who have spared no cost in gifting these gigantic umbrellas to the Kanchipuram Sri Varadarajaswamy Perumal Temple on the occasion of the annual "**Garuda sevai**". Likewise, for the Sri Veeraraghava Perumal temple in Tiruvallur too. We know that the temple administrators (*devasthaanam*) of these big temples also regularly lend out the service of these magnificent festive-accessories to other smaller temples and shrines in and around the province… which is a matter of pride indeed since it is a good use of the *"daanam'* made in the first place. Another similar kind of *daana* is made with temple horses too.

Finally, the *'daanam'* that reigns supreme over all other *"daana"* is what is called *"rathna daana"* --- the gift of priceless diamonds. But then even amongst such invaluable *"rathna daana"*, there is one that stands unequalled and unrivalled by any other and it is called *"jeeva rathna daanam"*.

What makes this *"jeeva rathna daanam"* unique and exceptional? Why are other forms of daana -- whether it is *"go-daanam, bhu-daanam, kannika daanam, sri-moorthy daanam, Sri Kosa daanam, vastra daanam"* – all never at par with *"jeeva rathna daanam"*? It is because all of them, while capable of yielding *"phalan"* of the highest order viz.: blessings, benediction or exquisite states of happiness in the realms of the highest heavens (such as *"brahma lokam"*, *"svarga lokam"*), their *phalan* nonetheless is tainted by the defect of impermanence and *"dukkhaanubhavam"* or ultimate grief that inevitably follows such a condition and must be experienced.

On the contrary, the resultant *"phalan"* which *"jeeva rathna daanam"* promises are eternal, limitless and capable of bestowing *"aanandam"* or ceaseless pure, unalloyed bliss in the realm called *"Sri Vaikuntam"*. Having reached that state, there is no question of returning to mortal or mundane existence ever again through endless cycles of rebirths. It means everlasting blissful coexistence with the Supreme One who has deigned to receive and accept such *"jeeva rathna daanam"*.

Now who is this recipient of such a gift called *"jeeva rathna"*? To whom should one be ready to make a gift of one's *"Jeevan"*? Let me explain:

Many are the different kinds and forms of *"daana"* that have been listed above. It should be understood that in making such several types of *"daanam"*, certain rules and procedure are to be abided. The gifts are to be made at the proper time, in the proper place and settings, with proper pre-qualifications and pre-conditions etc. This *"jeeva rathna daana"* (*Atma daana*), on the other hand, is a gift to be made solely to **our Lord Sriya: pathi Srimann Naaraayanan**, the only one who is fit and able to receive and accept such a supreme gift. It is He who being ever solicitous of the well-being of our *Atmaa* or soul, awaits expectantly, and constantly too, the moment when we ourselves are ready to go forward to make the final gift of *"jeeva rathna daana"* to Him and ascend to his abode in *Sri Vaikuntam* to thereafter enjoy eternal bliss in His Company. Such mortal souls are not differentiated in any manner at all: it is utterly immaterial to Him whether we mortals are men, women, belonging to either this or that caste, sect or denomination. So long as we truly make the ultimate gift of our "*Atma*" to Him, he is ever ready to accept the offered "*jeeva rathna*" of ours and bestows upon us everlasting experience of "*mukthaanandam*" or the Bliss of "*moksha*" upon us.

He who seeks "*moksha*" and is willing to make the supreme gift of "*jeeva rathna daana*" should understand that it cannot be made to gods other than Srimann Naaraayana who alone can bestow "*moksha phalan*". Offer of "*daana*" to please other deities such as Rudra or Brahma may at best secure for one the heavenly delights abounding in *Brahma-loka* or *Kailaasa-loka*. But then even those realms are impermanent and subject to "*pralaya*" or ultimate cosmic dissolution. The Creator of all the fourteen realms of all mortal existence (i.e., heaven and earth, matter and spirit, all spatio-temporal existence), the scriptures reveal to us, is none other than Naaraayana into which all gets finally subsumed.

To make the gift of such "*atma samarpaNam*" or "*jeeva rathna*" there is really no specific time or place designated, no occasion, personal status or qualification is required; no age is barred, nor is wealth or social standing a criterion; it does not matter whether one is healthy or afflicted by disease or disability; nationality does not matter nor does one's faith or even if one is atheistic… So long as one is possessed of a soul that finally recognizes Sriman Naaraayana as the one and only Ultimate Reality, and has gained true "*gnyaana*" of that Reality; and so long as such a soul has realized too that it is by gifting itself as "*jeeva rathna*" at the feet of Naaraayana it absolves itself of all taint and traces of sin, infirmity and defects, it gets welcomed and admitted into the company of the celestials and liberated souls who have already performed "*jeeva rathna daana*" to the Almighty; and together with all of them it delights in Sri Vaikuntam.

It must therefore be realized that nothing stands as an obstacle between us and the deed of "*jeeva samarpanam*": not religion, not caste, not country, not age, and nothing… no bar or exclusion of any kind! Just never forget that there is none other who can receive your final gift of "*jeeva rathna*" than this Sriman Naaraayana.

There is one other matter that must be underscored here:

Gifts are bestowed by a donor to the recipient usually through designated intermediaries who aid in the proper conveyance of the object of gift. In the case of the many aforesaid *"daana"* (such as *go-daana, kanya daana* etc.), the intermediaries are elected persons with sufficient competence in terms of good knowledge of *saastra, mantra* and *ritual*. For the gift of *"jeeva rathna daana"* those intermediaries may not possess the requisite qualifications or experience. So, one must be aware that one needs a proper and genuine guide and mentor, *"upaadhyaya"* or *"Acharya"*, who alone can show the way for one on how to bestow the great and profound gift of one's *Atma* through mantra, ritual and *saastra*-based procedure. By doing so, he who completes the *"jeeva rathna daana"*, secures release from all mortal bondage (of *"sukha"* and *"dukkha"*) and ascends to the supreme state of bliss and liberation. This is what is vouchsafed in that great doctrine called **Saranaagathi**.

To conclude, whatever may be the fruits of one's charitable deeds that one may expect to reap in life, one must realize that it is only through renouncing them – '*bharannyaasam*' – that they ultimately all get realized. But if it is *"moksham"* (or liberation from the eternal cycle of mortal rebirth) that one is seeking, then performing *"bharannyaasam"* alone is not sufficient. Sriman Naaraayanan bestows the grace of eternal salvation only on souls that have gifted him with renunciation of both the deed and as well of the fruits of the deed.

अत्र रक्षाभरन्यासः समः सर्वफलार्थिनाम् ।
स्वरूपफलनिक्षेपस्त्वधिको मोक्षकाङ्क्षिणाम् ॥

"atra rakshaabharannyaasaha samaha sarvaphalaarThinaam,
Svarupaphalanikshepaastvadhiko mokshaankshinaam."

***

-20-
On the Glorious Significance of "*Govinda Naama*"

Synopsis: *In this epistle, Mukkur Swamy waxes eloquent while explaining the beauty and significance of the name of "**Govinda**", the sweetest of all "naamas" by which Bhagavan Sriman Narayana is known to his devotees. The Acharya's keen sense of literary appreciation comes to the fore as one reads the passages in his discourse. Ten avatars of Vishnu – the "**dasaavatara**" – are evocatively described with reference to various creative ways in which the Sanskrit phonemic root of the word "govinda" can be employed or interpreted.*

Moved by her concern for the wellbeing of all creation, **Goddess Paarvathi** the consort of **Lord Paramashiva**, on an occasion asked her husband a very subtle question:

"Keno paayena laghunaa vishnornaama sahasrakam I
Pattyathe pandithaire nithyam srothumicchaam-yaham prabho"
II

*"My lord! I ask you this question on behalf of all our dear devotees and for the sake of their wellbeing and happiness… Please deign to give me a reply! When pundits, even being well versed in the scriptures, due to lack of time, however, find themselves unable to daily chant all the "**1000 naamas**" (sacred names) of the Lord of the entire universe, **Sriman Naaraayana**, which is the other easiest alternative they choose instead? Please enlighten me on that easy path, my Lord!"*

Heeding the request of his wife, *Lord Paramashiva* answered in these rather terse words:

"Sri raama raamethi ramey raamey manoramey II
Sahasranaama taththulyam raama naama varaananey II"

"My dearest Paarvathi, my beloved of indescribable, divine beauty! You ask a tantalizing question with a coy smile playing upon the corner of your lips! I am enchanted by it! And so I shall give you a clear answer: **I am not aware of how other pundits manage to easily overcome the problem of finding time for the daily chant of the Sahasranaama. But I can tell you how I myself daily chant the Sahasranaama in the easiest way and shortest time possible every day and what experience I gain thereby.** Listen...."

Sensing that her Lord might have been slightly irked by the unusual way she had queried him, Goddess Paarvati sought to assuage him by saying, *"My lord, I did not mean to pique you by posing my question in the roundabout fashion I know I did. I did so because I did not wish to abruptly ask what your opinion was regarding the matter. That's why I broached the matter in the way I did."*

Lord Paramashivan then went on to share his very own experience:

"Simply by chanting **"sri raama raama..."** *I am able to experience the same supreme divine bliss ("bhagavath anubhavam") that which even a single thought of Sri Rama -- or* **"manoraamey manoramey"** *-- can plunge one into and get him or her immersed in that oceanic feeling of joy that the very sight of Rama's person of the most enchanting smile ---* **"pumsaaam mohana roopaya"** *--- creates! Even when uttered just once, the sacred "naama" of "raama", absolutely and divinely pristine .... "tathulyam" ...., becomes the equal at once of the entire* **Sahasranaamam***! And that is the means by which, how and why I am able to experience the supreme bliss through the simple words* **"sri raama raama...**"*! Thus, from my own experience, I can say that the single "naama" of "raama" is without doubt the equal of the entire* **Vishnu Sahasranaama!"**

***

The above incident is widely known already to all of us. Let me now tell you about another similarly single sacred *"naama"* by chanting which one is able to easily contemplate upon all the ten different avatars that Lord Vishnu undertook in his descents on earth in different epochs. Many men of enlightenment in the past have expatiated upon it and I shall now share with you, their accounts. So please listen to me:

"Vedaanudharatey jagannavihatey bhugolamudhbhibratey

Daityam daarayatey balim chalayatey kshatrakshayam kurvatey;

Powlasthyam jayatey halam kalayatey kaarunyammaatanvatey

Mlecchaan moorchyatey dashaakritikrutey krishnaaya thubyam namah: "

The above *shloka* accounts for all the **ten divine avatars of Vishnu** -- *matsya, koorma, varaaha, narasimha, vaamana, parashuraama, raama, balaraama, krishna* and *kalki* --- and the *"govinda shabdham"* i.e., the mere phoneme "***Govinda***", indeed spells out and signifies all ten!

Let me now explain how….

(1) **Matsyaavataaram**: ***Brahmmaa*** (primordial Creator), once puffed up with great conceit, began to think of himself far too highly: *"Isn't it I alone who created the fourteen cosmic worlds? So, can there be anyone else superior to me! With my four faces, I am able to know and recite all four great Vedas all at once! The other gods like Rudra, Indra, and the like, all offer obeisance to me alone! Hence, there is really none who is my equal in all Creation!"*

Filled with such self-conceit and arrogance, *Brahmmaa* momentarily forgot that there was one who was his father, the supreme lord of the universe, **Sriman Naaraayana**.

As *Brahmmaa* lived thus absorbed in his own self-importance, one day an *"asura"* named *Sankan*, miniaturizing himself in form, entered the body of *Brahmmaa* as he was yawning away, unmindful of the demon that had already infiltrated him through the cavity of his mouth. The demoniac *Sankan* using his magical powers, thereupon, quickly succeeded in extracting all divine Knowledge of the four great Vedas that were embedded in *Brahmmaa's* body and mind and made good his escape with it. *Sankan* then forthwith went to the deepest quarters of the great, dark oceans to hide himself there.

Having been robbed of all his Vedic Knowledge, *Brahmmaa* was shocked out of his wits! He became completely perplexed and unhinged! He could no longer perform his cosmic functions of Creation and became utterly paralyzed. He sank into despair and woe. He began desperately looking out in sheer panic for rescue and aid. It was only then in that moment of crisis that *Brahmmaa* remembered his father again! And at once he beseeched him thus, *"Oh Lord, my father, I have no one else to turn to but you! Please do save me now!"*

Bhagavaan Naaraayana then took the form of a humungous fish (*"matsya"*), plunged into the oceanic depths to accost and slay the *asura*, *Sankan*, who had hidden himself there with the Vedas. The Vedas were then recovered and *Bhagavaan* restored them again to *Brahmmaa*.... There ends the story of the *"matsyaavataara"*.

Now this *"matsyaavatara"* is denoted by the word *"govinda"* which is derived from the Sanskrit phoneme **"gaava:"** and the phrase **vindayateeti govinda:"** The expression *"gaava:"* means the acoustical body of all Vedas. The expression *"vindayateeti"* refers to the deed through which *Brahmmaa* the Creator, who had lost all his *"braahmanam"* (i.e., the functionality of cosmic Creativity) was however quickly saved by restoring the Vedas again to him. And he whose deed it was that resulted in such restoration is denoted by the name *"govinda"* ... i.e., *Bhagavaan* **Govindan**.

(2) **Koormaavataaram:** At the time of the great primordial mining of the heavenly **Sea of Milk** (*"ksheeraabdi"*), the *Devas* and *Asuras* (the celestial gods and demons) collaborated in a titanic effort to extract from out of its depths the mythical ambrosia (*amrutham*), the elixir of immortality. For the purpose of the mining, the ocean itself served as their vast crucible or mortar. The massive mountain of Mandara served as a gigantic pestle. And the celestial serpent, Vaasuki, served as the long rope tethered to the pestle with which the churning and drilling of the sea-bed was carried out.

As they heaved the great mountain and churned it, the mountain began to sink and collapse deeper and deeper into the ocean floor and got stuck there. Both the *Devas* and *Asuras* grew thoroughly exhausted by the epic effort of extricating it. Finally, out of sheer desperation, they were about to give it all up in despair. In that moment, moved by his great compassion for his creation, *Bhagavaan* assumed the avatar of **koormaa**, the form of a tortoise as leviathan. The tortoise plunging deep into the waters, burrowed its way into the seabed under the collapsed *Mandara Mountain* and lifted it out to the sea-surface by bearing it on its hard-shell (the plastron and carapace of which is known even ordinarily to withstand high amounts of pressure, almost two hundred times the tortoise's own weight)!

Once the mountain stood again well balanced on the ocean-floor, it became possible then for the *Devas* and *Asuras* to recommence their churning and mining! It is thus that *Bhagavaan*, in his avatar as *"koormaa"* came to be known as **Govindan**.

In the context of the story of this avatar, the Sanskrit phoneme **"gobhi:"** followed by the expression **"vindayateethi"** makes up **"govinda:"** .... an apt description for this avatar! The term *"gobhi:"* refers to the form of a tortoise and *"vindateeti"* refers to such awe-inspiring form that was assumed by *Bhagavaan* while responding to the calls of desperate prayer the *Devas* and *Asuras* sent out to him in their moment of crisis and which he did in the nick of time!

(3) **Varaaha avataaram:** Once upon a time the most fearsome and cruel of celestial demons, the *Maha-asura* named **Hiranyaakshan**, was the sworn and implacable enemy of *Bhagavaan* and all other gods. Through awesome, irresistible powers gained by dint of his long and severe acts of spiritual austerities – *'tapas'* – the demon was able to abduct the entire earth to the dark and murky depths of the oceans where the tyrannical demon was able to hold the world in secret captivity as a hostage in an unknown and untraceable location.

Bhagavaan then assumed the gargantuan form of a white-complexioned wild boar, "**varaaha**" avatar, which then dived into the sea to the spot where Mother Earth was held hostage. The *varaaha* rescued her and restored her to her original location and condition amongst the heavenly realms.

From the context of this story of this avatar, from the Sanskrit phoneme "**gaam**" describing the Earth and *Bhagavaan* as "*vindayateeti*" i.e., he who saved Mother Earth, the phrase "*gaam vindayateeti govinda:*" is derived, a most apt name for the avatar.

(4) **Nrisimhaavataaram:** The name Govindan refers to the fiery and explosive mien or *"jwaala"* aspect of the avatar of **Narasimha** --- as denoted by the Sanskrit phoneme **"gohshu"** and the phrase **"vindayateeti govinda:"**

This term *"jwaala"* alludes to the great fiery waves emanating from flames to which glow-worms in the dark get fatally attracted. After dancing momentarily, the **dance of death** around the fire, they all get soon incinerated of their own accord.

Hiranyakashipu, the powerful and atheistic *"asura"* King who defied *Bhagavaan*, and to destroy whom the **Narasimha** avatar itself was assumed by *Bhagavaan*, sent 30 million of his troops to attack the Lord. They rushed towards *Bhagavaan* to slay him, but like a great swarm of glow-worms, they all only ended up being enveloped by the flames – "*jwaala*" -- and perished instantly.

The man-lion form as avatar was assumed by *Bhagavaan* when he emerged roaring, raging and snarling out of a stone-pillar that *Hiranyakashipu* had struck down with a single blow of his great mace. It was a challenge to his son *Prahlada's* belief that *Bhagavaan's* presence was all-pervading in the universe. To prove that he was indeed immanent even in a stone-pillar -- exactly as *Prahlada* had told his father about it -- **Narasimha** emerged and appeared out of the pillar and accosted the awe-struck *Hiranyakashipu*, who then ordered thirty million of his troops at once to overwhelm and overpower *Bhagavaan*. It was in that moment when *Bhagavaan's* mien began emitting terrible, searing and deadly waves of blazing "*jwaala*" flames that seemed to tempt and fatally draw all the troops in one fell swoop into a raging inferno, as it were, and from which there was no escaping death. Thus, did Lord *Narasimha* get his name, "***govinda***"

(5) The word "*govinda*" also refers to the avatara of *Bhagavaan* as **Vaamana** as portrayed in this *puraanic* story:

Balichakravarty, the grandson of *Prahlada*, was a great and virtuous King on earth. But having gained great physical powers through spiritual austerities and sacrifices, he became puffed up with overweening pride and ambition. He waged war against the first amongst the celestial gods, *Indradeva*, defeated him and annexed his heavenly empire to his own. The disconsolate *Indra* then went to *Bhagavaan* and pleaded for justice. *Bhagavaan* then undertook the avatar of **Vaamana**, disguising himself as a pygmy-sized *brahmin brahmachaarin*-boy (a bachelor Vedic acolyte).

One day, just as King *Balichakravarthy was* concluding the ceremonial rites of a great Vedic sacrifice (*yagnya*), *Vaamana* arrived there and in the usual customary way on such occasions, asked the King for a charitable donation. When asked what he wanted as charity, *Vaamana* told the King he wanted a gift of land admeasuring three yards! This very act of *Vaamana* in asking for alms is denoted by the apt Sanskrit expression, *"gaam vindayateethi govinda:"* ... *"gaam"* as Sanskrit phoneme signifying land!

The King granted it to the young *brahmin* boy. It turned out however that with merely two steps of his that were taken, *Vaamana* strode the entire world and the heavens! And for the third step, the completely humbled King asked *Vaamana* to place his feet on the sovereign's now un-crowned head to fulfill the charity! Vaamana did so and banished King *Balichakravarthy* into a short period of exile to the netherworld.

Not too long thereafter, the *Bhagavaan* in another avatar taken concurrently as **Trivikrama**, he granted eternal redemption to the king who by then had surrendered to him in the true spirit of *'saranaagathi'*. By this act too, the Sanskrit phoneme, *"gaa:"* means *"charanaananaravinda-sambhandha"* ... *"vindayateethi govinda:"* i.e., one who blessed the humbled King by placing his divine feet upon his head. It aptly describes the *Trivikrama* avatar too.

The word *"govinda"* also refers to the avatar of *Bhagavaan* as **Parashuraama** as referred to in the scriptural expression: *"akshathraam trissapthakruthva: kshiteem"*. Incensed with boiling rage over the humiliation that had been meted out by kings of the *"Kshatriya"* caste to his father, *Parashuraama* swore revenge upon them. He took a solemn but terrible oath that he would exterminate and rid the entire world of twenty-one generations of the *Kshatriya* royalty. Wielding his mighty axe as his weapon, he then went about slaughtering twenty-one generations of *"Kshatriya"* clans one after another. Thus, the Sanskrit phoneme **"gavi"** prefixing the phrase **"vindayateeti govinda"** is attributed to *Parashuraama*. The phomeme *"gavi"* denotes the world and *"vindayatheeti"* refers to the wailing of the *Kshatriyas* therein who became victims of the serial slaughter by *Parashuraama*.

(6) **Raamaavataaram:** The word *"govinda"* refers to the avatar of *Bhagavaan* as *Sitaaraaman*. The rationale for such attribution is as follows:

The *devas*, constantly harassed and tyrannized by **Raavana**, decided at last to go to Brahmmaa and implored him to put an end to *Raavana*. But *Brahmmaa* told them that *Raavana* could be slayed by no god or celestial but only by a human. On hearing Brahmmaa's words, the *devas* became very anxious and agitated. They began wondering how any human could ever be intrepid and able enough to put an end to the danger Raavana posed. It was then that, as revealed in the scriptures ... *etasmin antarey vishnuroopayaatho mahaadhyuthi:"* ... that the supremely effulgent *Bhagavaan*, bearing the conch (*sankha*) and discuss (*chakra*) in his hands, appeared on the scene as the savior and refuge of the gods who then surrendered unto him invoking these words: **"siddhagandharvayakshaas cha tatthas tvaam sharanam gathaa:..."** where the words themselves signify the Sanskrit expression "**gaam vindayati**".

Furthermore, in the context of the story, the Sanskrit root "*gaam*" also refers to Earth (*bhoomi*) restored again to *devas* by *Bhagavaan* in answer to their prayers to him. In the context of the events that occurred during the *raamaavataara*, the same phoneme has many other semantic meanings too explained below:

- "*gaa:*": refers to *Raama's* mastery over archery and other martial arts, as well as in the expertise of other disciplines such as *Vedaanta*;

- "*gaam*": refers to *Raama's* tutelage under Sage *Viswaamitra* and having thus attained under the guru's guidance, expertise of the highest order in the higher arts, sciences, crafts and in other advanced fields of learning ("*siddhaashrama*");

> to his triumphant return to the city of Ayodhya thereafter with his radiant bride, Sita;

> to his having readily accepted his father, Dasaratha's desire that he should succeed him as emperor to rule the empire;

- to then, however, his also acceding without demur to Queen Kaikeyi's desire that he should renounce the throne and retire in exile to the forests;

- to having anointed Bharatha at Chithrakoot and charging him with the heavy burden of responsibility for the office of Regent ruling the empire;

- to having granted pardon and redemption to the demon, Kaakaasuran;

- to having patiently resided for several months in the forests surrounding the city of Kishkinda;

- to have mobilized the apes and bears of Kishkinda to undertake the project of building a great causeway across the sea to the island of Lanka;

- to have conquered the highland territories of Lanka;

- to having accepted Vibheeshana's surrender and as per solemn promise given to him, as well as having also resolved of his own will to overcome and overthrow Raavana and install Vibheeshana instead on the throne of Lanka;

- And finally, to have returned in glorious triumph and splendour to Ayodhya to reclaim and ascend its throne as Emperor!

(7) **Balaraamavataaram:** The name ***Govinda*** also signifies the avatar of **Balarama.** Under the ostensible pretext of going about on a pilgrimage to various holy centers in the country (*teertha yaatra*), *Balaraama* also accomplished at the same time the principal mission of his avatar *viz.* to destroy a few evil demons (*asuras*) who were infesting the Earth, which as already seen above, is denoted by "*gaam*", the Sanskrit phoneme.

(8) **Krishnaavataaram:** It is well known that the word *Govinda* is most popularly associated with the avatar of **Sri Krishna.**

Unable to bear the cruel tyranny of evil-minded rulers of the world, the Goddess Earth (***bhoodevi***) beseeched the Creator *Brahmmaa* to intervene. *Brahmmaa*, along with other gods such as *Rudra* and *Indra*, then approached *Bhagavaan*, the Lord known as *"ksheeraabdi-naathan"*, to put an end to *Bhoodevi's* misery.

Bhagavaan descending upon the earth then in his avatar as the ruler of *Dwarka* kingdom and as the son of *Vasudeva*, defeated and destroyed all earthly tyrants and conferred upon *Bhoodevi* deliverance from evil. Thus, the apt Sanskrit phrase to describe all these events: **"gaam vindati"** ...

The phrase can also be taken to signify the fact that Bhagavaan in this avatar was a native of the hamlet of *Nandagokulam* where as a simple cowherd he protected and cared for all his cattle herds. But Krishna also cared for another sort of herd in the world – the herds of spiritually ignorant, ordinary people like us for whose benefit alone, but under the pretext of instructing Arjuna, Krishna delivered the invaluable lessons, reflecting the essence of the wisdom of the ageless Upanishads contained in the sermon of the **Bhagavath-Gita**. Moreover, Krishna became *Govinda* also because in the **Gita** he resolved to show all mankind an easy path to pursue the final goal of salvation through resorting to the doctrine of *"saranaagathi"*: "... **sharanam vraja sarva paapebhyo mokshaishyaami...**"

9.1 It is both significant and interesting to note here that in the *Raama* avatar, *Bhagavaan* was accompanied by *Lakshmana*, the very personification of *"seshatvam"* i.e., divine servitude. Likewise, in the *Krishna* avatar, *Balaraama* accompanied *Bhagavaan* as his constant *"seshan"* or servitor. In both these avatars, as the *saastras* reveal to us, *"seshaavataara"*, the very personification of divine servitude, was indeed manifest. But in the *Krishna* avatar there is yet another extraordinary facet of *"seshaavataara"*. It is this:

9.2 **Garuda** is the divine avian vehicle, *"pakshiraajan"*, of *Bhagavaan* in the heavenly spheres. He is known to be the personification of the Veda. *Garuda* too descended upon earth in the avatar as the offspring of his mother, *Vinata*, only to accompany and serve the Lord, as and when needed, as his earthly vehicle. This is a unique feature of Krishna avatar not seen in any other. Thus, the Sanskrit phoneme: **"gO"** refers to *Garuda* personifying the

Veda, while "***vim***" (as in "*go-* "*vin*"-*da*") refers to *Krishna* using *Garuda* as his vehicle during his avatar.

10. **Kalki-avataaram:** The name *Govindan* refers to the avatar, **Kalki**, also that *Bhagavaan* is believed will be taking in the future at the very end of the epoch or "*yuga*" known as **Kali,** when his mundane mission will be to annihilate all beings on earth that are inimical to the Vedas, that have abandoned all virtues and observances of "*varnaashrama*", go about living in depravity as mere animals such as dumb goats and cows, and that have abandoned all sacred rites and sacrifices. *Kalki* will thus save and redeem the world. The horse-borne *Kalki* avatar traversing across the length and breadth of this world will also be known as **Govinda**.

In view of all that has been explained above, it should be clear now that the Supreme *Sriman Naaraayana* in *parama padam*, who is celebrated by all the **Upanishads** as the immanent spirit of all creation, is none other than ***Govindan***.... "*gobhi: vindateethi*".

The truth behind such statement is evident from the fact that even those who might be ignorant about the significance of *Govinda-naama* nonetheless, while they are assembled to listen to the *Raamaayana* being discoursed upon at any public place or forum, or the *Bhaagavatham*, or the *Vishnupuraanam*, for that matter, or while being assembled at any other such religious congregations, all in unison do chant "***govinda, govinda, govinda***" right after the leader of the assembly loudly chants the phrase "***govinda naama samkeerthanam***...."! If you ask the question: "*At a public discourse on the epic Raamaayana, why should people assembled choose to chant the name of "Govinda"? Similarly, why chant "govinda" at public discourse on Srimad Bhaagavatam"?*" nobody will know the answer!

The probable answer can be only this: Since time immemorial, it has been custom and convention established by some wise sermonizer in the past, an adept in Vedanta and *Vyaakarana* (i.e. semantics and grammar), who with a view to secure for his audience, comprised of both laity and cognoscenti, the sublime blessings of divine grace of all the ten avatars of Vishnu combined, hit upon the brilliant idea to somehow contrive to make them all the chant the single *"naama"*, **Govinda!**

Talking of religious customs and established convention, let me also explain another matter here:

Before we commence any Vedic rite or ritual, instead of enjoining us all to chant *"naaraayana, naaraayana, naaraayana"* --- and only thereafter invoke the litany of *"sankalpa mantra"* which is to the effect that *"On this day, in this month, in this fortnight of this year and under this asterism and in this solstice of the year.... I do hereby solemnly resolve to faithfully perform the ritual that I am going to perform here and now, on the command and sole pleasure of the Lord Almighty, Sriman Naaraayana!"* --- why does the *saastra* instead enjoin us to chant "**govinda, govinda, govinda**"?! Such a ritual procedure is observed by one and all, irrespective of whether one is a pundit or a layman or whether belongs to the *Tenkalai* or *Vadakalai* sect, is it not? Why is it so that the ritual is commenced with the chant of *"govinda, govinda, govinda, asya sri bhagavatha:. Etc"* when it is patently being performed only for the sake of Lord *Naaraayana*?!

The answer to this question too has been given by our wise ancestors which I am summarizing briefly below:

The ritual might be conducted out of obedience to *Sriman Naaraayana's* command (*aagnyaa*) and at his sole pleasure (*preetyartham*), but the prayer to him is couched in apt expressions that effectively seek blessings and sublime grace from each of *Bhagavaan's* 10 avatars (*dasaavataara*) that are to be bestowed upon the ritual-performer in the same manner and measure as it had been bestowed upon devotees and protégés in the time of each such avatar of the past.

To conclude, let us all therefore resolve now that during our lifetime on earth we will constantly repeat the divine, sacred chant of **"Govinda naama samkirtanam"** on our lips and earn and enjoy thereby the blessings of every one of his ten different glorious avatars!

***

-21-
Eight Maxims of Life

Synopsis: In this concluding "arul mozhi", Sri Mukkur Azhagiyasingar we find has specially culled out eight scintillating aphorisms from different Vedantic scriptures and proceeds to uncover the truths and wisdom embedded therein in a truly masterly fashion. The eights maxims explained here are truly guideposts for finding fulfilment in one's life.

(1)

"anugantham sathaam varthma kruthsnam yadi na shakyathe I
Svalpamapyanuganthavyam maargastho naavaseedhathi II"

Every man and woman should aspire always to keep developing to attain high position or stature in life. However, to succeed in reaching such high stature, due efforts will be needed to be exerted and of which one is of particularly great importance. It is this: One must always closely observe how men of great noble qualities ("**mahaan**") conduct themselves and take cues from them. Also, one must pay heed to and embrace the exhortations and guidance of such *mahaans*. By doing so and following in their footsteps, we can be sure it will elevate us in life.

Even if we cannot fully embrace all the ways of the *mahaans* in either word or deed, we must nonetheless attempt do so at least partly to the extent possible for us. Gradually, those attempts will fructify and we will then be able to reach shore safely in life. One might not perhaps be able to walk the entire distance on a well-laid but very long road; but at least, even the little distance that may have been traversed would still make the journey worthwhile, would it not?

***

(2)

"Pratyaham pratyaveksheta narascharatimaatmana: I
Kim nu me pashubhisthulyam kim nu satpurushairithi II"

Every earthling that has taken human birth, as either a male or a female on this planet, must never fail to do this act daily viz. reflect deeply and silently within ourselves upon how, from dawn until bedtime, each day has been spent. "Has this day in my life been spent no differently than as mere goats or oxen live it? Or, has it been spent in accordance with what noble and wise elders of mine have always exhorted me to live by?" Why is such daily self-reflection necessary? Because making it a habit in life, we become wiser day by day, ever so slowly but then surely too.

How so?

The habit of such daily reflection will bring about self-awareness in us and keep us constantly on guard about how our days get spent. "If I continue to spend my days in life like a mere, unregenerate animal, what then could be the real purpose for which I have been given this birth as human being on earth? I might as well have been born an animal too, wouldn't I?"

Realizing thus, it would dawn upon one then that the real purpose of human existence lies not in aping animals but emulating those of human beings, nobler and superior to oneself, thereby becoming a better human being oneself. As one follows the path led by *mahaans* one finds oneself getting elevated, as learning from them the lofty lessons of wisdom found in Vedanta helps imbibe great values of life. When high values of life are practiced, then inevitably one ascends to high stature too in in the world. This is precisely the reason for which one must cultivate the habit of self-reflecting upon how each passing day in life has been spent. If a day has been spent well, then it must be a matter of satisfaction. If not, the day must be rued over as being wasted and duly regretted.

***

(3)

"Sadbhireva sahaasetha sadhbhi: kurveetha sangamam I
Sadhbhirvivaadam maitreemcha naasadhbhi:kichidhaachareth
II"

It should be one's endeavor to seek and strike relationships with the pious, the wise and the elderly at all times. One's knowledge of the many verities of life and the world must be deepened and broadened only through frequent interactions with such wise ones. Such interactions and relationship with them must be based on genuine attitude of personal friendliness and fraternity. Under no circumstances should one cultivate relations of any kind with those who harbor inimical feelings towards Vedas or else show atheistic tendencies or are otherwise ill-disposed towards the path of virtue and rectitude in life. If this advice is not heeded then there is every probability that such unsavory association can easily turn self-destructive. The perversity of the words and behavior of such persons can easily begin to slowly corrupt and degrade one's own sense of morality and uprightness.

It would all start something like this: At the beginning they would invite you to go with them outdoors to enjoy the fresh air. Then you will find they have brought you to a place of ill-repute. Once they have got you with them in that place of sleaze, they will tempt you into consuming substances that are taboo. They would tell you, "Try drinking this... nothing is wrong in enjoying it! Is there anything harmful if you enjoy drinking the sweet juice of tender coconuts? This here drink is to like tender-coconut water.... So, there's nothing wrong in enjoying it, come on!" Gradually, you will thus be led deeper and deeper into a sinking morass.... In the beginning you will spend a few hundred rupees every day in enjoyment... but by and by the addiction will grow and, in the end, you would have lost much of your wealth even! By then you would be turned into an utter satyr. Soon thereafter you would begin disowning all virtue and disrespecting even the good and elderly... The moral degradation would be complete.

Therefore, is it being overly stressed here that at no time, and under no circumstances, should one ever have any truck or company with persons of dubious character and morals.

***

(4)

"Na dvishanthi na yaachante paranindaam na kurvathe I
Anaahootha na chaayaanthi tenaashmaanopi devathaa: II"

One who desires to elevate his or her stature in life should never keep harboring ill-will or spite in the heart against anyone -- especially against one's mother, father, spouse, offspring, one's in-laws, or daughter-in-law, son-in-law, neighbors or community-elders – for any reason whatsoever. Such spite or hatred shown to others only ends up begetting reciprocal and equal ill-will and hatred from them in one form of harm and malice or the other. Vicious resentments shown towards one's community at large also can rebound on oneself even more viciously. While hatred towards governmental authority can invite swift reprisal, hatred shown towards divine authority will incur terrible retribution that might be delayed a little but is ineluctable. Therefore, one should never for any mindless reason show ill-will towards people from any walk of life, caste, class or creed.

Conversely, one should not also show go around pandering to all and sundry persons who might be considered high and mighty—nor be obsequious, bowing and scraping before them just to gain favors such as asking *"Please grant me charity... give me* **"go-daanam", "tila-daanam"** *or* **"uppu-daanam"** i.e., seeking alms from utterly unworthy donors. Similarly, one should not officiate as a funerary priest *("aama-shraadham")* in the homes of all and sundry out of greed for the donation of grocery ration such as bagful of rice, pulses and vegetables. Similarly, all sorts of people go to the seashore at Sethusamudram to perform rites and ceremonies in expiation of their mortal sins *(paapam)*; thereafter they take a ritual dip in the sea and discard all their clothes to jettison it in the waters. Such discarded clothes even if they are of the finest qualities should never be coveted. No one should go scavenging for such *'sari'* or *'veshti'*… or receiving it in charity … since such alms or donations will only envelop one in the tentacles of deadly Sins. Seeking alms in the form of any objects tainted by sin should always be abjured.

You should also abjure casting aspersions upon people, defaming them or being unduly judgmental about them. If you do so, then the retaliation from such people can be severely damaging and extremely prejudicially to ourselves. Such aggrieved people can lash back venomously at you by starting to rake up some real or alleged past misdemeanors committed in life not only by you but also by seven generations of your ancestry whose fair name too will get needlessly dragged into the gutter... i.e., you could soon turn victim of the same calumny that you yourself initiated in the first place.

Thus, you could end up being defamed as follows: *"Did you know this fellow's grandsire was a convicted felon! His grandmother was a scamster! His father was a leper! And do you know the horrible deeds this chap was up to in his youthful years? There was not a single nefarious house of sleaze and sin that he had not visited! And also, no one knows today for sure if his son is a male or a female!"* With such vehemence would the campaign of vilification be turned on to smear and tarnish your reputation and standing in society!

In the past there might have been one or two acts of misdemeanor or minor transgressions committed by you. However, as you grew and matured you might have totally forgotten them by putting them all behind you out of genuine regret. But they will all now be dredged up again to besmirch your good name. You will then have to face much embarrassment and social humiliation. This is the reason hence why one must think twice before speaking ill of others, or otherwise castigating them.

There is yet one other important matter to be emphasized here:

A man should never step into anyone's house, or into any social gathering for that matter, uninvited or as an unwelcome guest since the hosts, however gracious, will give him neither hospitality nor show courtesy. To make matters worse, the uninvited man might try hard to make himself acceptable in the company and go about talking too much about this and that... The host getting very irritated by the garrulousness of the gate-crasher will then only sharply rebuke him: *"Hey! why don't you keep quiet; attend to whatever business you came here for and then leave?!"* The unwelcome guest will then have to slink away in shame.

Some priests are known to at times to impose themselves on households where the religious fire-ritual such as the *"Aayush homam"* is ceremonially performed by the hosts. The priest would barge into that home announcing, *"I came to learn that this "homam" is being performed here! I thought you might be in need of the services of a* **"ghanapaatin***" (Vedic chanteur) like me! So, here I am!"* On listening to the uninvited priest, the embarrassed host would mutter bitterly under his breath, *"Why has this fellow intruded into my home like a* **"goodu-goodu paandi"** *without being invited! He has no decency?!"* (**Translator's Note**: Srimadh Azhagiyasingar employs here a very apt and impishly funny Tamizh metaphor! A *"goodu-goodu paandi"* is a minstrel dressed in garish costumes pulling a cow or bullock along with him, bedecked in equally garish costume, with jingling bells around its neck and with painted horns and tail; he usually appears unexpectedly out of nowhere in a village or town street with the animal tagging along, as he goes from door to door singing rustic ditties that foretell fortunes of the home or family; the wandering beggar is a harmless nuisance -- but a real nuisance, nonetheless). Thus, no matter where a man visits, if he goes there uninvited, he is sure to be mistreated.

To sum up, (a) one should never harbor ill-will, malice or rancor in the heart towards others; (b) never go about seeking alms or aid in any indecent or ungracious manner from all and sundry types of people and that too in the most inopportune of times and situations; (c) never defame or denigrate anyone; (d) and finally, never impose oneself anywhere in any company as an uninvited and unwelcome guest. If a man were to thus implicitly heed the above maxim, and go about minding his own business with the dignified behavior expected in his station in life, then he shall surely gain the respect of everyone around him. His stature will rise and he will attain positions of pride and honor. This is, in pith and substance, what this wise maxim, "**Na dvishanthi na yaachante.... tenaashmaanopi devathaa:** " conveys to us and to help us understand it better, it also illustrates it through an apt simile: A piece of granite stone remains ever mute and inert, fixed in one spot from where it never moves; it is silent witness to everything around it; it harbors no ill feelings towards anyone; it speaks ill of none. It is precisely because a piece of stone possesses such qualities that it soon turns divine in nature... the stone gets transfigured into a sacred idol such as those of Sri Ranganatha at Sri Rangam, Sri Srinivasa at Tirumala, Sri Varadaraja at Kanchipuram or as Sri Aravamudan at Tirukudanthai! Therefore, there should be no doubt at all that if we adhere to the 4 injunctions spoken about in the above maxim, we can make our lives sublime.

***

(5)
"Patatho naasthi moorkathvam japatho naasthi paathakam I
Mounina: kalaho naasthi na bhayam chaasthi jaagratha: II"

Those who choose to engage in serious and regular study of our scriptural texts such as the sacred puranas, the great Vedantic works of our traditional preceptors or the *"divya-prabhandham"* of the holy **Azhwars** can be sure that their general level of intelligence and wakeful-ness in life will never wane. Also, he who is steadfast in practicing daily meditation or *mantra-japam*, such as chanting *gaayatri, ashtaakshara* and other mantras, will never fall into sin. Even if there may be the taint of any past sins upon the person, they will all simply vanish in time and the person will soon begin to glow with a certain lustrous aura. If the person is also in the habit of observing on certain days a vow of silence (mouna vrata), then on such days he will be able to avoid all kinds of controversy and untoward happenings. Similarly, if a person trains himself to remain at all times very mindful and alert to all situations and occurrences that are happening in his life, he will be free of all anxiety and stress. For instance, a man who is planning for a wedding in the family, is mindful well in advance of what preparations are needed for the grand event, and goes about them in a thorough manner, where is the question of any anxiety or stress for him? Well before a wedding or an event is celebrated, if all sufficient resources have already been mobilized for the same, where then is any need to worry and fret over conducting it? Similarly, if one prepares oneself in life by acquiring thorough knowledge of all *"sastreeya"* truths or scriptural wisdom about surrendering unto Bhagavan, there will arise no angst over death or mortality (*"yama-bhayam"*). If the wealth earned by one and kept at home is well secured in safe custody, there will be little to fear about robbery or burglary. If one eats with due moderation, avoiding gluttonous overindulgence over food, disease can be prevented.

Thus, the moral of this maxim is: Be awake and very mindful of everything you do in life.

***

(6)
"Gatepi vayasi praahyaa vidyaa sarvaatmana budhai: I
Yadhyapi' syaanna faladha sulabha saanyajanmani II"

"Sir, I have now already crossed the age of 60 years… So, what then is the use of my trying to study or learn? It is too late now in life to acquire knowledge"! That is what some pensioners leading an easy, laidback life in retirement often quite nonchalantly go about telling everyone. They should not be thinking that way at all. They should to the extent possible shed all inertia and put in best efforts to acquire basic knowledge of our scriptures such as *Purusha Sooktham, Sri Sooktham, Vishnu Sahasranamam* and others with the guidance of an Acharya.

One should never say, *"What purpose or use is all that going to be to me now at my age?"* We must continue to chant and practice whatever little of the Vedas we may have learnt even if it fetches us no prospect of any pecuniary gain (*"sambhaavanai"*). We must persevere with it as a mark of gratitude offered to please Bhagavan who has blessed us with so much goodness in life. Even if such knowledge remains deficient in this lifetime (*'janma'*), it will effortlessly by itself grow, mature, blossom and surely fructify as beatific knowledge and wisdom in a future *'janma'*. So, one must never at any time slacken in the ardent and arduous effort to learn and acquire knowledge in life.

***

(7)
"Athidaanaadh balirbaddho hyathimaanaath suyodhana: I
Vinashto raavano lowllyaath athi sarvatra varjayeth II"

Those who wish for a life of happiness and comfort, should never try to get ahead in life through deeds, both good or otherwise, which contravene the ordainments of our *"sastras"*. You might now wonder and ask how could it be ever possible at all for a good deed to be in contravention of the *"sastra"*? Well, the same query was posed by Arjuna too in the first shloka of the **17ᵗʰ Chapter of the Srimad Bhagavath Gita** and for which Sri Krishna provided a lucid answer. You must go and read it. The question posed by Arjuna was this: If a man were to perform in all good earnestness a deed as ordained by *"sastra"* but was carried out at inappropriate time, or at the wrong place or in improper situation, or for the sake of unworthy persons, what will be the outcome? Krishna answered that however good and virtuous a deed may be that has been performed, if it has been performed in contravention of the "sastra", it can still rank only along with the deeds of *"asuras"* i.e., deeds qualifying as *"tamasic"*; in other words, deeds rendered bereft of any merit, mettle or meaning. Not only will such deeds not yield beneficial results, they may in fact produce only the maleficent. For instance, let us say a man solemnly performs the annual *"shraadham"* ceremony at home to propitiate the departed soul of his parents and ancestors. But then he performs it in the hour of midnight! And he also ensures the ceremonial procedures are done very scrupulously in accordance with the *'sastra'*--- i.e., he bestows upon the officiating priests (*"brahmana"*) due honors and the gifts of food, new clothes, money and even gold tokens!

Will the ritual offering yield the desired spiritual results for the man? *No, none whatsoever!* Why? Because as per the "sastra" the 'shraadha' rite must be performed during midday only. So, even if one conducts the ceremony spending elaborately on it in a midnight session, no spiritual benefit can ever accrue out of it. Similarly, imagine a man's home is in the middle of a neighborhood where there are butcheries too. He performs with great *"bhakthi"* and *"shraddha"* – piety and ardor – daily puja or *"tiruvaaraadanam"* to his household deity and thereafter even gives food offerings to household guests (*"thadhiaaraadanam"*). Will it bear any spiritual benefit for him? None whatsoever! Because, the *"sastra"* clearly advises against residing in such places of impurity. Again, the sastra enjoins that on the day before the rite of *"upanayana"* is performed in a home, the host must invite worthy persons to his house and please them with a ritual banquet (*"thadhiaaraadanam"*). But suppose the host insolently says,

"*Does it really matter who I invite for the ritual feast?!*" and does invite utterly unfit or impious persons to be the guests, will the "*upanayana*" ritual be deemed to have been conducted in proper manner? *Never!* Here is another example: Let us say a man wants to perform the "*shraadham*" ceremony at home but under the excuse of being unable to find any suitable "*brahmanas*" to officiate over the rite, he instead invites a wedded brahmin lady of virtuous character to do the same honors as the brahmin priests. He confers upon her all-due honors such as gifts of rich sarees and money... Will such a ceremony yield any spiritual benefit? *None at all!*

The above answers as gleaned from Sri Krishna's reply to the question Arjuna posed have only this clear message: A man who performs good deeds thinking he is being virtuous but then performs it in contravention of the "*sastra*", can not only not expect to gain any benefit out of the deed but, on the contrary, may perhaps suffer detrimental consequences from such performance.

The "*sastra*" exhorts us never to fail to offer our Acharya or guru "*Dakshina*" i.e., generous gifts of gratitude. But even that gift or offering to the preceptor must not be given other than in accordance with modalities prescribed in the '*sastra*'. Just to please the guru or acharya, one should not offer one's family wealth thereby depriving one's children what is rightfully theirs as heirs. Likewise, you can offer an over-abundance of the delicious jackfruit as "*nivedanam*" or offering to the household deity and thereafter wolf it all down with greedy gusto! You will surely suffer and die from suggestion, even though you have consumed only offerings ritually made to Bhagavan. That is why the Vedas say, **"anname mruthyu: anname amrutham**...." Gluttony leads to death; moderation leads to healthy sustenance. Moderation in everything act in life is necessary. Excess in even giving charity leads to peril as the story of *Mahabali* illustrates. Intemperance and ego, similarly led to the complete downfall of Duryodhana when he arrogantly rejected the efforts of wise men like **Bhishmacharya** and **Sri Krishna** to mediate an amicable settlement between the warring families (*Kaurava* and *Pandava*) — "*soochyakram naiva daasyaami*" ... *oosi munaiyum idang koden*...." *I shall bow down to none, and I shall concede not even as much as a pin-head!*". And out of sheer hauteur and hubris, uncontrollable lust seized Ravana who had dared to abduct Sita; it made him stubborn in refusing to release her as his hostage; and in the end he lost his entire empire of Lanka.

This maxim thus teaches us this: Whether it is a good or bad one, neither should ever contravene the *"sastra"* ... *"ati sarvatra varjayeth, atikramya sarvatra"* – i.e., what goes against *'saastra'* must be abandoned.

***

(8)
"Vrutha Vrishti: samudreshu vrutha truptasya bhojanam I
Vrutha daanam samarthasya vrutha deepo divaapi cha II"

As a general rule in life, no one should undertake any work that has neither value nor purpose. Such work earns appreciation from nobody; and it may in fact be the cause of much troubles. If a man is seen to be going about daily just loitering idly on the street, he is likely to be the first suspect in case there is a burglary in any house on that street. If a man is seen often lurking in and around doing nothing inside an empty quarter, he could be the target of all kinds of suspicions. If a man is seen to be stalking another and also found to be waving his hand for no reason at all at the other, there can be no doubt what people might think of him. Likewise, if one were to aimlessly keep pelting stones, just out of idle fun, up a tree-top, sooner or later, one day it is probable that a stone will fall on the head of a passerby causing grievous injury. If a man were to needlessly shower himself or dunk himself in a bath for ten times or more in a day, one can imagine what his state would be...

It is through some of the above simple illustrations that the above conveys to us the important lesson that we should never engage idly in purposeless, frivolous activities that are of no use to anyone. What is the use if dark, huge rain-bearing clouds drifting or hovering over the horizon offload their entire supply of copious rainfall on the ocean mass? Would that be any different from the wealthy man who instead of feeding the poor and hungry many living around him, invites home the few already well-to-do and well-fed friends of his and force-feeds them at a rich banquet? Likewise, the actions of a man who proudly goes on piling again and again lavish gifts (e.g., *go-daanam*, etc.) upon his already well-to-do kith and kin, are as only as wasteful and purposeless as those of the man who walks out in broad daylight on to the street with a lamp in his hand, intending to further brighten the day! Would the man gain anything real from showing such munificence? Only if it rains upon arid land that has been seeded with grain would there be then real cause to celebrate the arrival of the monsoon. The crops too would then flourish. Similarly, if charity is done unto an indigent Vedic pundit, his impoverished family would surely flourish. If a starving man were to be served sumptuous food, the pangs of hunger would be removed. If one were to lit a lamp in darkness, light would then brighten the room bringing in at least a mood of good cheer…. Thus, whatever maybe a man's deeds in life, he must always make sure they all have some purpose, some use and some worth.

❋❋❋

It has been shown by men of very great wisdom, that anyone abiding by the above *8 maxims* can surely attain very great heights of fulfilment in life.

-END-

Acknowledgements

The Translator of this book wishes to place on record his deep gratitude to the following institutions for the support extended to its publishing:

1. *Sangitha Kalanidhi*, **Dr. Smt. Mani Krishnaswami Foundation, Chennai** for sponsoring the costs of publication.
2. **Sri Nrsimha Priya Charitable Trust**, Chennai, for permission to use their copyright over the Tamil original of the *"Arul Mozhi"* of Srimadh Mukkur Azhagiyasingar.
3. *"Nrsimha Priya"* **(English)** magazine which serialized the English translations in 2021 through 2023.
4. *"Vainavan Kural"* **(English)** magazine which serialized the English translations in 2021 through 2023.

About the Translator

M. K. Sudarshan is a graduate of the Madras University from Loyola College, Chennai, and a qualified Chartered Accountant and corporate executive by profession. After a 37 year-long and successful international career in corporate finance, he now lives with his wife in Chennai, pursuing wider interests in Indian philosophy, world history and comparative religious literature, studies, and prolific writing and blogging on a variety of subjects. His related interests are classical South Indian music, the history of Hindu temples in India and travelling worldwide.

Sudarshan is the author of two other published books on Sri Vaishnavism which have earned critical and popular acclaim worldwide: *"The Unusual Essays of an Unknown Sri Vaishnava"* (2016: *Partridge India*/2018: *StoryMirror*/2021: *Mainstream Publishers USA*/2022) and *"The Nondesript God: Abstraction or Paragon?"* (2022: *BlueRose Publishers*). His third book published in July 2023 is on the history of Sri Vaishnavas under the title *"A Tale of two cities: the Decline and Fall of the "ubaya-vedantins: A history of the Sri Vaishnavas of Tamil Nadu that was never written"*. *(All the books are available on the Amazon and Flipcart online platforms and in Kindle Editions also).*

Sudarshan regards the renowned Sri Vaishnavite scholar and Vedantic exponent, **U.Ve. Sri Mukkur Lakshminarasimhachariar** *(1944-2000CE)* as his spiritual mentor. He also imbibed values from his mother, the well-known classicist Carnatic Music artiste, (*Padma*

Shri) **Smt.Mani Krishnaswami (1930-2002)** and from his father **Madabushi Sri. M. Krishnaswami (1926-2013)** who hailed from a religious family in the ancient and sacred temple city of Tirumala-Tirupati. Sudarshan is a *sishya* of Sri Ahobila Matham.

Sudarshan has penned several published articles on a wide variety of subjects – both professional and religious – in newspapers and magazines (*The Hindu, Business World, New Horizon (UK), Sri Nrsimha Priya, Vainavan Kural, Tattvaloka* and others). He is also a prolific blogger on his website:

www.unknownsrivaishnava.wordpress.com.

www.ingramcontent.com/pod-product-compliance
Ingram Content Group UK Ltd.
Pitfield, Milton Keynes, MK11 3LW, UK
UKHW020247240426
12048UKWH00027B/1654